Teaching the Daode Jing

AAR
AMERICAN ACADEMY OF RELIGION

TEACHING RELIGIOUS STUDIES SERIES

SERIES EDITOR
Susan Henking, Hobart and William Smith Colleges

A Publication Series of

The American Academy of Religion
and
Oxford University Press

TEACHING LEVI-STRAUSS
Edited by Hans H. Penner

TEACHING ISLAM
Edited by Brannon M. Wheeler

TEACHING FREUD
Edited by Diane Jonte-Pace

TEACHING DURKHEIM
Edited by Terry F. Godlove, Jr.

TEACHING AFRICAN AMERICAN RELIGIONS
Edited by Carolyn M. Jones and Theodore Louis Trost

TEACHING RELIGION AND HEALING
Edited by Linda L. Barnes and Inés Talamantez

TEACHING NEW RELIGIOUS MOVEMENTS
Edited by David G. Bromley

TEACHING RITUAL
Edited by Catherine Bell

TEACHING CONFUCIANISM
Edited by Jeffrey L. Richey

AAR
AMERICAN ACADEMY OF RELIGION

Teaching the Daode Jing

EDITED BY

GARY D. DEANGELIS

WARREN G. FRISINA

OXFORD

UNIVERSITY PRESS

2008

OXFORD
UNIVERSITY PRESS

Oxford University Press, Inc., publishes works that further
Oxford University's objective of excellence
in research, scholarship, and education.

Oxford   New York
Auckland   Cape Town   Dar es Salaam   Hong Kong   Karachi
Kuala Lumpur   Madrid   Melbourne   Mexico City   Nairobi
New Delhi   Shanghai   Taipei   Toronto

With offices in
Argentina   Austria   Brazil   Chile   Czech Republic   France   Greece
Guatemala   Hungary   Italy   Japan   Poland   Portugal   Singapore
South Korea   Switzerland   Thailand   Turkey   Ukraine   Vietnam

Copyright © 2008 by The American Academy of Religion

Published by Oxford University Press, Inc.
198 Madison Avenue, New York, New York 10016

www.oup.com

Oxford is a registered trademark of Oxford University Press

Library of Congress Cataloging-in-Publication Data
Teaching the Daode Jing : edited by Gary Delaney DeAngelis
and Warren G. Frisina.
    p. cm.—(Teaching religious studies series)
Includes bibliographical references and index.
ISBN 978-0-19-533270-4
1. Laozi. Dao de jing. I. DeAngelis, Gary Delaney, 1943–
II. Frisina, Warren G., 1954–
BL1900.L35T35 2007
299.5'1482071—dc22   2007011732

9 8 7 6 5 4 3 2 1

Printed in the United States of America
on acid-free paper

Preface

Warren G. Frisina

The *Daode Jing* (*DDJ*) enjoys an enviable place in college and university curricula. It is a staple in courses on Asian and East Asian intellectual history and culture. Over the past thirty years it has also made its way into philosophy, history, religion, and theology courses as well as broader "great books" courses that are designed to introduce students to seminal ideas in the humanities and social sciences.

As the *DDJ* points out, however, fame and acceptance are always mixed blessings! Many of those who teach the *DDJ* do not have specific training in its history, language, and cultural context. More often than not we find ourselves reaching beyond our graduate and professional preparations as we try to introduce our students to a text whose brevity belies its complexity. On such occasions the conscientious among us dutifully head off to libraries, where we are confronted with a list of translations that seems to grow exponentially, along with a secondary literature whose size precludes even a cursory attempt to scan its horizons.

The essays included in *Teaching the Daode Jing* aim to facilitate the nonspecialists' efforts to prepare to teach the *DDJ*. This book will also be of interest to sinologists, since its contributors include some of the leading scholars in the field. Still, readers should know that editorial decisions were made with an eye toward the needs of the nonspecialist. The contributors were asked to write clear, accessible essays that would help someone who is about to use the *DDJ* in the classroom.

We have included ten essays by scholars who teach the *DDJ* on a regular basis. In assembling the list of contributors we had two goals in mind. First, we wanted readers to have up-to-date information about contemporary approaches to understanding the *DDJ*. For that reason, some of the essays speak about the current state of *DDJ* scholarship. At the same time, however, we also wanted to give our readers concrete examples of how different scholars have approached the *DDJ* in their classrooms. Thus, some of the essays undertake specific descriptions of particular assignments, classroom exercises, and a variety of other ideas that have been put to use by our contributors.

As is true of any classic text, the *DDJ* is capable of generating heated scholarly debate. On the assumption that nonspecialists should be alerted to some of these debates we've deliberately included essays by scholars who disagree with one another. Our thought was that by presenting both sides of an issue we could allow our readers to assess the options and make their own choices. To take just one example, some of our essayists applaud the use of material from popular culture (e.g., the *Tao of Pooh* and the *Star Wars* movie series), while others counsel against it, arguing that these materials confuse more than they clarify. *Taken as a whole, this volume does not aim to make any progress in settling such questions.* As editors we are interested in providing teachers with a handy collection of resources. We are not trying to advance *DDJ* scholarship. This volume is not even a comprehensive survey of the range of options currently in play. It is easy to imagine a *Teaching the Daode Jing II or III* as there are many voices not yet represented in this small collection.

Of course, to say that we have deliberately included conflicting points of view is not the same as saying that we are advocating an "anything goes" attitude about the *DDJ*. Each of the essays is grounded in an intellectual tradition which currently plays an important role in contemporary debates over how the *DDJ* ought to be interpreted. Moreover, all of the contributors present closely argued defenses of their interpretive claims and their pedagogical techniques.

In sum, this volume brings together an eclectic group of well-respected scholars whose essays provide the reader with grist for reflection about how to approach the *DDJ*. We believe that this open-ended approach is the best way to begin providing tangible support to those who are wrestling with this wonderfully complicated text.

To help orient readers to what is coming, we offer brief summaries of the essays in the order of their appearance. Before turning to those summaries, however, it would perhaps be useful to say a word or two about transliteration and why we chose not to render all of our essays into one of the two standard formats. Most everyone who has spent any time reading Chinese material in translation is aware that we are in the midst of a transition. The older Wade-Giles system is what most of the more senior scholars learned as graduate students and is still in use today. The newer, pinyin system is gaining fast and will likely supplant Wade-Giles in time. At the moment, however, we are betwixt and between. All Chinese Romanization is rendered in pinyin throughout the text. The exceptions to this are in citing published works that use the Wade-Giles system and in citing published Chinese authors whose names are rendered in Wade-Giles.

Part I: Approaching the *Daode Jing*

Part I of this volume presents five different ways of approaching the *DDJ* as one prepares to use it in class.

"Third-Person and First-Person Approaches to the Study of the Laozi*" by Harold Roth*

In the opening essay of this collection Harold Roth takes up questions important to all scholars who deal with ancient texts. He asks, "How is it possible to be both historically accurate and yet nonreductionistic? How is it possible to both respect the ideas and underlying experiences found in ancient religious texts, yet also be critical of their authors' understanding of themselves and their traditions?" Eschewing both the uncritical faith stance of Daoism's apologists as well as the reductionist tendencies among some contemporary secularists, Roth preaches a middle path. Since the *Daode jing* draws from a meditative tradition that utilizes breath control, he suggests that our teaching include a mix of both *third-person analysis* (where we rely on the traditional tools of scholarship such as historical-textual research, hermeneutical analysis, and contemporary philosophic reflection) and *first-person analysis* (where we encourage our students to engage in simple meditation and breathing exercises that are tied to specific chapters and that add an experiential dimension to their study). He suggests this combination as a way of both discharging our scholarly responsibilities and demonstrating a healthy respect for the integrity and coherence of this ancient text.

"The Dao *and the Field: Exploring an Analogy" by Robert G. Henricks*

It could be argued that a great deal of teaching involves locating analogies that successfully mediate between student's expectations and what a text is actually saying. For many years Robert Henricks has used the image of an untended field to help his students understand what the *DDJ* means by the *Dao*. Henricks's field is not a farmer's field but a natural field that is "barren and deserted in the winter but filled with a host of different wildflowers throughout the spring and summer." Henricks's extended meditation on this analogy leads him into a discussion of central themes: the *Dao*'s rhythmic cycles from tranquility to activity and back; the need to remain "rooted" in the *Dao*; the true nature of morality; and what the *DDJ* might mean by immortality.

"The Daode jing *and Comparative Philosophy"*
by David L. Hall

The pedagogical aims of comparative philosophers teaching in an American or European context are both similar to and different from the aims of historians. Like historians, the comparative philosopher is concerned that students be made self-conscious about Western conceptual assumptions that mask or render obscure Chinese texts like the *DDJ*. Beyond awareness, however, comparative philosophers are also engaged in cultivating constructive responses to the challenges implicit in competing philosophical visions. In this essay, David Hall discusses the way the *DDJ* contradicts or even subverts some of the more prominent assumptions about ontology, cosmology, and the self in the Western philosophic and religious traditions. Where many Western philosophers describe being as "a common property or a relational structure," the *DDJ* seems not to posit any such "superordinate One to which the Many reduce." Similarly, where many Western thinkers portray the self as a collection of competing and sometimes conflicting faculties (e.g., reason, appetite, and will), the *DDJ* does not. Bringing students to an awareness of these differences is, Hall argues, an excellent way to introduce them to the advantages of a comparative approach to philosophic reflection.

"Mysticism in the Daode jing*" by Gary Delaney DeAngelis*

While its "exotic" language and cultural assumptions may make students prone to overly mystical interpretations of the *DDJ*, there is no denying that it is a mystical text. In this essay Gary DeAngelis outlines the way he employs the *DDJ* in a course on comparative mysticisms. Beginning with Ninian Smart's definition of mystical experience as a "state of consciousness . . . 'where one acquires a fundamental insight into the nature of reality,'" DeAngelis leads students into a discussion of how the *DDJ* responds to two basic questions:

"What is the nature of ultimate reality? and How may one experience that reality?" These questions lead students to explore basic epistemological issues as they come to a deeper understanding of what the *DDJ* may mean by saying that it is possible to "know" a *Dao* that is itself "unknowable."

"The Daode jing *in Practice" by Eva Wong*

As many of the essays in this volume point out, we all feel an obligation to help our students catch at least a glimpse of the historical and cultural contexts that gave rise to the *DDJ*. With that objective in mind we often find ourselves combating the twin tendencies to make the text seem either too familiar or too strange. One way of navigating between these extremes is to turn students' attention away from abstract ideas and philosophical principles to show them what the text looks like through the lens of Daoist practices. In this essay, the contemporary Daoist practitioner Eva Wong explains that many of the *DDJ*'s most puzzling passages make perfect sense when seen in the light of specific Daoist activities and exercises. Specifically, she argues that phrases like "stilling the mind," "nourishing the soul," "infant breathing," and "cleaning the subtle mirror" point to particular kinds of actions that early (and in many cases contemporary) Daoists believed would lead one to live a life more nearly in accord with the *Dao*.

"Imagine Teaching the Daode jing*!" by Judith Berling, Geoffrey Foy, and John Thompson*

This essay is a collaborative effort between an experienced teacher-scholar and two graduate students at the very beginning of their careers as teachers. The authors present three "overlapping" strategies for teaching the *DDJ*. The first emphasizes situating the *DDJ* within the context of Zhou Chinese intellectual struggles and proceeds by student-led discussions about thematically grouped chapters. The second contrasts contemporary expectations regarding gender language with the *DDJ*'s own use of feminine metaphors in order to help students uncover what the text may mean when it uses those metaphors in the way that it does. The third approach aims to turn the *DDJ*'s notorious ambiguity to the teacher's advantage. By leading students through a series of re-readings of the text from different points of view the teacher can help students to see (a) how their understanding of the text changes with each rereading and (b) that all interpretations are context-dependent.

Part II: Recent Scholarship and Teaching the *Daode jing*

In part II of this volume, the focus of the essays shifts to current trends in *DDJ* scholarship. While each contains its own pedagogical suggestions, readers should view these essays as a way of listening in on the contemporary scholarly debates over the *DDJ* and how it ought to be interpreted.

"My Way: Teaching the Daode jing *and* Daoism *at the End of the Millennium" by Norman J. Girardot*

In his essay, Norman Girardot reflects on his own history of teaching the *DDJ* at American colleges and universities from the early 1970s through to the end of the twentieth century. Along the way, he describes scholarly and cultural changes that have had an impact on what he does in the classroom, especially his use of popularized presentations of the *DDJ* both as a way of opening students to the text and as a reference point to be criticized once he has led them to a fuller understanding of its historical and cultural context. Girardot also describes his "growing appreciation for the nature and role of performative ritual in teaching and knowing." These rituals include classroom exercises, writing itself, and, on one memorable day, a college-wide "phantasmagoria" called *Dao*-day.

"The Reception of Laozi" by Livia Kohn

Livia Kohn urges teachers of the *Daode jing* to take seriously their responsibility to help move students from a singular image of the *Daode jing* as an Americanized version of the "go-with-the-flow philosophy of life" to an appreciation of the multifarious history and ongoing reception of this text and the traditions it has helped spawn. In particular she urges that students come to understand the textual history of the *Daode jing*'s development (as revealed via recent archaeological finds), the historical reality surrounding the text's creation (e.g., warring states politics, competing philosophic views), and the role the *Daode jing* has played in the development of Daoist rituals and practices. Following suggestions made by Harold Roth in the opening essay of this volume, she also suggests that students would benefit from an appreciation of the religious dimensions of Daoism, especially an understanding of the meditative and cultivation practices that seem so critical to the early Daoist communities and the development of Laozi from legendary antagonist of Confucius to the status of a divine being.

*"Hermeneutics and Pedagogy: Methodological Issues
in Teaching the* Daode jing*" by Russell Kirkland*

Russell Kirkland describes his approach to teaching the *DDJ* as "contrarian."
He argues that most textbooks do a credible job of presenting the *DDJ* as it has
been inherited through both Confucian and Western conceptual lenses, but
that such a view fails to see the *Daoist* as they saw themselves. Like LaFargue he
challenges students to "ponder the alienity of ancient China" before making
assumptions about what the text is trying to accomplish. By focusing their
attention on early Daoist religious practices and the status of the *DDJ* as a
Daoist scripture, Kirkland aims to cultivate in his students an appreciation for
both the original aims of the text and the way hermeneutical models are
developed, challenged, and clarified.

*"Hermeneutics and Pedagogy: Gimme That
Old-Time Historicism" by Michael LaFargue*

Drawing directly on techniques developed in biblical hermeneutics, Michael
LaFargue aims to cultivate in students a capacity to see the *DDJ* from the point
of view of its many literary forms and implied interlocutors. By exploring the
structures of proverbial sayings LaFargue leads students away from the tendency to take its statements too literally, a tendency that typically makes the
DDJ seem more obscure and mysterious than it is. Setting aside hypermystical
readings that he attributes to the needs of contemporary Western interpreters
rather than the text itself, LaFargue encourages his students to ask, What
"pragmatic implications" of the *DDJ*'s statements can we reasonably attribute
to the early Daoist practitioners who both produced and made use of this text?
This leads, he argues, to a historicist understanding of the *DDJ* that is rooted
in questions quite different from those that a contemporary Western reader
would typically bring to the text.

Contents

Contributors

JUDITH BERLING is a China specialist who teaches East Asian religions at the Graduate Theological Union in Berkeley, California. She is a past president of the American Academy of Religion and is a founding coeditor of the journal *Teaching Theology and Religion*. Her latest publication is *A Pilgrim in Chinese Culture: Negotiating Religious Diversity*.

GARY D. DEANGELIS is the associate director of the Center for Interdisciplinary and Special Studies and teaches Asian religions in the Department of Religious Studies at Holy Cross College. His latest publications include "Myamoto Musashi and the Book of Five Rings" and the China and Japan entries in a forthcoming *Dictionary of Religious Studies* for undergraduates. He can periodically be found running and sailing in Rhode Island.

GEOFFREY FOY is the assistant director of continuing education at Central Washington University. He has a PhD in Chinese religion from the Graduate Theological Union.

WARREN G. FRISINA teaches at Hofstra University in the Department of Philosophy and Religious Studies and is the acting dean of Hofstra's Honors College. He is particularly interested in exploring points of contact between Chinese and American philosophic traditions. His latest publication, *The Unity of Knowledge and Action: Toward a Nonrepresentational Theory of Knowledge*, is a constructive attempt to explore the implications of Wang Yang-ming's slogan *chih hsing ho-i* (the unity of knowledge and action) for American philosophy.

NORMAN J. GIRARDOT is the University Distinguished Professor of Humanities at Lehigh University and teaches Asian religions in the Religious Studies Department. His publications include *Myth and Meaning in Early Taoism* and *The Victorian Translation of China: James Legge's Oriental Pilgrimage.*

DAVID L. HALL was a professor of philosophy at the University of Texas at El Paso. He passed away in 2001. In addition to three books on the philosophy of culture, a book on Richard Rorty, and a rather salacious novel, *The Arimaspian Eye*, he published four books in comparative Chinese and Western thought with Roger Ames. At the time of his death Hall and Ames were at work on a philosophically sensitive translation of the *Daode jing.*

ROBERT G. HENRICKS is a specialist on ancient China and is Professor Emeritus of Chinese Religions in the Department of Religion at Dartmouth College. His publications include *Lao-Tzu Te-Tao Ching*, *The Poetry of Han-shan*, and *Lao Tzu's Tao Te Ching: A Translation of the Startling New Documents Found at Guodian.* When he isn't reading old Chinese texts he is said to spend inordinate amounts of time and money on fly-fishing.

RUSSELL KIRKLAND is a professor of Asian studies at the University of Georgia specializing in historical and interpretive issues spanning diverse phases of the Taoist tradition. His publications include *Taoism:The Enduring Tradition*, numerous articles and encyclopedia entries on Daoist topics, and a variety of entries in the forthcoming *Encyclopedia of Taoism*, edited by Fabrizio Pregadio, and *Handbook of Daoism*, edited by Livia Kohn.

LIVIA KOHN is a professor of Religion and East Asian studies at Boston University. She has written and edited numerous books, including *Early Chinese Mysticism*, *Daoism and Chinese Culture*, and *Cosmos and Community: The Ethical Dimension of Daoism.* She is also a longtime instructor of Qigong.

MICHAEL LaFARGUE is the director of East Asian studies at the University of Massachusetts and teaches Asian religions in the Department of Philosophy and Religion. His publications include *The Tao of the Tao Te Ching*, *Tao and Method*, and *Lao-tzu and the Tao-te-ching* (coedited with Livia Kohn). He is known to be a passionate kayaker.

HANS-GEORG MOELLER is an associate professor in the Philosophy Department of Brock University, St. Catharines, Ontario, Canada. He has published numerous books and articles on Chinese and comparative philosophy, including *Daoism Explained* and *The Philosophy of the Daode jing.*

HAROLD D. ROTH is a professor of East Asian studies at Brown University and the author of *The Textual History of the Huai-nan Tzu, Original Tao: Inward Training (Nei-yeh) and the Foundations of Taoist Mysticism,* and *A Companion to Angus Graham's Chuang Tzu: The Inner Chapters,* as well as several books' worth of articles in scholarly journals in the field. When not engaged in doing his part to destroy forests through publishing so many dubious theories, Roth enjoys the world of baseball (playing, coaching, fanning) and encourages his sons to "get a life" and not become academics.

JOHN THOMPSON has a PhD from the Graduate Theological Union with a dual focus in Buddhism and Chinese religion and philosophy.

EVA WONG is a practitioner of the Daoist arts and is initiated into the Hsien-t'ien wu-chi and the Wu-Liu sects of Daoism. She has also learned from the Complete Reality School in China and Taiwan and the Kun-lun sect in Hong Kong. She is the author of more than ten books on Daoism, including *Seven Tao ist Masters, The Shambhala Guide to Taoism, Teachings of Taoism,* and *Harmonizing Yin and Yang.*

Teaching the Daode Jing

Introduction

Hans-Georg Moeller

The essays included in this volume present a variety of experiences in teaching the *Daode jing*, a text being taught by an increasing number of scholars in many fields in the humanities. While each paper naturally presents an individual perspective and a personal approach, there are nevertheless some recurring themes that are addressed in most, if not all, reports. I will try to identify three of these recurring themes, because it seems that they can be relevant to anyone who teaches the *Daode jing*. Of the three themes I discuss, two are hardly contentious while one is highly so—and I will leave this one for the end of this introduction.

Academic and Popular Approaches

When one is going to teach a class on the *Daode jing* to undergraduate students who have no background in Chinese studies, one can nevertheless expect that many of the students will have heard of this text, if not read it (in translation), or at least texts that are related to it. Most essays in this volume deal with this specific situation that a teacher of the *Daode jing* is likely to be confronted with. There will be certain preconceptions of the subject that are not academically grounded but are premeditated by the mass media and popular culture. Daoism in general, and the *Daode jing* in particular, have become some kind of Asian or Chinese "icons" in the multicultural pattern of contemporary North American society, and some students will un-avoidably have been exposed to them. The Dao is referred to, as many authors point out, in blockbuster movies (*Crouching Tiger, Hidden Dragon, Hero*), it is dealt with in various popular practices such as martial arts and feng shui, and it is sold in best sellers by, for instance, Benjamin Hoff (*The Tao of Pooh*) and Stephen Mitchell (*Tao Te Ching*). All contributors to this volume seem to agree that a course or a class on the *Daode jing* will have to take this phenomenon into account, and while there are different opinions on the usage of such popular materials in the classroom, no one seems to suggest that one can simply ignore their existence.

Since a university class is inescapably part of an educational setting there arises naturally a sort of tension between a popular and a more academic ap-proach to the text—and this tension can be made use of for arousing students' interest as well as for challenging them to question and extend their knowledge of the subject. Norman Girardot, for instance, asserts, "It's not that I think Mitchell's Zennish pseudo-translation of the *Laozi*, Hoff's New Age Pooh Bear Dao, or Kevin Smith's Silent Bob are intrinsically evil. They assuredly are not, and I have used both Mitchell's and Hoff's works in the classroom. When employed strategically and contextually, they constitute an effective way to begin and end a course on Daoism." There seems to be a consensus among authors that popular Daoism cannot simply be dismissed as trash or snobbishly ignored altogether. It constitutes a reality, and to deny this would not be very productive. All authors, however, make it explicitly or implicitly clear that a university class on the *Daode jing* cannot just be a lecture on New Age Daoism. In an academic context it is therefore prudent, as many contributors point out, to introduce the *Daode jing* within a historical framework and to make it clear that there is a substantial difference between contemporary America and ancient China. A course on the *Daode jing* will hardly avoid dealing with this difference—or, as Judith Berling, Geoffrey Foy, and John Thompson say, "Some contextualization is required to engage students fruitfully with the text." Teaching the *Daode jing* academically necessarily involves such a contextualization, including informa-tion on the cultural background and the philological peculiarities of this text.

The potentially productive tension between popular and academic ap-proaches to the *Daode jing* thus immediately relates to another, also potentially productive, tension that is perhaps most neatly captured by Michael LaFargue's hermeneutical distinction between the attempt to reconstruct what the text "meant to its original authors and audience" and what it can mean to a con-temporary reader. This distinction between "them" and "us" grants each ap-proach its own specific validity and legitimacy on the one hand, while, on the other hand, it also strongly cautions against a conflation of their different reading strategies. Both reading strategies make sense, but because they are methodologically so far apart it is very unlikely that they will concur. Both approaches, the academic and the popular, the historical and the "contemporary," can coexist—in the real world as well as in the classroom. This coexistence implies that neither approach should be forced on the other. Popular Daoism can certainly not claim a monopoly on reviving the true spirit of the *Daode jing* that is supposedly lost in, for instance, "dry" philological translations, but neither can academic research claim the *Daode jing* as an exclusive object of scholarly investigation. To put it in the words of the famous butterfly dream allegory in the *Zhuangzi*: There is a man, and there is a butterfly, and "so there is necessarily a distinction between them." To ignore this distinction, to try to blur it or even it out, or to claim that it is a hierarchical one, is neither very Daoist nor, so the authors of this volume seem to agree, didactically rewarding.

Which Text, Which Translation?

A second issue that is brought up—again, if not explicitly then at least implicitly—in virtually all contributions to this volume is the practical problem of having to use English translations when teaching the *Daode jing* (outside the field of Chinese studies). The majority of teachers who discuss the *Daode jing* in their classes will not be trained scholars in Ancient Chinese language—and the same will certainly be true for the students taking these classes. This situation leaves teachers and students dependent on the sources that are used in class. The very choice of the translation(s) of the *Daode jing* will substantially determine the image of the text that the course will produce.

In the case of the *Daode jing* the problem of translation has a much deeper dimension than with many other great books. The *Daode jing* is a text without an identifiable author or authors, without a specific date or time of creation, and without a definite form. It is, moreover, a book that, most likely, was originally none; present-day sinological scholars mostly assume that the text had oral origins. Many essays in this volume talk about the extremely complex textual history of the *Daode jing*: it emerged over centuries, and the early manuscripts discovered in relatively recent excavations show different versions of the text at different times. The choice of one or more English translations of the *Daode jing* is thus not only a choice of one or more particular renderings, but it is also necessarily a choice of one or more editions or versions of the text on which the translation is based. There are translations of the "standard edition" of the text by Wang Bi that goes back to the third century C.E. (although recent scholarship has shown that, most likely, even the text that is transmitted as the Wang Bi edition is different from the text that Wang Bi actually worked with), with or without Wang Bi's commentary in English. Then one finds, though much more rarely, translations based on other editions (such as the one ascribed to Heshang Gong, third century C.E.?). Then there are translations on the basis of the various manuscripts found, respectively, in Mawangdui (around 200 B.C.E.) and Guodian (third or fourth century B.C.E.). And there are also translations—often the most popular ones—that do not identify any specific Chinese edition as their source. Translations of the *Daode jing* presuppose a choice of one or more Chinese "original" text(s), which are, paradoxically enough, never truly originals because there simply exists no authentic *Urtext* to work with. Sinological translators will typically not only have subjectively decided on one or more Chinese editions as their source(s), but they will also rely on one or more specific Chinese commentaries of their choice. To translate the text, for instance, on the basis of the Wang Bi edition does not mean only to follow Wang Bi's wording of the *Daode jing*, but also to be at least influenced by Wang Bi's interpretation. Thus, to decide, for instance, between the Wang Bi and the Heshang Gong editions is not only a philological, but also a hermeneutical decision for the translator—and this decision is inevitably repeated by the teacher who then decides for one of these translations for his or her class.

The *Daode jing* is not only different from other great books by, philologically and historically speaking, not precisely meeting the characteristics of many other books; it is also very unique in style. This adds to the difficulties involved in its translation. As many essays in this volume point out, it works more often than not on the basis of imagery (Henricks and others), proverbial sayings (LaFargue), and poetic devices (Hall and others). Such linguistic and rhetorical features are often hard to translate. Accordingly, translations vary greatly not only in regard to their textual source, but also in how they deal with the literary aspects of the text.

Generally speaking, the authors of this volume distinguish between two kinds of translations: academic and popular. The differences between these approaches have already been discussed in the preceding section, and teachers of the *Daode jing* will hardly avoid taking these differences into account. (Typically, the academic translations are more literal and less appealing to a general reader, while the opposite tends to be the case with the popular ones.) Several authors, however, address internal differences among the academic or expert translations. Some of these translations are so expert that they are hardly readable anymore—and are completely unusable in an undergraduate class outside Chinese studies (see, for instance, Norman Girardot, note 7). Others, however, even though certainly also expert and produced by eminent scholars, are highly interpretative in a way that often remains hidden to the non-sinological instructor. I would like to explain this with the help of one example. The line from the *Daode jing* quoted most often in the present volume (and probably not only here) is the first line of the first chapter. Robert G. Henricks cites it in Wing-tsit Chan's translation: "The *Tao* that can be told of is not the eternal *Tao*." David Hall translates: "The Way that can be spoken of is not the constant Way."[1] Semantically speaking, the most important difference between these two renderings is the difference between "eternal" and "constant." Whereas "constant" is a rather colloquial word, the term "eternal" is resplendent with theological and philosophical connotations. Strictly speaking, these two words, although close in their meaning, belong to very different "language games." Chan's translation of the *Daode jing* was a major, and highly successful, effort by this eminent scholar to present the text, as he states in the preface, "from the perspective of the total history of Chinese philosophy" and to integrate it into the discourse of Western academia. As a Chinese professor at an American university, he was among the most important proponents of Chinese thought and culture in his time and worked for its establishment within the curricula of the West. With his translations of Chinese classics he attempted to introduce Chinese texts as serious materials deserving the full attention of Western scholars and, particularly, philosophers.[2] So he used a highly metaphysical vocabulary to demonstrate the philosophical and religious status and significance of texts like the *Daode jing*. His translations thus contributed considerably to the academic respect that the *Daode jing* has gained in North America (as reflected, for instance, in the publication of this present volume), while they also cemented a sort of metaphysical interpretation of the *Daode jing* that more recent authors like David Hall tried to overcome or correct in their studies and translations. In this way, all translations reflect to a certain degree the agenda of their translators. This is, to use Norman Girardot's expression once again, certainly not "intrinsically evil," but it is something that those who teach the *Daode jing* in English translation will have to consider. Many translations and interpretations thus function, as Russell Kirkland says, not as a window "into the text itself, but merely into *the mind of the translator*."

Is the *Daode jing* a Religious Text?

In regard to the two issues discussed above, I could not detect substantial disagreements among the contributors to this volume. But this is decidedly not so in regard to the third problem that is persistently addressed (again, if not explicitly then at least implicitly) in these essays: the question as to which academic discipline can rightfully claim for itself the *Daode jing* and, for that matter, Daoism. This text is a volume in a series on teaching classic texts in *religion*, and accordingly, a majority of the contributors teach in departments of *religion*, and, again accordingly, most contributors either explicitly or implicitly take the *Daode jing* to be a religious text. But this opinion is not shared by all contributors, and it is more likely not to be shared by those who do not have a background in religious or theological (biblical) studies. Some contributors are practical teachers, others are philosophers. Particularly the latter tend to not understand the *Daode jing* as a (primarily) religious text. I find this an important controversy, particularly because it is likely to also reflect a diversity among the readership of this book: not every reader will teach the *Daode jing* as a "classic text in religion"; some will teach it, I suppose, as a classic text in philosophy, others may teach it as a classic text in literature, and others may perhaps teach it as a classic text in breathing (see Roth). This situation may be summarized by rephrasing the statement by Russell Kirkland quoted above—in a less psychological and more sociological manner: Our way of reading and teaching the *Daode jing* may thus serve not so much as a window "into the text itself, but merely into *the education and institutional affiliation of the instructor*."

The dispute over what the *Daode jing* is and, more broadly, what Daoism in general is has a long history. This dispute is, one might say, an episode within the history of modern Western academic politics, or even, to use Edward Said's influential concept, an episode within the history of Orientalism. The background of this dispute is aptly depicted by Norman Girardot:

> I spent considerable time tilting at windmills concerning the assumed two, and utterly distinct, forms of Daoism (the so-called *daojia* "philosophical" and *daojiao* "religious" forms). Thus throughout most of the 1970s, the dominant scholarly and popular construct of Daoism was that it was an interesting, but relatively obscure and certainly minor, sinological subject which, according to both native Chinese and Western scholarly opinion, rather neatly divided itself into an early classical, elite, or philosophical phase and a later ritualistic, superstitious, popular, or religious tradition.

It is a fact that until recent decades modern Western and Eastern scholarship on Daoism largely applied such a schema, and that this schema was not only classificatory, but also evaluative: Daoist "philosophical" texts (i.e., the *Daode jing* and the *Zhuangzi*) were normally viewed as quite respectable works of universal importance that deserved a certain recognition as great books; that is, they were seen as somewhat on par with what in the eyes of dominating Western values could be counted as theoretically or historically significant. On the other hand, the various forms of Daoist religion that have been so important throughout Chinese history and the vast number of texts included in the Daoist canon (*Daozang*) tended to be viewed as objects of mere anthropological interest or as relevant only for research on popular culture; they were not granted high-culture status on the basis of the dominating Orientalist criteria. Due to the efforts of a number of scholars (particularly in France, North America, and Germany), however, this one-sided view is, fortunately, no longer generally held. Daoist religion has not only been emancipated as a major factor in Chinese society, both historically and culturally, but, in the course of this emancipation, the traditional distinction between Daoist religion and Daoist philosophy has largely been torn down. It is now widely accepted that the Daoist classics had, from the beginning, their religious or practical aspects and that Daoist religion was not merely a degeneration of an earlier blossoming but a development in its own right that not only incorporated the classic texts but continued to produce new texts and other significant cultural products and practices.

Even though the former Orientalist hierarchy and distinction between Daoist philosophy and religion is no longer in place, the wounds have not been completely healed, as is obvious in many contributions to this volume. Some of the essays seem to indicate an attempt to reverse the former hierarchy and to establish Daoism as a primarily religious tradition, to portray the *Daodejing* as a primarily religious text and, consequently, to teach Daoism exclusively so. Livia Kohn, for instance, states very explicitly, "It is important, therefore, to make it clear from the beginning of the class that Daoism is first and foremost a religion and that, while philosophical ideas bandied about in its name have their place in this religion, they are far from dominant in it." Similarly skeptical or dismissive of a philosophical reading of Daoism, and particularly the *Daodejing*, is Russell Kirkland: "The evidence of the text [the *Daodejing*], unsystematic in any perceptible sense, demonstrates either that its composer had no philosophical positions or that, as some analysts today suggest, he was too stupid to understand or explain his own philosophy." Earlier scholars attempted to cleanse Daoist philosophy from religion, but this tide seems to have turned.

There are other contributions to this volume—although clearly the minority—that obviously do not take the *Daode jing* as a primarily religious text. David Hall, for instance, was a comparative philosopher and read the text accordingly in a philosophical way. But he concluded his essay by saying, "In closing I should note that . . . I certainly do recognize that the philosophical import of this work by no means exhausts its significance. Its poetic value, for example, is clearly as significant as its philosophical worth."

How one conceives of the *Daodejing* and Daoism, and particularly how one teaches it, is influenced by the department one is employed by or was educated in. I am unable to come up with a statistical survey, but it seems to me that the provenience of the contributors to this volume is, by and large, representative for where and how the *Daode jing* is taught in present-day North America. It is now pretty common to have experts on Eastern religions in departments of religious studies, or to even have positions for teaching Asian religions. It is very telling that we are now academically used to speaking of religions and literatures in the plural, inclusive of non-Western ones. This is not yet so common when it comes to philosophy: How many departments of philoso-ph*ies*, not to mention Asian philosophies, are there? Here, Daoism and the *Daode jing* are not yet as emancipated as in religious studies. Still, the *Daode jing* is taught in an increasing number of introductory and even advanced courses outside of Chinese and religious studies.

It is hard to definitely say what kind of text the *Daode jing* is. I suppose that the *Daode jing* in itself is not accessible, and none of the contributors to this volume seems to claim such an access. Even historically, however, the *Daode jing* was approached—in China and elsewhere—in very different ways, and the imposing of labels such as philosophy, religion, or literature is, in-evitably, an effect of the present academic discourse that issues, and cannot but issue, such labels. The *Daode jing*, historically speaking, did not come with any of them. Like the Dao, it does not speak. It is our lecturing and writing, for better or worse, that makes it speak.

NOTES

1. Both Henricks and Hall come up with very different versions of this line in their respective English translations of the whole text.

2. His well-known *Source Book in Chinese Philosophy* (Princeton: Princeton University Press, 1963) is still reprinted and widely used in North American universities.

PART I

Approaching the *Daode Jing*

Third-Person and First-Person Approaches to the Study of the *Laozi*

Harold D. Roth

As a scholar, teacher, and sometime reconstructor of the religious thought of the early Daoist tradition whose academic position has been housed for two decades in a department of religious studies, I have done a considerable amount of thinking of late about how best to approach the study and teaching of the textual materials that are my primary sources. Because of the considerable exegetical literature on the *Daode jing* that has accumulated over two millennia, it has been necessary to bring a degree of organization to this material and to develop some clarity about the perspectives that can be found in this hermeneutic corpus before presenting it to a modern audience. Moreover, given the context in which we teach in recent times, it is also important to deeply consider how we are to approach the thought found in ancient religious texts in a manner that both utilizes recent historical scholarship and respects the integrity of the ideas and the experiences that led to them that are found in these texts.

The academic study of Asian religious traditions in North America has, in the past several decades, taken a turn in the direction of the social sciences as a corrective to the tendency among some in earlier generations to idealize them (when they weren't excoriating them for being inferior to Christianity or seeing them as odd variants of it), and this is certainly a welcome development.[1] However, far too often extreme forms of historicism, the doctrine that knowledge of human affairs has an irreducibly historical character, and of social constructionism, the claim that all human phenomena are socially constructed artifacts, have been applied in a far from unbiased fashion by scholars with their own personal axes to grind against specific Asian religious traditions or by scholars who want to lump these traditions together with the Christian and Jewish traditions that they have personally rejected. Deluding themselves into thinking they have an objective or scientific viewpoint, they have established their entire careers on "debunking" the religious thought, practices, and underlying experiences of Asian religious traditions without the slightest bit of awareness about the methodological or personal axes they are grinding or the extent to which they remain confined within an essentially Western religious *Problematik* that is far from scientific or objective.[2]

One of the foundational assumptions of this body of reductionistic scholarship on Asian religious traditions is that practitioners, including the authors of the religious texts we study, are essentially deluding themselves and their followers when they assert that there is an ineffable transcendent or sacred dimension to human experience (viz., "The Way that can be spoken of is not the constant Way").[3] Yet since most Asian religious traditions affirm the interpenetration of the sacred in the secular, to begin by denying it and then look for reductive explanations for why it cannot be possible is to approach the study of these Asian traditions from a perspective that is deeply partial and flawed.[4] It is a perspective, however, with which we are extremely comfortable because it is a foundational element of the worldview in which most Western scholars have been raised. Yet it is an element whose dogmatic origins remain largely unexamined. In the traditional ontologies of the Abrahamic religions, there is a fundamental division between Creator and Creation, sacred and secular. Thus there can be nothing sacred in the secular. Whether or not one believes in a transcendent sacred realm, there can be nothing sacred in the everyday world of mundane experience that we all inhabit. Thus both believers and nonbelievers make the same unexamined assumption. To have this as part of one's system of religious beliefs is one thing, but to have it guide one's "objective" scholarship is, to paraphrase Sartre, *mauvaise foi* of the highest order. Yet this assumption has come to dominate the study and teaching of Asian religious traditions in North America, greatly to our detriment.

From my own perspective, I am interested in the possibility that there is something more to the "sacred" than either believers think or reductionist scholars automatically deny. For me there is the distinct possibility that the ancient Daoist texts that have come down to us contain insights into the nature, activity, and context of human consciousness that just might be applicable to modern human beings. Toward this end I myself have practiced meditation within several Asian traditions—Hindu, Buddhist, and Daoist— with an eye toward identifying their techniques of training of the attention and imagination and personally examining their effects. Rather than biasing my research with unprovable religious doctrine, as some religious studies scholars would suggest, this has given me an additional methodological tool for conducting a fair and balanced analysis of the very insights into consciousness that others assume to be false and dogmatic.

The question I want to return to is this: How is it possible to be both historically accurate yet nonreductionistic? How is it possible to both respect the ideas and underlying experiences found in ancient religious texts, yet also be critical of their authors' understanding of themselves and their traditions? In recent years in my teaching I have begun to develop a philosophy of how to approach these texts. I frame the problem in terms of what might be called third-person and first-person methods of studying religious texts and traditions.

The modern North American academy is dominated by what we might call third-person learning. We observe, analyze, record, and discuss a whole variety of subjects at a distance, as something "out there," as if they were solely objects and our own subjectivity that is viewing them doesn't exist. Certainly there are exceptions: in public speaking one both reads books about the subject and actually practices it; in studio art, a course wouldn't go very far if students didn't have the chance to practice on paper or canvas what they are being taught. The same is true for some courses in music: theory is appreciated so much more by actually playing the music that exemplifies it. The experimental sciences are all about applying third-person learning in controlled laboratory settings; at least in physics, the effect of the subjectivity of the observer who sets up the experiments is known to be an integral part of the results.

In many of the humanities we tend to value third-person learning at the expense of all other forms. Yet do we not find that when students are called on, for example, to reflect on what a famous poem means to them, they derive a deeper understanding of its meaning? Or when students are challenged to apply ethical theories to problems in their own lives, that they learn useful tools and see the relevance of these formerly abstract theories?

In my teaching I have done rather extensive experiments in what I would call critical first-person learning. I say "critical" because in many forms of first-person learning in the contexts of religion, one must suspend critical judgment and believe in the truth of the tradition one is embracing. There is an important place for this form of committed first-person learning, but we should be careful to not require that kind of commitment from any of our students in a secular university. But why not allow them to get some firsthand experience of, for example, such practices as Buddhist insight meditation or Confucian adherence to family rituals or Daoist energy circulation (*daoyin*) in a totally secular context, in which the need to believe in a creed is removed, in which students simply need to be willing to conduct simple observations in the only laboratory we always carry along with us wherever we go: our Beings? Why not attempt to use this experience as a basis for reconstructing the worldview of the people who created these texts, rather than assuming that it is totally impossible to do because human experience is totally determined by culture and hence incommensurable across cultures and times?

I would like to suggest that one way of approaching the study and teaching of Asian religious traditions that is both sympathetic and critical is to combine first- and third-person approaches to them. Toward this end I present some ideas on how to do this while studying the *Daode jing*.

Third-Person Approaches to Studying the *Daode jing*

I teach the *Daode jing* in a number of lecture courses and advanced seminars, from a "Foundations of Chinese Religions" course that includes everything from oracle bones to the *Huainanzi*, to a "Laozi and the *Daode jing*" advanced seminar in which the occasional student is able to read classical Chinese. I try to remain consistent in the overall approaches I use to study the text if I am not always able to follow each approach to the depth I would like. These three approaches are:

1. History: presenting the best understanding of the historical context of the text
2. Historical hermeneutics: uncovering the worldview—the practices, experiences, and beliefs—of those who created the text
3. Relevance: responsibly retrieving insights from the text into our modern context[5]

The methodological approaches I use to do this are primarily of the kind I have called third-person, but I also use a critical first-person approach that I call "reconstructive meditation" in helping to give my students some insights into both the historical hermeneutics and the contemporary relevance of the *Laozi*.

History

The foundation of any enlightened study of the ideas in the *Daode jing* is a thorough grounding in what we can establish about its actual history. The primary source for this is the text itself in its various redactions and other closely related texts that were rough contemporaries, such as *Guanzi's Neiye*

(Inward Training) and related texts and certain parts of the *Zhuangzi, Lush-iqunqiu, Huang-Lao po-shu,* and *Huainanzi.*[6]

The textual history of the *Laozi* is complex and, to my way of thinking, absolutely riveting. Until the publication of Rudolph Wagner's *A Chinese Reading of the Daode jing* in 2003, the best way for nonspecialists to read about the various recensions and redactions of the text and its major commentaries was in several scholarly essays written by Wagner and William Boltz.[7] Brief introductions to the excavated recension from Mawangdui (ca. 200 B.C.E.) and to the "proto-*Laozi*" from Guodian (ca. 310 B.C.E.) by Lau, Henricks, Mair, and Henricks, respectively, touch upon some of these major issues as well; that of Lau is the most detailed.[8] However, Wagner's book is by far the most thorough, especially his meticulous reconstruction of the most important commentary ever written on the *Laozi,* that of Wang Bi (226–249 C.E.) and the redaction of the *Laozi* text on which it was based. In establishing a critical edition of this lost redaction, Wagner provides textual variants from the excavated recensions and from major redactions in the *textus receptus* (received text) that, although it was transmitted with the Wang Bi commentary, was actually primarily a text associated with another early commentary more closely allied with Daoist religious practice, that of Heshang Gong (n.d.).[9]

I often have the students in my *Laozi* seminar get a feel for these textual variants by having them compare translations of some of the major chapters between the Mawangdui and received recensions, but it is only those few who can read Chinese that really get a good sense of this. This is because translations of the received text alone vary so much that it is difficult for a non–Chinese reader to know when the differences are caused by genuine textual variants or by the translators' varying understandings of the text. One translation that can potentially overcome this difficulty is the bilingual *Tao Te Ching* of D. C. Lau, which contains his translation of the received text in part 1 and that of the Mawangdui recension in part 2. However, as the book's dust jacket notes state, on occasion "the translator has taken the opportunity to give the translation an overdue revision." Unfortunately, he places those corrections in his translation in part 2, thus negating its use for comparative purposes.[10] In these cases I have to fall back on my own knowledge of Chinese to guide students past this problem.

While one must go to a variety of mainly Chinese sources to learn about the Mawangdui excavations and texts, there is a superb source for the details of the excavations from Guodian that yielded several texts with many parallels with the extant *Laozi* recensions. This is *The Guodian Laozi: Proceedings of the International Conference, Dartmouth College, May, 1998,* edited by Sarah Allan and Crispin Williams.[11] Consisting of essays based on papers presented at the conference and of a record of the discussions that ensued therein, it presents details of the tomb excavations and contents; details of the three bundles of bamboo slips that contain parallel material to the extant recensions of the *Laozi* and their textual significance; early discussions of a short, heretofore unknown text included in bundle 3, "Vast Unity Generates Water" (*Taiyi shengshui*); and it concludes with Edmund Ryden's critical edition of the texts contained in the three bundles.[12] This is essential reading for advanced students. Although some have argued that these Guodian parallels to all or part of thirty-three *Laozi* verses are an anthology taken from an already complete eighty-one-verse text, I have concluded that in light of the textual variations internal to the parallels, the total lack of alternative corroborating evidence to the existence of a complete *Laozi* until at least sixty years after the tomb was sealed, the eleven partial parallels, and the many variations in characters, order, and structure between the Guodian texts and their parallels in the extant recensions, this scenario is highly unlikely.[13] Instead, these Guodian *Laozi* parallels constitute an early attempt to assemble a coherent text from a more general body of "Daoist" philosophical verse, a corpus of probably originally oral material that was also drawn on to create "Inward Training." Whether these Guodian texts represent a kind of intermediate stage to the extant *Laozi* (a "proto-*Laozi*," if you wish) or simply an early failed attempt to draw from this corpus out of which the complete eighty-one-verse *Laozi* was later assembled cannot be determined at this time.

The next task in studying the textual history of the *Daode jing* is to identify its literary genre and to derive the historical evidence it might yield. The early research of Bernard Karlgren pointed out the verse nature of much of the text, but it is the masterful essay by William Baxter for a collection entitled *Lao-Tzu and the Tao-te-Ching*, edited by Livia Kohn and Michael LaFargue, that specifies with a great deal more precision the types of verse, its dating relative to other early Chinese poetic sources, and its larger literary and philosophical context that links it to "Inward Training" and the three other "Techniques of the Mind" texts in *Guanzi*.[14] Baxter's analysis of the rhetorical structures and the phonological characteristics of the *Laozi* in comparison to those of these *Guanzi* texts and to the *Book of Odes* and *Elegies of Ch'u* indicate a mid-fourth-century B.C.E. date for it and that "the *Lao-tzu* and similar texts emerged from a distinctive tradition of philosophical verse with strong oral elements and little concept of individual authorship" (249). The literary genre he identifies contrasts with the narrative genre found in the other major sources of early Daoist thought, *Zhuangzi* and *Huainanzi*, a point that should not be overlooked. Baxter's essay is very important for intermediate and advanced students, and even those without Chinese can get some valuable insights from it.

Further conclusions on the date and origins of the *Daode jing* and the myth of its reputed sixth-century B.C.E. author are found in A. C. Graham's "The Origins of the Legend of Lao Tan."[15] Therein he conclusively demonstrates how a Confucian story of Master Kong being given instruction in the Rites from a Zhou historiographer by the name of Lao Dan became the basis for the attribution of the text of the *Laozi* to this same figure at some point in the first half of the third century B.C.E. It was a masterful stroke to make the founder of their main rival's tradition a student of their own, and it bespeaks a conflict between Confucians and proponents of the *Laozi*, wherein they both were competing for political power and influence at a local state court (perhaps the Qin court of Lu Buwei). Writings from both traditions are certainly found in the philosophical work produced there in about 240 B.C.E., the *Lushiqunqiu*, and it is in this text that we have the earliest clear statement that Lao Dan taught Confucius.

Despite the historical origins of the text, the legend of a sixth-century B.C.E. founder of the Daoist tradition has persisted into modern times and has been elaborated on in both the literati tradition and in the organized Daoist religion. Livia Kohn's essay "The Lao Tzu Myth," gives a valuable overview of the various legends that have developed surrounding Laozi and draws on the insights of Anna Seidel's important and detailed study, *La divinization de Lao-tseu dan le Taoisme du Han.*[16]

So, to wrap things up, what I find important to communicate to my students about the historical context of the *Laozi* are the following:

1. An understanding of the *Daode jing* must be grounded in its textual history.
2. The legends surrounding the book are influential and must be understood.
3. It is a collection of mostly rhymed verse that contains some framing, and it was built up in a number of stages that cannot now readily be ascertained.
4. It is representative of a literary genre of "Daoist" didactic poetry that also includes *Guanzi*'s four "Techniques of the Mind" texts.
5. A complete eighty-one-chapter recension seems to have been established by the middle of the third century B.C.E., and not earlier.

Historical Hermeneutics

A decade ago Michael LaFargue published his monumental study of the hermeneutics of the *Laozi*, entitled *Tao and Method: A Reasoned Approach to the Tao Te Ching*, and in a single stroke reestablished the legitimacy of the attempt to reconstruct the original meaning of the text, or at least the series of ideas shared by its compilers and their audience (its "competence").[17] This work, seriously underappreciated by sinologists, at one and the same time drives a stake into the heart of postmodernist claims that the text is nothing more than the personal understandings of its readers and of modernist claims that the *Laozi* supports one or another of their own personal philosophical beliefs. Although I might not agree with all the ideas he identifies as significantly constitutive of the philosophical milieu of the text (especially his Mencian emphasis) or with every single literary genre he identifies in its eighty-one verses, his insights, derived initially from methods he learned as a New Testament textual scholar, have advanced the historical hermeneutics of all early Chinese philosophical texts.

Agreeing with the importance of the attempt to establish the original meaning of the *Laozi* to its authors, compilers, and audience, I have looked instead to a group of early texts that I conclude constitute an early Daoist tradition that was centered on the cosmology of the Way and on methods of "inner cultivation" by which to directly access the Way in one's everyday existence.[18] By using a methodology based on identifying a constellation of key technical terms in each of these works and organizing them into three basic categories—cosmology, inner cultivation, and political thought—I have been able to build on the insights of Graham and Liu Xiaogan to argue that the early Daoist tradition consisted of a series of loosely connected master disciple lineages, all grounded in the meditative practice of inner cultivation.[19] The texts in these lineages all share a common cosmology and inner cultivation vocabulary but differ in their political philosophy. Elaborating on Graham's divisions that he applied only to the *Zhuangzi*, I have argued that there are three aspects to early Daoist tradition: individualist, primitivist, and syncretist.[20] I do not think these are really three distinct and separate lineages but rather three aspects of a loosely organized tradition that coalesced into what we might call a philosophical school (rivaling the Confucians and the Mohists) only in the middle of the third century B.C.E. under the syncretist aspect, which might also, with some confidence, be identified by the terms used a century and a half later by the Han historians Sima Tan and Sima Qian as both Daojia (Daoist school) and Huang-Lao. It is quite possibly to this group that we owe the establishment of the myth of Confucius's "teacher," Lao Dan, as the author of the *Laozi* and the founder of their tradition. *Laozi* is a text from the primitivist aspect, although its advocacy of *wu-wei* government and critiques of Confucian values are much less strident than the other sources in this category, chapters 8–10 and the first third of chapter 11 of the *Zhuangzi*.

While the political philosophy of the *Laozi* is interesting, for me the challenge is to understand the role of inner cultivation in the text. Much of the insights about it seem couched in deliberately opaque or metaphoric language, designed to be understood within a small circle of practitioners yet, ironically, destined to be used for centuries by those who had no idea of its basis in breath cultivation. A good example of this is chapter 56, which begins with a sentence that is usually translated this way:

1. One who knows does not speak; one who speaks does not know.

I recall a former professor of mine (and he is certainly not alone in this) who used to love to point out the hypocrisy in Laozi saying this and then writing a text of five thousand characters. But this misses the entire point of the verse, which can only be understood by reading on:

2a. Block the openings;
2b. Shut the doors.
3a. Blunt the sharpness;
3b.Untangle the knots;
3c. Soften the glare;
4. Let your wheels move only along old ruts.
5. This is known as the Profound Merging (*xuan tong*).

Reading this passage in the context of the apophatic inner cultivation techniques of reducing sensory stimulation (2a+b), perceptual distinctions (3a), emotional bonds (3b), and intellectual activity (3c) that leads to relaxed breathing (4) and eventual union with the Dao, the first two lines take on a very different meaning. They indicate that what follows is an esoteric teaching that must be learned through personal instruction from an adept and can be truly understood only through the experience of inner cultivation. This, in turn, provides the justification to accept the textual variants of the Mawangdui recension of the first line, leading to a more precise translation: [21]

1. Those who understand it [i.e., the following saying] do not talk about it; those who talk about it do not understand it.

This is just one example of how an understanding that the intellectual milieu of the *Laozi* was conversant with inner cultivation practices can help us to get a sense of the hidden meaning in some of its more obscure passages.[22]

Another compelling insight of LaFargue is that each of the eighty-one *zhang* (chapters) of the *Daode jing* is a unique individual composition whose elements are distinct literary genres he identifies. To a certain extent Lau had pointed the way to this insight decades earlier in the way he chose to format his translation, clearly indicating (p. xl) rhymed verse by indentation and single lines and subdividing each chapter into component sections that could stand on their own.[23] Interestingly enough, the Guodian *Laozi* parallels confirm this general insight: eleven of the thirty-two passages are complete syntactic and semantic units that are fragments of whole chapters in the major extant recensions, and many of these correspond to subdivisions in the Lau and LaFargue translations. Here are two examples related to inner cultivation practice:

Guodian A XII

The space between heaven and earth, is it not like a bellows?
Empty it out and it is not exhausted;
Activate it and it continues to come forth.[24]

This is one of three distinct units for Lau (four for LaFargue) in chapter 5 of the received text, famous for statements about "straw dogs" (which the director Sam Peckinpah found compelling). Donald Harper has found a similar bellows analogy in early macrobiotic hygiene literature, where it refers to a type of breathing in which the *qi* is circulated in the body. I agree with him in asserting that it has this meaning in the *Laozi* as well.[25]

Guodian A XIII

Attaining emptiness is the apogee (of our practice)
Holding fast to the center is its governing mode.[26]

The myriad things arise side by side
And residing here, I see them slowly return
The forms of heaven are great in number
But each returns to its root.[27]

LaFargue sees these as two distinct units, the first a general comment about self-cultivation and the second a description of what one does in meditation.[28] Lau, however, sees the following lines as being part of the same semantic unit:

Returning to one's roots is known as stillness.
This is meant by returning to one's destiny.
Returning to one's destiny is known as the constant.
Knowledge of the constant is known as discernment.

There is further material in this chapter that is clearly from a different textual unit. In light of the Guodian parallels it appears as if this latter unit is a commentarial addition that was perhaps created in the composition of this chapter.

The Guodian *Laozi* parallels clearly demonstrate that the chapters in all extant recensions of the text were built up from smaller independent units of verse, commentary, and framing. It is extremely important to keep this in mind when teaching the *Laozi* to even introductory audiences. For my advanced courses I include a reading of Robert Henricks's careful translation of these textual parallels, which may or may not constitute an independent text in their own right.[29] I sometimes have students read these Guodian parallels before they read the received text of *Laozi* and ask them to analyze it without reference to the latter. They invariably see about as much coherence to them as they do to the received text.

Hence, historical hermeneutics is an extremely important tool in the pedagogy of *Laozi*. Establishing as much as we can about the intellectual milieu of its creators can help control the tendency among many of us who have embraced the text to interpret it as a support for a wide variety of quite modern intellectual positions.

Contemporary Relevance

To a great extent, much of what has been written throughout the ages about the philosophy of the *Laozi* falls under this heading. This includes all the major and minor commentaries, from *Huainanzi*'s "Daoying" (Responses of the Way) essay in the second century B.C.E. to Yuan Emperor Taizu in the fourteenth century C.E.[30] Alan Chan's essay in the Kohn-LaFargue anthology gives a solid comparison of the two most influential commentaries, the Heshang gong and Wang Bi, while Isabelle Robinet's essay in the same volume provides an excellent overview of the later and virtually unknown commentaries.[31] This approach also includes the many modern philosophers who attempt to explain the ideas of the text in terms of ideas from the intellectual contexts in which they are working. There are too many thinkers in this group to inclusively list here, but a few of the most prominent are Fung Yu-lan, Chad Hansen, Liu Xiaogan, A. C. Graham, Benjamin Schwartz, Roger Ames, and numerous authors whose work has been published in *Philosophy East and West* over the past five decades. The *Religious and Philosophical Aspects of the Laozi*, edited by Mark Csikszentmihalyi and P. J. Ivanhoe contains some interesting examples of such philosophical interpretations. And then there are the scores of modern Chinese thinkers who we could include and the myriad uses in popular Western culture such as the *Tao of Pooh* and George Lucas's "Force." Julia Hardy's essay, "Influential Western Interpretations of the *Tao-te-ching* in the Kohn-LaFargue volume provides a thorough overview of major Western interpreters of the *Laozi*.[32]

While some of these modern interpreters, such as Liu Xiaogan, clearly state that they are adapting the *Daode jing* for modern uses because of the deep insights it contains into the human condition, many interpreters and all traditional commentators assert that they are uncovering the true meaning of the text. Despite this, I would argue that many, in their use of philosophical perspectives from their own intellectual milieu, are in reality interested in the contemporary relevance of the text. That is, they wish to retrieve responsibly the ideas in the text they find most relevant today. I could not agree more with the following assertion by Robinet:

> They [the commentaries] develop a sense of contemporality that can be received by people of their own time and is relevant to their world, a world more likely than not dominated by a vastly different kind of thinking, such as Confucianism and Buddhism. To dissolve the distance between the period and culture, in which the text evolved, the reader of another time must either make the text contemporaneous to the reader or make the reader contemporaneous to the text. This is the task commentaries typically set for themselves, aiming at translating the text into a more current language while circling around its obscurities, lessening its paradoxes, and reducing its originality. They reshape the document for a newer taste, frequently using syncretistic forms of interpretation.[33]

In teaching the *Laozi*, one of the absolutely essential things to keep in mind is to clearly distinguish between contemporary interpretations of the text and whatever we can establish of the text's original meanings through historical hermeneutics. There is absolutely nothing wrong with discovering something of value for our contemporary world in the ideas of the *Laozi*. Indeed, I think its teachings on inner cultivation contain valuable insights for us. But it is important to differentiate between what we can reasonably establish about the "original meaning" of the text through careful examination of its history and its larger intellectual context and the contemporary philosophical positions we use to interpret it.

A Critical First-Person Approach: Reconstructive Meditation

I would like to close with a section about a new approach I have taken in teaching the *Laozi* that adds the critical first-person element I advocated in my introduction. This is engaging students in what I call reconstructive meditation, the logic of which runs as follows:

1. The creators of the *Laozi* practiced a form of breath meditation that led them to deeper and deeper states of tranquility and to what they asserted was an eventual merging with the Way.[34]
2. They applied the clarity of mind developed through this meditation to the tasks of everyday life, hence developing, for example, the notion of "effortless action" (*wu-wei*).[35]
3. Despite vast differences in cultural contexts, human beings in the third century B.C.E. in China had essentially the same physiology of body and mind as do modern humans. This assumption is widely accepted in evolutionary biology and neuroscience.[36]
4. Thus, practicing breath meditation should have largely similar physiological effects on us as it did on them, although we, of course, conceive of the underlying mechanisms in entirely different fashions.

Based on these assumptions, I have developed a series of reconstructive meditations for students linked to passages in the *Daode jing*. Herewith two examples:

Bellows Breathing

The space between heaven and earth, is it not like a bellows?
Empty it out and it is not exhausted;
Activate it and it continues to come forth

Laozi 5 speaks of the space between heaven and earth being like a bellows. Early Chinese physiological hygiene texts linked this bellows to the natural movements of the diaphragm as it inhales and exhales.

Instructions: Sitting upright in a comfortable position and with eyes closed (remember: "The Five Colors blind men's eyes"; *Laozi* 12), imagine your diaphragm to be a bellows and simply follow its movements as you inhale and exhale. Do this for ten (or more, depending on prior experience of students) minutes, then stop.

Observing Consciousness While "Holding Fast to the Center"

Attaining emptiness is the apogee (of our practice)
Holding fast to the center is its governing mode.

The myriad things arise side by side
And residing here, I see them slowly return
The forms of heaven are great in number
But each returns to its root.

Laozi 16 recommends gradually emptying out consciousness through a process of "holding fast to the center." I interpret this to mean concentrating on the feeling of inhaling and exhaling as you experience it in the center of your body, somewhere in your abdomen. For some of you it may be as high as the solar plexus; for others it may be as low as the spot later called the "cinnabar field," three finger-widths below your abdomen.

Instructions: Sitting upright in a comfortable position, concentrate on your breathing and determine where it is centered in your abdomen. Carefully follow your breathing through its cycles of inhalation and exhalation. This is "holding fast to the center."

When you are established in this breathing, open your focus to allow in the various thoughts and feelings that inevitably arise when attempting to sit quietly. Pay careful attention to where they come from. Notice how they arise and invariably pass away. Pay attention to where they go to. Do not follow them; do not react to them; always maintain an awareness of your center of breathing and simply continue watching thoughts and feelings as they arise and pass away. This arising of something out of nothing is basic to your consciousness as microcosm and to the entire cosmos as macrocosm.

Conclusions

These reconstructive meditations help give students a sense of the experiential basis underlying not a few passages in the *Laozi* and start to provide some insight into the possible origins of the cosmology for which the text is renowned. I do not by any means wish to assert that these reconstructions are the exclusive original meaning of these passages; I only wish to assert that they may point to their possible experiential bases. In the end, reconstructive meditation is just another wrench in the toolbox of the scholar and teacher of the *Laozi*, another way to approach its meaning without reducing it to a series of ideas intended to deliberately confuse its audience and reinforce some very Western biases about the essentially rational and profane nature of human experience. It can provide new insights into the history of the text, the "competence" of its authors, composers, and audience, and can also contribute some insights into the nature of consciousness that some may find of contemporary relevance. It is in these ways that reconstructive meditation can augment the other three approaches.

NOTES

I wish to thank Henry Rosemont Jr., Erin Kline, and Michael Slater for their helpful criticisms of this manuscript but absolve them of all blame for whatever questionable assertions and contentious opinions I decided to retain.

1. R. C. Zaehner, *Mysticism, Sacred and Profane* (Oxford: Oxford University Press, 1961), argues that Christian mysticism is superior to all other forms. James Ware, *Alchemy, Medicine and Religion in the China of* A.D. *320: The Nei Pien of Ko Hung* (New York: Dover, 1963), consistently translates Dao as "God."

2. Propriety (*li*) prevents me from being any more specific about this except to say that most of the scholars I have in mind do *not* work on Daoism. And that is an interesting phenomenon in itself!

3. For a good example of this, see Wayne Proudfoot's assertion in *Religious Experience* (Berkeley: University of California Press, 1987), 128–130, that the *Daode jing* uses paradoxical statements about the nature of the Dao to establish its ineffability, which is thus a feature of grammar and not of experience. By implication, the Dao is not a genuine power or force but a product of the linguistic manipulations of its inventors and the subsequent beliefs of its followers.

4. Of course, Herbert Fingarette got it right in his field-revising study of the *Analects: Confucius—The Secular as Sacred,* 2nd ed. (Prospect Heights, Ill.: Waveland, 1998).

5. The categories of "historical hermeneutics" and "contemporary relevance" are found in the writings of Michael LaFargue. The most accessible is "Recovering the *Tao-te-ching*'s Original Meaning," in *Lao-tzu and the Tao-te-ching,* ed. Livia Kohn and Michael LaFargue (Albany: State University of New York Press, 1998), 231–254.

6. For a detailed discussion of the relationship between the *Daode jing* and *Neiye* and these other texts, see my book *Original Tao: Inward Training (Nei-yeh) and the Foundations of Taoist Mysticism.* New York: Columbia University Press, 1999, in particular 144–153, 185–190.

7. Rudolph G. Wagner, *A Chinese Reading of the Daode jing: Wang Bi's Commentary on the Laozi with Critical Text and Translation.* (Albany: State University of New York Press, 2003). See also the following essays: Rudolph G. Wagner, "Interlocking Parallel Style: Laozi and Wang Bi," *Journal Asiatiques* 34, no. 1 (1980): 18–58; William Boltz, "The Religious and Philosophical Significance of the 'Hsiang erh' *Lao Tzu* in the Light of the Ma-wang-tui Silk Manuscripts," *Bulletin of the School of Oriental and African Studies* 45 no. 1 (1982): 95–117; William Boltz, "Textual Criticism and the Ma-Wang-Tui Silk Manuscripts," *Harvard Journal of Asiatic Studies.* 44, no. 1 (1984): 185–224; William Boltz, "The *Lao Tzu* Text That Wang Pi and Ho-shang Kung Never Saw," *Bulletin of the School of Oriental and African Studies* 48, no. 5 (1985): 493–501. The best overview of the text and commentaries of the *Laozi* is Boltz's *Lao tzu Tao te ching,* in *Early Chinese Texts: A Bibliographical Guide,* ed. Michael Loewe, Early China Special Monograph Series no. 2 (Berkeley: Institute for East Asian Studies, University of California, 1993). For a succinct summary of the textual issues relevant to *Laozi* and other early philosophical texts, see Harold D. Roth, "Text and Edition in

Early Chinese Philosophical Literature," *Journal of the American Oriental Society* 113, no. 2 (1993): 214–227.

8. D. C. Lau, *Chinese Classics: Tao Te Ching* (Hong Kong: Chinese University Press, 1982); Robert Henricks, *Lao-Tzu: Te Tao Ching* (New York: Ballantine, 1989) Victor Mair, *Tao Te Ching: The Classic Book of Integrity and the Way* (New York: Bantam, 1990); Robert Henricks, *Lao Tzu's Tao Te Ching* (New York, Columbia University Press, 2000) (translation of Guodian *Laozi* parallels).

9. For an excellent and detailed study of the contrasting approaches of the Wang Bi and Heshang gong commentaries, see Allan Chan, *Two Visions of the Way: A Study of the Wang Pi and Ho-shang-kung Commentaries on the Lao-tzu.* Albany: State University of New York Press, 1991.

10. For details, see my review in *Philosophy East and West* 35, no. 2 (1985): 213–215.

11. Sarah Allan and Crispin Williams, eds., *The Guodian Laozi: Proceedings of the International Conference, Dartmouth College, May, 1998,* Early China Special Monograph Series no. 5 (Berkeley: Institute for East Asian Studies, University of California, , 2000).

12. Edmund Ryden, "Edition of the Bamboo-Slip *Laozi* A, B, and C, and *Tai Yi Sheng Shui* from Guodian Tomb Number One," In Allan and Williams, *The Guodian Laozi,* 187–231.

13. Harold D. Roth, "Some Methodological Issues in the Study of the Guodian *Laozi* Parallels." In Allan and Williams, *The Guodian Laozi,* 71–88.

14. William Baxter, "Situating the Language of Lao-tzu: The Probable Date of the *Tao-te-ching,*" in Kohn and LaFargue, *Lao-tzu and the Tao-te-ching,* 231–254.

15. A. C. Graham, "The Origins of the Legend of Lao Tan," 1981, in *Studies in Chinese Philosophy and Philosophical Literature* (Singapore: Institute for East Asian Philosophies, 1986), 111–124. An edited version appears in Kohn and LaFargue, *Lao-tzu and the Tao-te-ching,* 23–40.

16. Livia Kohn, "The Lao-Tzu Myth," in Kohn and LaFargue, *Lao-tzu and the Tao-te-ching,* 41–62; Anna Seidel, *La divinization de Lao-tseu dan le Taoisme du Han* (1969; Paris: École Française d'Extrême-Orient, 1992).

17. Michael LaFargue, *Tao and Method: A Reasoned Approach to the Tao Te Ching* (Albany: State University of New York Press, 1994). LaFargue earlier published a summary of his arguments from this volume together with a radically rearranged translation in Michael LaFargue, *The Tao of the Tao Te Ching* (Albany: State University of New York Press, 1992).

18. For further details, see Roth, *Original Tao,* chap. 5.

19. A. C. Graham, "How Much of *Chuang Tzu* Did Chuang Tzu Write?," in *Studies in Chinese Philosophy and Philosophical Literature* (Albany: State University of New York Press, 1990), 283–321; Liu Xiaogan, *Classifying the Zhuangzi Chapters,* trans. William Savage (Ann Arbor: Center for Chinese Studies, University of Michigan, 1994).

20. Graham initially proposed the latter two categories to represent two major authorial voices in the *Zhuangzi.* Liu Xiaogan preferred the categories "anarchist"

and "huang-lao" to Graham's "primitivist and "syncretist," but, unlike Graham, he related these voices in *Zhuangzi* to larger intellectual movements. In this aspect, I follow Liu. For the references, see the previous note.

21. I accept the Mawangdui variants of *fu yan* and *fu zhi* instead of the received text's *bu yan* and *bu zhi*. The negative adverb *fu* implies a direct object, whereas the adverb *bu* does not and is therefore more vague. The received text contains many examples of this sort, where a relatively clear text has been made vaguer and thus more "mystical." See Lau, *Chinese Classics*, 218, 80.

22. For examples of this kind, see my essay "The *Laozi* in the Context of Early Daoist Mystical Praxis," in Mark Csikszentmihalyi and P. J. Ivanhoe, eds., *Religious and Philosophical Aspects of Laozi* (Albany: State University of New York Press, 1999, 59–96. This is an excellent collection and provides a philosophical complement to the Kohn and LaFargue collection.

23. Lau, *Chinese Classics*, p. xl.

24. Ryden, Edition of the Bamboo-Slip *Laozi*, 206.

25. Donald Harper, "The Bellows Analogy in *Laozi* V and Warring States Macrobiotic Hygiene," *Early China* 20 (1995): 381–392.

26. Ryden, Edition of the Bamboo-Slip *Laozi*, 207.

27. I read the last character in the line, *tu* (sincere, serious, solid), as a loan for *tu* (also sincere, but can mean supervisor, to inspect, to correct), which when combined with the character *mai* (meridian) in Chinese medicine refers to the central supervisory meridian that controls the flow of *yang qi* in the human body. This is the reading in the Mawangdui recension. I interpret this passage to mean that the dominant mode by which emptiness is attained is by concentrating on the center. I think the center here refers to the center of the body where breathing is experienced, and thus the passage commends focusing on breathing in order to attain emptiness.

28. LaFargue, *Tao of the Tao Te Ching*, 62–63.

29. Henricks, *Lao Tzu's Tao Te Ching*.

30. The twelfth essay of the *Huainanzi*, "The Responses of the Way," consists of a series of narratives presented to illustrate various statements from the *Laozi*. Each narrative ends with the formula, "And so the *Laozi*, says . . ." This "reverse commentary" genre is also found in the "Commenting on *Laozi*" and "Explaining *Laozi*" chapters of the *Hanfeizi*.

31. Allan Chan, "A Tale of Two Commentaries: Ho-shang-kung and Wang Pi on the *Lao-tzu*," in Kohn and LaFargue, *Lao-tzu and the Tao-te-ching*, 89–118, is a summary of his book on the same subject. Isabelle Robinet, "Later Commentaries: Textual Polysemy and Syncretistic Interpretations," in Kohn and LaFargue, *Lao-tzu and the Tao-te-ching*, 119–142, is a masterful essay in which the late Professor Robinet provides insights from many *Laozi* commentaries that are virtually unknown to modern scholarship, both East Asian and Western.

32. Julia Hardy, "Influential Western Interpretations of the *Tao-te-ching*," in Kohn and LaFargue, *Lao-tzu and the Tao-te-ching*, 165–185.

33. Robinet, "Later Commentaries," 121.

34. The justification for this is detailed in my essay "The *Laozi* in the Context of Early Daoist Mystical Praxis."

35. This is one example of a more pervasive pattern of early Daoist meditation. For further details, see my essay "Evidence for Stages of Meditation in Early Taoism," *Bulletin of the School of Oriental and African Studies* 60, no. 2 (June 1997): 295–314.

36. Evolutionary biology posits that all human beings (*Homo sapiens*) share a common genetic pool, whether they live in North America or in China, whether they live today or three thousand years ago. According to geneticist F. S. Collins, human beings are "99.9% genetically identical." "Genome Research: The Next Generation," in *The Genome of Homo Sapiens*, ed. Bruce Stillman and David Stewart (Cold Spring Harbor, N.Y.: CSHL Press, 2003), 50. Geneticists Y. Sasaki et al. state, "*Homo sapiens* is a unique organism characterized by its highly developed brain, use of complex languages, bipedal locomotion, and so on. These unique features have been acquired by a series of mutation and selection events during evolution in the human lineage and are mainly determined by genetic factors encoded in the human genome. "Human versus Chimpanzee Chromosome-wide Sequence Comparison and Its Evolutionary Implications," in Stillman and Stewart, *The Genome of Homo Sapiens*, 455. This common genetic heritage leads to the common physiology and neurophysiology that distinguishes human beings from the other higher hominids.

The *Dao* and the Field: Exploring an Analogy

Robert G. Henricks

Several years ago while looking for a way to explain to a class the meaning of Laozi's *Dao* (the Way, literally a road or a path), I hit upon an analogy that has proved to be quite fruitful. It is an analogy that provides us with a model for understanding the nature of the *Dao* and the nature of its operations. It also provides us with a way to understand Laozi's moral philosophy, and it may help us understand what Laozi believed with regard to life after death/immortality.

The analogy is drawn between the *Dao* and a field—not a farmer's field which is groomed and cultivated for the purpose of raising a single, hybrid crop, but a "natural" field, one left untended, one that is barren and deserted in the winter but filled with a host of different wildflowers throughout the spring and summer.

The appropriateness of this analogy and its usefulness for understanding the thought of Laozi will become clear once we see what Laozi himself said about the *Dao*. And to begin this task there is probably no better place to start than with the beginning of the book itself, the opening lines of chapter 1:

> The *Dao* that can be told of is not the eternal *Dao*:
> The name that can be named is not the eternal name.[1]

A cryptic start to a cryptic book. Laozi tells us that anything he says about a *Dao*, after all, will not be about a true, eternal, or constant *Dao*. But at the same time he seems to confirm, in this backward way, that there is some such reality. Whatever the *Dao* might be, it is eternal and abiding. Moreover, there might be a name that is appropriate to it, a name that is equal to its reality, an eternal name, but the names we use do not qualify for such status.

All in all, the opening lines seem to suggest what is often suggested in mystic literature: that there is a transcendent, eternal reality, with which we may come into contact but that lies beyond the realm of precise description. All attempts to talk about it somehow fall short of conveying a true sense of what it is. That this is Laozi's meaning seems to be confirmed, as a matter of fact, in the very next line of chapter 1, where he calls the *Dao* the "Nameless." He adds, moreover, that in this aspect it is the origin of the phenomenal world, the beginning of all things: "The Nameless is the origin of Heaven and Earth."[2]

But the label "Nameless" can be understood in two different ways. It can mean, as we have suggested, something for which an appropriate name cannot be found. But it might also refer to a time or a condition of things—undifferentiated reality—when distinct phenomenal forms had not yet appeared, a state lacking nameable realities. The Chinese for "Nameless" (*wu ming*) allows both of these interpretations (i.e., not having a name and not having names), and as it turns out the *Dao* for Laozi is "nameless" in both ways. The *Dao* is that elusive, difficult to describe, single reality that existed prior to, and gave rise to, all other existing things.

Thus in chapter 14, where problematically "names" are assigned to the *Dao*, we find the following:

> We look at it and do not see it:
> Its name is The Invisible.
> We listen to it and do not hear it;
> Its name is The Inaudible.
> We touch it and do not find it:
> Its name is The Subtle (formless).
> These three cannot be further inquired into,
> And hence merge into one.[3]

And in chapter 25 we have this:

> There was something undifferentiated and yet complete,
> Which existed before heaven and earth.
> Soundless and formless, it depends on nothing and does not change.
> It operates everywhere and is free from danger.
> It may be considered the mother of the universe.

I do not know its name; I call [or, I would style it] *Dao*.
If forced to give it a name, I shall call it Great.[4]

This is a telling statement on the nature of the *Dao*. It reports motifs that we already know: that the *Dao* is eternal, undifferentiated, the source of the phenomenal world, and something vague and elusive. But to this is now added the sense that the *Dao* is a reality that continues to be functional after creation, insofar as it is something that operates everywhere, and of course this also tells us that it is omnipresent. Moreover, the distinction that is made here between "name" (*ming*), which we do not know, and "style" (*zi*—Wing-tsit Chan "calls it"), is informative. In China a person's name (personal name, that is, not surname) is given at birth; it is personal and rarely used in direct address. But the "style" is taken at capping age (around 20), and it is less personal, more publicly used, and less a part of that person's reality—who he or she really is. The word *Dao* has this "style" kind of relation to the reality at hand.

Laozi does venture here, when forced of course, to find some name to use for this reality, choosing the word *da*, the Great. But Kaltenmark has probably caught the import of this when he says, "It is clear that he [Laozi] is using *da* in an absolute sense: the Immense, the Incommensurable."[5]

There is one more thing that Laozi tells us in chapter 25 which is important for our understanding of the nature of the *Dao*. He says, "It may be considered the mother of the universe." When we move into the realm of image and metaphor, we find that Laozi depicts the *Dao* as a very feminine reality indeed. And to be more precise, as the line here makes clear, as something like a mother.

Three kinds of evidence can be called forth to support this and draw it out. To begin with, Laozi explicitly refers to the *Dao* as the "Mother" in no fewer than five different chapters. In addition to the reference already noted in chapter 25, in chapter 1, picking up the text where we left off, we find: "The Named is the mother of all things [literally, the ten thousand things]."[6] In chapter 20 Laozi laments that he alone values "drawing sustenance from Mother (*Dao*)."[7] Chapter 52 begins, "There was a beginning of the universe, Which may be called the Mother of the universe."[8] And in chapter 59 the statement is made, "He who possesses the Mother (*Dao*) of the state will last long."[9]

Second, the *Dao* is often pictured as womblike or vagina-like in its capacity as the source and originator of all forms. At the end of chapter 1, womb and vagina symbolism are both quite explicit. The *Dao* is said to be "deeper and more profound, the door of all subtleties."[10] An inexhaustible womb is the image portrayed at the opening of chapter 4: "*Dao* is empty (like a bowl). It may be used but its capacity is never exhausted."[11] As a womb the *Dao* would contain all things in essence or seedlike form, and chapter 21 seems to me to support this:

> The all-embracing quality of the great virtue follows alone from
> the *Dao*.
> The thing that is called *Dao* is eluding and vague.
> Vague and eluding, there is in it the form [or forms].
> Eluding and vague, in it are things.
> Deep and obscure, in it is the essence.
> The essence is very real; in it are evidences.[12]

Chapter 6, without question, is the best chapter to cite in this regard. Called here the "spirit of the valley," the valley itself being a symbol of constant fertility, the *Dao* is again described in terms of womb and vagina. But again in contrast to its mammalian counterpart, this is a source that can never be used up, one that will last forever:

> The spirit of the valley never dies.
> It is called the subtle and profound female.
> The gate of the subtle and profound female.
> Is the root of Heaven and Earth.
> It is continuous, and seems to be always existing.
> Use it and you will never wear it out.[13]

The third point to be made on behalf of the maternal nature of the *Dao* is that the *Dao* not only contains all things and brings them forth to life, but it also continues to function in a maternal way in the rearing of its children. That is to say, it nourishes them and protects them and brings them to maturity and completion. And in providing sustenance and care for all things, it has no favorites. Yet in contrast to its human counterpart, it does not seek to control and direct that growth, nor does it ever claim credit for the work it has done.

There are two chapters in the text that make this point, chapters 34 and 51. Chapter 34 reads:

> The great *Dao* flows everywhere.
> It may go left or right.
> All things depend on it for life, and it does not turn away from them.
> It accomplishes its task, but does not claim credit for it.
> It clothes and feeds all things, but does not claim to be master
> over them.
> Always without desires, it may be called the Small.

All things come to it and it does not master them; it may be called
    the Great.
Therefore (the sage) never strives himself for the great, and there
    by the great is achieved.[14]

In chapter 51 two points of interest are added: the *Dao* and its virtue (really
Power) are "naturally" honored and esteemed for what they do even though
they promise no reward (in contrast, perhaps, to the honor and esteem ac-
corded state rulers), and the involvement of the *Dao* in the *complete* life cycle of
its children is neatly underscored:

The *Dao* brings them to life and virtue nourishes them.
Substance gives them form and ability completes them.
Therefore the 10,000 things honor the Way and esteem virtue.
No one rewards this honoring of the Way and esteeming of virtue.
And yet they are constantly so of themselves.
The Way brings them to life, nourishes them, develops them, rears
    them, rests them, makes them secure, cares for them, and protects
    them.
It brings them to life, and yet it does not possess them.
It brings them to action, and yet it does not make them dependent.
It brings them to completion, and yet it does not rule over them.
This is called the Profound Virtue.[15]

We may now turn with benefit to explore the analogy. My contention is
that in the model of a *field of wildflowers passing through the seasons* we have an
almost perfect model for grasping the nature of the *Dao* in its totality—we can
see it, as it were, prior to, during, and after creation.

Let us approach it this way. Were we to go to an untended field in the midst
of the winter, we might see no form of life whatsoever. There would be nothing
but a still, silent void, with nothing for the senses to grasp. Did we not know
better, we would presumably conclude that there was no relationship whatsoever between this inert mass and the variety of forms, sounds, and smells that
we know as summer life.

But were we to return to that field sometime in mid-June, we would find
that the most marvelous of transformations had occurred. The very same field
that had been barren and still is now the scene of bustling activity, covered with
ten thousand (as it were) different forms of life. There are sunflowers and
nightshade and butter-and-eggs and chicory, hundreds of kinds of wildflowers,
all different shapes and colors and sizes, some tall and some short, some with
one big flower, others in tiny clusters, to say nothing of the many nonflowering

grasses. And just as there seems to be an infinite number of kinds, there is as well an infinite number of each kind.

It would now seem clear to our minds that what had appeared to us in winter to be an inert, sterile void was in reality a fecund, perhaps inexhaustible womb, containing the seeds for all forms of life. Had we dug into the earth in winter, of course, we would never have detected these forms—there would have been only one, undifferentiated, homogeneous earth. And yet somehow, mysteriously, in the most minute, infinitesimal forms, the seeds of all these many plants, as yet indistinguishable, were there all the time.

The work of the field does not stop with springtime creation. Just as it made no distinctions in bringing forth a variety of forms, so too it remains impartial through the summer in providing support and nourishment for all, bringing all of the plants to completion of their natural life cycles. It does this all, however, somewhat mysteriously, with no sign of any "action" on its part at all. It, like the *Dao*, does indeed do everything by seeming to do nothing at all.[16] And the marvel of it all is that though none of this would have come to be without the soil—the earth—the field itself never claims any credit. Instead, it remains in the background, assuming a low and withdrawn position. We lose sight of the real source for all this beauty; our senses are captivated by the variety of forms and colors and smells. After all, the field, in contrast, is drab and uninteresting.

In discussing our field point for point have we not in fact also been talking about Laozi's *Dao*? They are both, before they give birth, still and tranquil, the undifferentiated one. They might appear to be lifeless but are in fact fecund wombs. They both bring into being a multitude of forms and provide nourishment for all alike. They bring all things to completion but claim no credit and act without force. It is only in its cyclical character that the field seems to vary from the *Dao*. The field passes through cycles of creation and destruction, of evolution and devolution of plant life. But although the *Dao*'s forces may wax and wane, total cosmic reabsorption, a swallowing up periodically of even Heaven and Earth, does not seem to be part of its movement.

We can continue with the analogy. Although the field makes no demands on the plants for which it provides, there is one obvious condition that must be met for any flower that wants to realize its given nature, destiny, and life span, that condition being that it must keep its roots in the ground. A sunflower will never realize its "sunflowerness" and will never live the four to eight weeks possible for its species if it forgets its origins and tries to make it on its own, uprooting itself from its very source of sustenance.

It is the same for man, I think, in Laozi's terms. The only way for a man to realize his particular way of being human, and to realize his given span of years, is somehow to keep his roots planted in the *Dao*. Laozi himself tells us (in chapter 20) that he, at least, values drawing sustenance from the Mother. And in chapter 52 he talks of holding on to the Mother, even after we have become aware of her sons, and he says that one who does so will remain free from harm throughout his life:

> There was a beginning of the universe
> Which may be called the Mother of the universe.
> He who has found the mother (*Dao*)
> And thereby understands her sons (things),
> And having understood the sons,
> Still keeps to its [their] mother,
> Will be free from danger throughout his lifetime.[17]

Our analogy, however, perhaps breaks down at this point, in that Laozi seems to assume that this is precisely what most people do not do. In contrast to our flowers in the field, people can and do go against the natural way of things: they turn their backs on the mother and become uprooted. Or, to put it another way, as Laozi does in chapter 53, people ought to stay on the Great Way, a road that is broad and smooth, but somehow they all delight in bypaths.[18]

Thus, in the case of man a rupture occurs. And if a man is to be what he can be, if he is to realize his nature and destiny, a return must be made: he must get back to the highway, get back to mother *Dao*. Laozi speaks of returning to the roots in chapter 16, and perhaps this is what he means:

> Attain complete vacuity.
> Maintain steadfast quietude.
> All things come into being,
> And I see thereby their return.
> All things flourish,
> But each one returns to its root.
> This return to its root means tranquility.
> It is called returning to its destiny.
> To return to destiny is called the eternal (*Dao*).
> To know the eternal is called enlightenment.
> Not to know the eternal is to act blindly to result in disaster.[19]

The fitness of the field analogy for understanding the nature of the *Dao* ought to be clear by now. That it works so well might not be all that remarkable. One of the names used for the *Dao* at certain places in the *Zhuangzi* is in fact the "great Clod" (that is, the great lump of earth).[20] And the *Dao* that Laozi talks about sounds in many ways like the Mother Earth deities that we find in other cultures at other times. To take but one example, when the Sioux holy man Black Elk speaks of the earth in the following passage, we are reminded of things Laozi says about the *Dao*: how it is the source for all things and how he himself draws nourishment from it.

> Is not the sky a father and the earth a mother and are not all living things with feet or wings or roots their children? And the hide upon the mouthpiece here [Black Elk is describing a holy pipe],which should be bison hide, is for the earth, from whence we came and at whose breast we suck as babies all our lives, along with all the animals and birds and trees and grasses.[21]

Of course, the *Dao* is not exactly the same as Mother Earth. For example, in Black Elk's statement at least, the fecundity of the Earth is in some part dependent on the sky-father: life-giving rain and the heat of the sun come from him. Conversely, the *Dao*'s creativity seems to be self-contained, and the *Dao* as a conception of ultimate reality is both more transcendent and more universal than that which we find in the Earth Mother.[22] The *Dao* is an eternal, unchanging, invisible reality that is somehow present everywhere, not localized in space. And the *Dao* gives birth to the entire universe, including Heaven and Earth, not just to man, the animals, and plants. Moreover, the use of the name *Dao* or Way for this reality underscores the identity of it with the ongoing process of change and transformation in the universe as a whole, just as it underscores the fact that there is *a Way* for man to live, that is, to remain in touch *with the Way*.

Still, the correspondence of *Dao* and Mother Earth is interesting, and it is tempting to think that somewhere behind Laozi's conception of the *Dao* lies an earlier belief in or veneration of a Mother Earth deity in China. However, we find little indication of this in the religious beliefs and practices of dynastic times. There is, apparently, evidence in the oracle bones of Shang (c. 1766–1122 B.C.) of sacrifices to the Earth, and the Zhou (c. 1122–249 B.C.) did offer periodic sacrifices to the Earth, or at least to the Gods of the Land, at the *she* altars.[23] But in both cases, that is, in both the Shang and the Zhou, the masculine deities in the heavens, Shangdi (the Lord on High) and Tian (Heaven), and the royal ancestors held center stage.[24]

This is a question that could be further explored. Perhaps this is simply another indication of Laozi's southern origins; the goddess form and the sacredness of the earth were perhaps more important in Chu.[25]

I claimed at the start that the field analogy also sheds light on other aspects of Laozi's thought, and I would like to show how this works with two issues in particular: morality and immortality.

Although there are passages in the *Laozi* that could be interpreted to suggest that Laozi's ideal sage is harsh, calculating, and inhumane,[26] the overall tenor of the text is moral. To put it more precisely, Laozi seems to have little quarrel with the Confucian ideal of the "good man," namely, the man who is filial to his parents, compassionate to his children, loyal to his prince, and genuine in all his relationships. Laozi's quarrel with the Confucians is rather one of method. He implies that left alone, people would *naturally* manifest these traits, and that consciousness of virtue—that there is a "good" way to act that needs to be cultivated—in fact destroys the possibility of genuineness and spontaneity, without which there can be no true virtue.

This is what I conclude from reading the two passages where he attacks the Confucian virtues of humaneness (*ren*), righteousness (*yi*), and propriety (*li*), first in chapters 18 and 19 (which should be read as continuous) and then in chapter 38. From chapter 18:

> When the great *Dao* declined,
> The doctrine of humanity and righteousness arose.
> When knowledge and wisdom appeared,
> There emerged great hypocrisy.
> When the six family relationships are not in harmony,
> There will be advocacy of filial piety and deep love to children.
> When a country is in disorder,
> There will be the praise of loyal ministers.

From chapter 19:

> Abandon sageliness and discard wisdom;
> Then the people will benefit a hundredfold.
> Abandon humanity and discard righteousness;
> Then the people will return to filial piety and deep love.
> Abandon skill and discard profit;
> Then there will be no thieves and robbers.

From chapter 38:

> The man of superior virtue is not (conscious of) his virtue,
> And in this way he really possesses virtue.
> The man of inferior virtue never loses sight of his virtue,

And in this way he loses his virtue.
The man of superior virtue takes no action,
but has no ulterior motive to do so.
The man of inferior virtue takes action,
And has an ulterior motive to do so.
The man of superior humanity takes action,
But has no ulterior motive to do so.
The man of superior righteousness takes action,
and has an ulterior motive to do so.
The man of superior propriety takes action,
And when people do not respond to it, he will stretch his arms
   and force it on them.
Therefore when *Dao* is lost, only then does the doctrine of
   virtue arise.
When humanity is lost, only then does the doctrine of righteous-
   ness arise.
When righteousness is lost, only then does the doctrine of propri-
   ety arise.
Now, propriety is a superficial expression of loyalty and faithful-
   ness and the beginning of disorder.
Those who are the first to know have the flowers of *Dao* but are
   the beginning of ignorance.
For this reason the great man dwells with the thick, and does not rest
   with the thin.
He dwells with the fruit, and does not rest with the flower.
Therefore he rejects the one, and accepts the other.[27]

The analogy to the field might make this clearer. I interpret Laozi to be saying that all people feel and express compassion, filial piety, loyalty, and humaneness, and perhaps righteousness and propriety, just as all black-eyed susans have yellow flowers with a brown cone, daisylike heads of ten to twenty rays, and hairy stems of one to three feet in length. This is the natural condition of things, and just as in the natural field black-eyed susans grow this way spontaneously, unaware of it, in a sense effortlessly, so too, when the *Dao* has not declined, do people feel and express these attitudes spontaneously, effortlessly, and without self-consciousness.

However, that is not to say that they all do so in the same way at the same time. Just as black-eyed susans differ from one another in their number of petals, in their length of stalks, and even perhaps in their shade of color, so too do people differ in their degree of feelings and their modes of expression.

But the evaluation of certain feelings and actions, the labeling of them as good, brings about self-consciousness and inevitably leads to the defining of a standard. The cultivation of virtue, like the cultivation of a field, aims at developing a hybrid crop by weeding out variety. This means that one way of expressing loyalty will be set up as the true way; there will be only one true way to be filial in any given situation. And it would be comparable to saying that all black-eyed susans ought to have, say, fifteen petals, stems of two feet, and a dark shade of yellow to be "good" black-eyed susans.

If flowers are anything like people the results of this would be (a) conflict, as each flower takes its own properties as the standard for all to follow; (b) hypocrisy, as flowers deny their given properties and try to become something they are not; and (c) discontentment, dissatisfaction with one's given condition when it does not match the norm.

All of this could be avoided by maintaining the variety, spontaneity, and natural harmony of the uncultivated field—that is, by returning to the *Dao*.

On the problem of afterlife/immortality, Laozi never comes right out and says that there is or is not life after death, or if there is, what it would be like. One can reach different conclusions on this point, depending on how one understands certain passages.

To begin with there are several places where Laozi claims that those who live in accord with the *Dao* will live out their life free from harm. At the end of chapter 16 we find: "Being one with Nature, he is in accord with *Dao*. Being in accord with *Dao*, he is everlasting, and is free from danger throughout his lifetime."[28] In chapter 32 we find: "It is by knowing when to stop that one can be free from danger."[29] This is repeated in chapter 44: "He who knows when to stop is free from danger. Therefore he can long endure."[30] Chapter 52 reads: "He who has found the mother (*Dao*) and thereby understands her sons (things), And having understood the sons, Still keeps to its [their] mother, Will be free from danger throughout his lifetime."[31] And finally in chapter 59 we find the conclusion: "He who possesses the Mother (*Dao*) of the state will last long. This means that the roots are deep and the stalks are firm [note the relevance to the analogy], which is the way of long life and everlasting vision."[32]

Since no more than freedom from harm is claimed here, the conclusion seems to be that for the Daoist, long life—or at least to reach one's natural or destined end—is the limit of expectation. However, the words "he is everlasting" (chapter 16) and "he can long endure" (chapter 44) in these passages could be read as suggesting an unnaturally long life, or even continued life, either physical immortality or life beyond the limits of the body.[33]

Physical immortality may be found in chapter 50, where we hear about one who is good at preserving his life:

> I have heard that one who is a good preserver of his life will not meet
>   tigers or wild buffaloes,
> And in fighting will not try to escape from weapons of war.
> The wild buffalo cannot butt its horns against him,
> The tiger cannot fasten its claws in him,
> And weapons of war cannot thrust their blades into him.
> And for what reason?
> Because in him there is no room for death.[34]

In later Daoism, when it was thought that one could transform his body into something refined and subtle, and thus impervious to harm, through breathing exercises, drugs, and other means, these lines would be taken quite literally. And I do not know that we can conclude for sure that Laozi himself did not have that in mind. However, the lines are certainly open to other interpretations. For example, that tigers and buffaloes and weapons of war could not harm such a man might come about because he lives cautiously and avoids dangerous situations.[35] Or it could be that he adapts to the natural tendencies of things and thus knows how to act with wild animals and soldiers so that they are not moved to anger.[36] That there is in him "no room for death" might only mean that he is not vulnerable in the ways that others are, that he will not be *easily* killed. Or it could mean that to the true Daoist "death" is not really "death"; he does not dwell on or fear it as others do, and he can thus better avoid it.

The end of chapter 33 is also a problem area. There we have the lines: "He who does not lose his place (with *Dao*) will endure. He who dies but does not really perish enjoys long life." What does this last line mean? On the surface of it, it seems to say that life can go on (perhaps in a spiritual way) even after the body dies, and that this is *true* long life (i.e., not simply a matter of living many years). But maybe the death he speaks of refers to dying in a spiritual sense, a dying to the old ways, that is, and a rebirth to a life lived in accord with the Way. Or perhaps "perish" means to die an "unnatural" death, to come to an end before one's time: to reach one's natural end, then, is long life. Or finally, one could follow Wing-tsit Chan on this, who reads this as speaking of an immortality of virtue; so long as one is remembered by future generations one does not really perish.[37]

There would seem to be three ways to read Laozi on the problem of afterlife/immortality: (1) he believed in physical immortality, continual life in the body for those who had lived right and learned how to preserve their lives; (2) he believed in some form of life after death (not specified) for those who had become one with the *Dao*;[38] and (3) he recognized death as final for all: the Daoist hope was for a long, natural life, free from danger and harm.

Moreover, the possibility of life after death may be understood in two different ways. It could be understood in a mystical sense. Insofar as the *Dao* is that one, eternal reality that gives rise to everything else, and insofar as the Daoist in some sense becomes one with the *Dao*, he could, at death, become fully identical with it—one with the eternal and unchanging. But in a more materialistic sense, insofar as the *Dao* is in some sense equivalent to the on-going process of life and material change, the Daoist could see death as just a stage in that process, and by developing matter and energy he does continue on.

The analogy of the field does not solve this problem; it does not show us for sure what Laozi thought. But it does help us visualize several distinct ways in which the problem could work out. The analogy does not, so far as I can see, support a notion of physical immortality; wildflowers do not continue on past their season. But that option aside, there are three different views to which it could point. One is that at death we merge once again with that storehouse of matter and vitality, the *Dao*, and that as matter and energy we are constantly recycled, reemerging in new forms of life, forms other than the human—in the analogy, the stuff of this year's sunflowers, bluebells, dandelions, and so on.

This is a view that other Daoist texts seem to draw out,[39] and it is presented as the natural way of things, a prospect that we ought to be willing to accept and perhaps even look forward to. For example, in chapter 6 of *Zhuangzi* when a certain Master Li is on the verge of dying, his friend Master Lai says to him, "How marvelous the Creator is! What is he going to make out of you next? Where is he going to send you? Will he make you into a rat's liver? Will he make you into a bug's arm?"[40] And he continues:

> The Great Clod burdens me with form, labors me with life, eases me
> in old age, and rests me in death.
> So if I think well of my life, for the same reason I must think well
> of my death. When a skilled smith is casting metal, if the metal
> should leap up and say "I insist upon being made into a Mo-yeh!"
> he would surely regard it as very inauspicious indeed.
> Now having had the audacity to take on human form once, if I should
> say, "I don't want to be anything but a man!—Nothing but a man!,"
> the Creator would surely regard me as a most inauspicious sort
> of person.[41]

Second, the field of flowers analogy could also lead to a transmigration of souls theory. That is to say, we could argue that the essence of each plant is contained in the seed, and that this provides a continuum of identity in the different plants that appear each year (i.e., the seeds from this year's black-eyed susans will give rise to next year's).

I do not know of Daoists ever developing this possibility, but it was used by an early Chinese convert to Buddhism, Mouzi, to explain rebirth:

> The spirit never perishes. Only the body decays. The body is like the roots and leaves of the five grains, the spirit is like the seeds and kernels of the five grains. When the roots and leaves come forth they inevitably die. But do the seeds and kernels perish? Only the body of one who has achieved the Way (here the Buddhist Way) perishes.[42]

Finally, one could also conclude from looking at the field that unique forms of life are unique forms of life, that this year's flowers will live and die to be replaced by a totally new crop next year. In short, one might conclude that death is final, and that the best one can hope for is a long life of health, natural growth, and a natural end.

NOTES

This essay first appeared in *St. John's Papers in Asian Studies* series, no. 27, in 1981. It is reprinted with kind permission of St. John's University, Institute of Asian Studies.

1. Wing-tsit Chan, *Sourcebook in Chinese Philosophy* (Princeton: Princeton University Press, 1963), 97. This is Chan's translation. Note that where I cite Chan's translation, words in parentheses are his own; my own comments or suggested variant translations are included in brackets. This article was written before I completed my own translation of the *Laozi*: Robert G. Henricks, tr., *Lao-tzu Te-tao ching: A New Translation Based on the Recently Discovered Ma-wang-tui Texts* (New York: Ballantine Books, 1989).

2. Ibid., 97. The silk texts of the *Laozi*, read differently here. They both say, "The Nameless is the beginning of the 10,000 things." The silk texts (there are two, designated *chia* and *I*) were discovered in 1973 in a Han dynasty tomb at Mawangdui in Changsha. They are the earliest known versions of the *Laozi*, dating from the first half of the second century B.C. While the content of the texts is generally the same as other known versions, there are occasional interesting variations, and I note some of these in the pages that follow. The silk texts are now readily available to Chinese scholars in book form in *Laozi: Mawangdui Han mu bo shu* (Peking: Wen-wu, 1975), hereafter cited as *Laozi: Mawangdui*. For the references to chapter 1, see p. 82.

3. Chan, *The Way*, 124.

4. Ibid., 152.

5. Max Kaltenmark, *Lao Tzu and Taoism*, trans. Roger Greaves (Stanford: Stanford University Press, 1969), 29.

6. Chan, *The Way*, 97. This is literally the "10,000 things"; in some of my own translations below I use that term. The term is a comprehensive way to refer to all forms of life.

7. Ibid., 134.

THE DAO AND THE FIELD   45

8. Ibid., 192.

9. Ibid., 205.

10. Ibid., 97.

11. Ibid., 105.

12. Ibid., 137.

13. Ibid., 110.

14. Ibid., 160. The silk texts read somewhat differently, and the lines about "clothing and feeding" are not present at all. My translation of the silk texts is as follows (for the Chinese, see *Laozi: Mawangdui*, 93):

The Way floats and drifts.
It can go to the left or right.
It accomplishes tasks and completes affairs,
And yet it does not have a name.
The 10,000 things entrust their lives to it,
And yet it does not act as their master.
And therefore it is constantly without desires. [This line seems out of place.]
It can be named with the things that are small.
The 10,000 things entrust their lives to it,
And yet it does not act as their master.
It can be named with the things that are great.
Therefore the Sage's ability to accomplish the great,
Comes from his not playing the role of the great.
Therefore he is able to accomplish the great.

15. This is my own translation of the silk texts. For the Chinese, see *Lao-tzu Ma-wang-tui*, 70. The line I translate "It brings them to life," however, is missing from both texts and is supplied from other versions. See Chan, *The Way*, 190, for an alternative translation of this line.

16. *Wuwei*, acting by not acting, is one of the traits of the *Dao* and the Sage. The opening line of chapter 37 in the *Laozi* is "Dao invariably takes no action, and yet there is nothing left undone." Chan, *The Way*, 166.

17. Chan, *The Way*, 192.

18. Ibid., 194.

19. Ibid., 128.

20. See especially chapter 6 and the phrase: "The Great Clod burdens me with form, labors me with life, eases me in old age, and rests me in death." Burton Watson, *Chuang Tzu: Basic Writings* (New York: Columbia University Press, 1964), 76. The *Dao* as the "great Clod" is the subject of H. G. Creel's essay "The Great Clod," in Herrlee G. Creel, *What is Taoism? And other Studies in Chinese Cultural History* (Chicago: University of Chicago Press, 1970), 25–36.

21. From John G. Neihardt, *Black Elk Speaks: Being the Life Story of a Holy Man of the Oglala Sioux* (Lincoln: University of Nebraska Press, 1961), 3.

22. We quite often find the combination of Sky-father and Earth-mother as world parents. However, there are instances of the Earth Mother herself giving birth out of

her own fecundity. On this see Mircea Eliade, *The Sacred and the Profane* (New York: Harper & Row, 1967), 144–145.

23. The dates here given are traditional. Our evidence from the Shang oracle bones actually accounts only for the period 1324–1225 B.C., the reign of Wu Ding. H. G. Creel *The Birth of China* (New York: Frederick Ungar, 1937), 180–181. The *she* and *fang* sacrifices were offered to the god(s) of the land and the spirits of the four quarters, respectively, in the spring and summer for aid in the growing season. Lester J. Bilsky, "The State Religion of Ancient China" (PhD diss., University of Washington, 1971), 59–62.

24. *Shangdi* is the name given to the supreme deity in the oracle texts of the Shang; Heaven, or *Tian*, is more commonly used by the Zhou, although they at times also use the name Shangdi. Both names refer to a deity of the "sky-god" type, an all-powerful, supreme deity who is constantly watching what goes on below. Both can and do intervene in human events; with Heaven this is done for moral purposes: he gives a mandate to a ruler, a contract to rule, and intervenes to remove this if the conditions are not upheld. Shangdi and Tian could be two distinct deities, the former of the Shang and the latter of the Zhou. Or it could be that Tian is another name for Shangdi, or a Shangdi who has been transformed. The best reading on this problem is found in D. Howard Smith, *Chinese Religions from 1000 B.C. to the Present Day* (London: Holt, Rinehart and Winston, 1968), 12–21, and H. G. Creel, *The Origins of Statecraft in China*, vol. 1: *The Western Chou Empire* (Chicago: University of Chicago Press, 1970), 81–100, 493–506.

25. Both Laozi and Zhuangzi are reported to have come from the state of Chu, an area whose customs and beliefs are well known to have differed markedly from those of the Zhou states to the north.

26. I have in mind the controversial lines in chapters 5 and 3. Respectively they read: "The sage is not humane. He regards all people as straw dogs"; "Therefore in the government of the sage, He keeps their hearts vacuous, Fills their bellies, Weakens their ambitions, And strengthens their bones." Chan, *The Way*, 107, 103.

27. Ibid., 131, 132, 167.

28. Ibid., 128.

29. Ibid., 157.

30. Ibid., 179.

31. Ibid., 192.

32. Ibid., 205.

33. That the Chinese here is *jiu* ("long time") in the first case and *chang jiu* (much the same meaning) in the second suggests to me life's coming to an end at some point.

34. Chan, *The Way*, 188. It is interesting to note that in the Mawangdui copies of the *Laozi*, the opening line of this chapter has "one who is good at *holding on to life (zhisheng),*" instead of "one who is a good preserver of his life *(shesheng).*" *(zhisheng).* See *Laozi: Mawangdui*, 69.

35. In chapter 17 of the *Zhuangzi* we have a passage where this kind of interpretation of how the Daoist avoids harm seems to be implied. Either that, or the

Daoist simply does not see harm as harm and accepts whatever comes his way. The passage reads: "And he who knows how to deal with circumstances will not allow things to do him harm. When a man has perfect virtue, fire cannot burn him, water cannot drown him, cold and heat cannot afflict him, birds and beasts cannot injure him. I do not say that he makes light of these things. I mean that he distinguishes between safety and danger, contents himself with fortune and misfortune, and is constant in his comings and goings." Watson, *Chuang Tzu*, 104.

36. In chapter 4 of the *Zhuangzi* we read of the tiger trainer who succeeds by not going against the fierce dispositions of the tigers: he does not give them anything alive that they would have to kill, or anything whole that they would have to tear up. Ibid., 59.

37. Chan, *The Way*, 159. The silk texts would seem to support this since they substitute "not forgotten" (*bu wang*) for "not perish" (*bu wang*). But since the character for "forgotten" is made by adding the "heart" element to the character for "perish," and since the adding of an element to the *correct* character is common in the silk texts, "perish" might still be the intended word. See *Laozi: Mawangdui*, 93.

38. I should note that in addition to the evidence already cited, there is one other thing that could support this. Ellen Ch'en, in her essay "Is There a Doctrine of Physical Immortality in the *Tao-te-ching*?," *History of Religions* 12, no. 3 (1973): 231–247, notes the phrase *mo shen bu dai* (in chapters 16 and 52), which she translates as "to lose the body without coming to an end." Unfortunately this phrase is open to interpretation. Chan translates it as "free from danger throughout his lifetime" in both places. Arthur Waley has "though his body ceases is not destroyed" in chapter 16, which supports Professor Ch'en, but "and to the end of his days suffers no harm" in chapter 52. See Arthur Waley, trans., *The Way and its Power: A Study of the Tao Te Ching and Its Place in Chinese Thought* (New York: Grove, 1958), 162, 206.

39. In addition to the *Zhuangzi* passages cited below, the *Liezi* follows this line and specifies what is involved. Man is a combination of dense *qi* (breath, energy) from the earth (his body), and subtle, active *qi* from heaven (his breath and vital energies). At death these *qi* return to their sources and are then recycled. See A. C. Graham, trans., *The Book of Lieh-tzu* (London: Lewis Reprints, 1973), 14–15, 18–20, 20–23, especially the anecdotes.

40. Watson, *Chuang Tzu*, 81. I would not take "Creator" here in a literal sense. I think it is used by Zhuangzi as another way to talk about the creative work of the *Dao*; natural transformation is all that is involved.

41. Watson notes that Mo ye was a famous sword of King Helu (reigned 514–496 B.C.) of Wu.

42. William Theodore deBary, *The Buddhist Tradition in India, China and Japan* (New York: Random House, 1972), 134–135. From a text called *Mouzi li huo lun* (Mouzi Settling Doubts), which is traditionally believed to date from the end of the second century A.D.

The *Daode Jing* and Comparative Philosophy

David L. Hall

The Confucian asks, "Master Lao, you say that 'the way that can be spoken of is the constant way.' Why, then, do you offer so many words which speak of the Way?"

To which Laozi replies, "I make for you a golden embroidery of drakes and pass it along for your enjoyment. I cannot, however, show you the golden needle by which it was made."

Before beginning any classroom discussion of the *Daode jing* I always recount this apocryphal exchange as a means of making a point about the language of that work and, indeed, of language generally. That cautionary tale is useful in warning us not to mistake the embroidery, however fine, for the "golden needle" that permits its creation. And, of course, the Daoist would believe that the sentiment of this story suggests the mood with which we might well approach language itself.

Words, the Daoist might say, serve as both signposts and barriers. It is as if the very sign that tells us where to go stands in the way of our getting there. Were I, for example, to encounter a sign in the form of a roadblock across the only highway leading into town that read "El Paso 99 Miles," I would know that I was heading in the right direction but would be prevented from going home.

Knowing this, we may be reconciled to the fact that traveling along the way that can be spoken of is the only means whereby we may celebrate the Nameless *Dao*. Its ability to provide its readers important experiences of the evocation of meaning beyond any words is what makes the *Daode jing* one of the most provocative of all the texts of world literature.

My first encounter with this book was as oblique as is the language of the work itself. As a high school student, I was on a long bus trip across the western states. While at a rest stop in Pecos, Texas, I was browsing through books and magazines displayed at the bus depot. Amid the usual examples of romance and detective fiction were two books whose titles immediately caught my eye: The first was A. N. Whitehead's *Adventures of Ideas*; the second was a work entitled *The Way of Life*. Its subtitle was *The Tao Te Ching*. I recall being fascinated by both works, each of which promised to transform my rather dull bus trip into a far more exciting journey. I had only enough money for one book, however, and so had to make a decision. After several minutes, I finally selected *Adventures of Ideas*.

I have come to believe that my encounter with these two books was more significant than I initially thought. For, some years later, as a graduate student, I selected the philosophy of Whitehead as the subject of my dissertation research. And it was not long after I began teaching that I found myself extending my interest in process philosophy by comparing Whiteheadian thinking with the Daoist sensibility through a consultation of the *Daode jing*.

Comparative Philosophy as a Collaborative Enterprise

Before discussing the manner in which I use the *Daode jing* in the classroom, it might be useful to address another issue concerning the pedagogy of that text. For those such as I who do not read classical Chinese, the question arises as to how one might approach the work. I assume that relatively few of those who employ this text in undergraduate teaching are expert in Chinese language and culture. In my experience, this is particularly true of those who use the work as a philosophical text. I would like to ask, therefore, by way of introducing the remainder of my remarks: "What is the role of the Western philosopher in furthering the appropriate use of classical Chinese texts in the classroom?"

The first thing to be said is that, quite obviously, if a translation of the *Daode jing* is to be relevant to the Western context, it is not enough that the translator be expert in only Chinese thought and culture. A reasonably subtle understanding of the Western philosophical tradition is presumed in every adequate translation of that work into Anglo-European languages. In the absence of this combination of sinological and Western philosophical skills in a single individual, the translation of the *Daode jing* into an English-speaking context suggests the need for collaboration between Chinese and Western specialists. Often this collaboration is minimally accomplished when the individual ignorant of the Chinese language consults a number of different translations of a given text and seeks some broad understanding of the history and culture of the period that contextualizes the work he or she is seeking to understand. Without some such concern, the Western interpreter of texts such as the *Daode jing* is likely to present either a superficial or a distorted interpretation. By the same token, when the sinologist seeks to translate a Chinese classic into English, he or she has the responsibility of gaining some understanding of the general cultural context into which he or she is seeking to translate the given work. Nothing is more disappointing than to pick up a copy of the *Daode jing*, the *Zhuangzi*, or the *Analects* translated by someone who, however subtle his or her sinological skills, is relatively innocent of the Western intellectual tradition. The result is always a travestied, trivialized, and unteachable text.

My own understanding of Chinese texts has benefited significantly from a collaboration begun some fifteen years ago with the sinologist Roger Ames of the University of Hawai'i. Ames's expertise in classical Chinese language and Chinese philosophical texts, combined with my knowledge of Western philosophy and the methodology of comparative cultures, has provided each of us with a more solid foundation from which to communicate the language of Chinese philosophy to undergraduate and graduate students.

Moreover, it is important to note that, though I am not trained in Chinese language, the speculative interpretation of Daoism contained in some of my earliest published writings has in fact influenced the translation of key terms in the more specialized treatments in subsequent works by Ames and me. Moreover, that interpretation is elaborated in our discussions of Daoism in our recent work, *Thinking from the Han*, as well as in articles on the subject of Daoism by the two of us in the *Routledge Encyclopedia of Philosophy*.

My intent here is really not to boast about my understanding of Daoism. I merely wish to correct what I consider to be a serious misunderstanding that affects the appropriate exercise of comparative Chinese/Western thought. In the case of texts such as the *Daode jing*, Western-trained philosophers have, on the whole, a great deal more to contribute to the translation of Chinese intellectual culture into Western cultural contexts than they might otherwise believe. Making sense of texts such as the *Daode jing* within an Anglo-European philosophical milieu is, first and foremost, a collaborative effort. Until this fact is endorsed by both (sometimes) overly confident sinologists and (often) all too timid Western specialists, the translation of Chinese philosophical texts into Anglo-European contexts will never reach the most desirable level.

The *Daode Jing* and Comparative Philosophy

As one of my principal philosophical interests is comparative thought, I most often have recourse to the *Daode jing* in classes devoted to Chinese and Western comparisons. The strategy of such a course is to suggest some fundamental assumptions of Western thought that might not be common to mainstream Chinese cultural sensibilities. The method involves attempting to bracket these assumptions in order better to understand the presuppositions of Chinese intellectual culture. There are, of course, many possible topics for such "uncommon assumptions." Chinese and Western classical cultures originate from alternative assumptions that shape dramatically contrasting senses of ontological and cosmological issues, such as the nature of "being" and "existence," the sense of "cosmos" or "world," the understanding of "natural laws" and "casual relations." In addition, classical Chinese approaches to such Western philosophical topics as "self," "truth," "transcendence," "reason," "logic," and "rhetoric" are quite distinct from the dominant family of Western understandings of these topics.

I have found that the *Daode jing* is helpful in making all of these important cultural comparisons. In what follows I wish merely to highlight a few of these issues as a means of demonstrating the value of the *Daode jing* as a text in comparative philosophy.

The first topic permits a contrast of Chinese and Western treatments of "Being" and the sources of world-order. The second involves the general treatment of the person construed in terms of the tripartite structure of the *psyche* originating in Plato, a model of "personality" that has been central to our tradition since that time. These two issues allow for a general understanding of some striking differences among concepts of "self and world" found in Chinese and Western cultures.

This approach is relevant beyond the efforts merely to train philosophers. Issues fundamental to the way we commonsensically think about the world are sedimented in the patterns of thought and expression of every reasonably educated person. Unless we seek to uncover at least some of our "uncommon assumptions," we shall err in our interpretation of alternative cultural sensibilities through the unthinking presumption that our common sense is universal.

Ontological and Cosmological Issues

In the Western metaphysical tradition, "Being" is most generally thought to be either a common property of things, in the sense of a universal applying to all things, or a container that relates things by placing them within its own structure. Metaphysical notions of Being are generally associated with the concept of ground; the relation of Being and beings, then, is thought to be that of indeterminate ground and determinate things. Nonbeing is characterized as the negation of Being either in a simple, logical sense, or as the *Nihil*, the Void, the experience of which, as in Heidegger's philosophy, evokes a sense of existential angst or dread.

The disposition of the Chinese from the beginning to the present is highly inhospitable to fixed forms of asymmetrical relations such as is expressed by the relation of Being and nonbeing. The Chinese existential verb *you* ("being") overlaps with the sense of "having" rather than the copula, and therefore *you*, "to be," means "to be present," "to be around," while *wu*, "not to be," means "not to be present," "not to be around." This means that *wu* does not indicate strict opposition or contradiction, but absence. Thus, the *you/wu* distinction suggests mere contrast in the sense of either the presence or absence of *x*, rather than an assertion of the existence or nonexistence of *x*.

Thus, if one translates *you* and *wu* in chapter 40 of the *Daode jing* as being and nonbeing, respectively, the following translation might result: "The things of the world originate in Being. And Being originates in Nonbeing." Such language can be most misleading if taken in the classical Western senses of Being and Nonbeing. Following the general preference of the *Daode jing* for reversing certain classical contrasts, *wu* appears to be given preference over *you*, as is *yin* ("passive,") over *yang* ("active"). Interpreting *wu* as "Nonbeing" would, then, suggest a preference for Nonbeing over Being, and this has led to some rather ridiculous mystical speculations to the effect that the Nihil or the Void, as Nonexistence, has priority over Being-Itself. Such an assumption of the senses of being and nonbeing deriving from the metaphysical contexts of Western philosophy can lead to total misunderstanding of the text. For, as a Chinese saying has it: "If one is off an inch at the bow, then one will be off several feet at the target." Thus in place of the claim that, for the Daoist, nonbeing is superior to being, it would be best to claim that nothing takes precedence over something. An alternative translation—ironically, with strong Marxist overtones—would be: "not having" is superior to "having."

The distinctive character of the *you/wu* problematic in the *Daode jing* allows for an interesting discussion of the presently topical postmodern critiques of reason. For one of the implications of the absence in that work of any notion of Being as existence per se is that there is no notion of Being as ontological ground and no need for a metaphysical contrast between Being and beings. There is no need to overcome the logocentrism of a language of presence grounded in ontological difference if no distinction between Being and beings, or beings and their ground, is urged by the classical Chinese language and its philosophical employment. A Chinese language of presence is a language of making present the item itself, not its essence.

Language that does not lead one to posit ontological difference between Being and beings, but only a difference between one being and another, suggests a decentered world whose centers and circumferences are always defined in an ad hoc manner. The mass of classical Chinese philosophical discourse, then, is in no need of deconstruction since the senses of *you* and *wu* within the Chinese sensibility do not lead to the creation of texts that could legitimately be targets of the deconstructor.

One may gain greater insight into this rather unusual sense of the being/ nonbeing relation in Chinese thought through an interpretation of the famous first lines of the *Daode jing*:

> The Way that can be spoken of is not the constant Way.
> The name that can be named is not the constant name.
> The nameless is the beginning of the ten-thousand things.[1]

Nameless Dao is best construed here, not as ontological ground, but merely as the noncoherent sum of all possible orders. The natural cosmology of classical China does not entail a single-ordered cosmos, but invokes an understanding of a world constituted by myriad unique particulars: "the ten thousand things."

An important implication of the *you/wu* relationship in Chinese intellectual culture is that the relevant contrast is not, as in the West, between the cosmological whatness of things and the ontological thatness of things; rather, it is a contrast between the cosmos as the sum of all orders and the world as construed from some particular perspective—that is, any particular one of the orders.

In the absence of a sense of Being as a common property or a relational structure, the world is not coherent in the sense that a single pattern or telos could be said to characterize its processes. It is not a whole, but many such wholes. It is not the superordinate One to which the Many reduce. Its order is not rational or logical, but aesthetic; that is, there is no transcending pattern determining the existence or efficacy of the order. The order is a consequence of the particulars comprising the totality of existing things.

This interpretation of being of the world makes of it a totality not in the sense of a single-ordered cosmos, but in the sense of the sum of all cosmological orders. Any given order is an existing world that is construed from the perspective of a particular element within the totality. But, as a single world, it is a selective abstraction from the totality of possible orders that are presently not around. The being of this order is not ontological in a foundational sense, but "cosmological" in the sense that it concerns, not Being-Itself, but the "beings" of the world and their relational order. Such an abstracted, selected order cannot serve as fundament or ground. Thus, the Chinese sense of being entails the notion, rather striking from our Western perspective, that all differences are cosmological differences.

The Chinese understanding of the *you/wu* relationship has profound implications for the manner in which philosophic discourse is shaped throughout the Chinese tradition. Without recourse to the senses of "Being" associated with Western speculative philosophies, assumptions we take for granted as conditions for philosophizing are simply not present. The proper understanding of "being" in the Chinese tradition helps us to account for the fact that there is no real "metaphysical" tradition in China if we mean by metaphysics anything like a universal science of first principles or a study of Being-Itself. In fact, within the strictly Chinese philosophical tradition there is little interest in asking about what makes something real or why things exist.

When we address distinctly cosmological issues—such as "What kinds of things are there?" or "What are the basic categories that make up the world as we know it?"—the situation is the same. Although it is true that Chinese thinkers, particularly the Daoists, ask about things, they do not ask about *categories* or *kinds* in any manner that would suggest that things have logical essences or constitute natural kinds. Because there is nothing like "Being" that shines through the beings of the world—because there are only the beings of the world—there is no effective impulse to handle cosmological issues by asking after the logos of the cosmos.

The principal reason Chinese thinkers are not apt to ask after the logos of the cosmos is that they lack a dominant concern for approaching what we term the "cosmos" as a single-ordered Whole. The term, often used in the *Daode jing*, that qualifies the Chinese understanding of what we term the "cosmos" is *wan wu*, "the ten thousand things," or, as D. C. Lau often renders the term, "the myriad creatures." Thus, "the nameless is the beginning of the ten thousand things. The named is the mother of the ten thousand things."

The Chinese stress on locutions such as "ten thousand things" suggests the same insight we encountered in terms of our discussion of the *you/wu* relationship. Without a viable notion of Being as ground, there is no basis on which one can presume the existence of a single-ordered world, a cosmos. Thus the testimony of the *Daode jing* is that the world is to be seen as a plurality: a many, not a one. Such an understanding of the world precludes the notion of cosmos, insofar as that notion entails either a coherent, single-ordered world or a congeries of entities with essential features or essential modes of connection.

The Wu-forms of Daoism

One of the more fascinating aspects of the discussions of the *Daode jing* is the doctrine of *wuwei*, literally "no-action." "Do that which consists in taking no action, and order will prevail" (3). "The Way never acts yet nothing is left undone" (37). Sentiments such as these express a doctrine of the art of rulership in which the "the best of rulers is but a shadowy presence to his subjects" (17). But from the perspective of the comparative philosopher, it is interesting to note that it is not only Western understandings of "action" that are problematized by the *Daode jing*, but the allied notions of knowledge and desire also receive a "reversed" interpretation in the forms of *wuzhi* ("no knowledge") and *wuyu* ("no desire").

The reason this is especially interesting with respect to Chinese/Western comparisons is that the understandings of knowing, acting, and desiring in the Western tradition have been strongly influenced by the tripartite model of the psyche deriving from Plato and perpetuated subsequently in various forms in the Western tradition. Contrasting understandings of the modalities of knowledge, action, and desire in the *Daode jing* with the manner in which they are construed in the philosophical traditions influenced by the Platonic psyche can provide a host of productive insights into the differences of Chinese and Western cultures.

The first thing to say about the general approach to philosophical anthropology in the West is that dominant theories of the self are shaped in accordance with a model of personality in which the self is seen as internally conflicted, that is, at war with itself. In Plato, the primary conflict is between reason and the passionate and volitional elements of the soul. This conflict is ramified with the confluence of Hebraic and Hellenic sensibilities, coming to be expressed in the words of St. Paul: "The good that I would do, I do not do; the evil that I would not do, that I do." This understanding of the soul in conflict receives a famous modern interpretation with Hume's claim that "reason always shall be a slave to the passions." The Humean interpretation is in turn reflected in the traditional conception of Freud's personality theory as based on the conflictual dynamics of id, ego, and superego.

The tripartite model of the self undergirds the institutionalization of the division between theory and practice that has characterized so much of our intellectual culture; it has influenced, for example, the search for scientific objectivity which has urged a separation of reason and the passions. In addition, conflict between the dynamics of power and justice in political culture is a consequence of writing large the tensions between volitional and rational components of the soul.

One can readily see from this that making comparisons between Chinese and Western understandings of knowledge, action, and desire might lead to extremely important insights into these contrasting cultures. The general lesson is that it is of some benefit to be aware of the uncommon assumptions on this issue of "the soul at war." Otherwise, we shall surely misconstrue Chinese understandings of the self and the relevance of those understandings to larger social and cultural contexts.

When we turn to the *Daode jing* to discover Daoist contributions to these issues, we see that there are terms such as *zhi*, *wei*, and *yu* that initially seem to correlate rather closely with what we call knowing, acting, and desiring. But it is important to realize that the understanding of knowledge, action, and desire found in the *Daode jing* is by no means based on a model of the self that presumes an internal struggle of reason against the obstreperous passions or will. The Daoists do not "slice the pie," as is done in the West; effectively, there are no faculties of knowing, doing, and feeling that can be distinguished one from the other, and there is no division between the modalities of reason on the one hand and appetite and will on the other.

If the Daoist self is not divided in the manner of the Western model of the tripartite soul, how are we to account for these three modalities? The *wu*-forms must be thought of simply as activities that establish the deferential relations that give rise to the self at any given moment. They are not faculties; they form no coherent psyche.

In discussing the *wu*-forms of Daoism it is essential that we call attention to the absence of a mind/body dualism in classical Chinese thought. It is this dualism, after all, that determines the principal conflict within the self between reason and the affective and volitional components.

In the absence of a mind/body dichotomy in Daoist understandings of the self, the basis for the conflictual dynamics of the psyche is not present. Further, because the distinctions among the affective, volitional, and rational components are not made in terms of a unified model of the self, the idea of a self at war with itself doesn't make much sense to the Chinese.

The best way of understanding the Daoist self is as a function of its relations with its world shaped by *wuzhi*, *wuwei*, and *wuyou*. To see this in the most productive manner, however, it is necessary to provide interpretations of the *wu*-forms that take account of the philosophical significance of the terms. Doing so has led me to translate these terms in the following manner: I render *wuwei* as "nonassertive action," *wuzhi* as "unprincipled knowing," and *wuyu* as "objectless desire."

Wuwei, often translated as "no action" or "nonaction," involves the absence of any action that interferes with the particularity of those things within one's field of influence. Actions untainted by stored knowledge or ingrained habits are unmediated, unstructured, unprincipled, and spontaneous. As such, they are consequences of deferential responses to the item or event in accordance with which, or in relation to which, one is acting. They are *non-assertive* actions.

It would be a mistake to interpret the modes of disposition named by the *wu*-forms as passive. The deferential activities underlying these modes are shaped by the intrinsic excellences of those things calling forth deference. Deference is deference to recognized excellence. The assumption must be that the Daoist sage sees beneath the layers of artifice that mask the naturalness of persons and things and responds to the excellence so advertised. Further, deference is a two-way street. The excellence of the realized Daoist calls forth deference from others. The *wu*-forms operate within a context of yielding and being yielded to. The model of the sage-ruler in the *Daode jing* is described in terms of *wuwei*. Thus the sage says, "I am non-assertive [*wuwei*] and the people are transformed of themselves" (57). Further, the sage-ruler "constantly causes the people to seek 'unprincipled knowing' [*wuzhi*] and to be objectless in their desires [*wuyu*]. In simply acting non-assertively [*wuwei*], everything is properly ordered" (3).

An interesting illustration of *wuwei* is found in the "push-hands" (*duishou*) exercise associated with the Chinese exercise form known as *taijiquan*. Two individuals facing one another perform various circular movements of the arms while maintaining minimal hand contact. The movement of each individual mirrors that of the other. *Wuwei* is realized when the movements of each are sensed, by both parties, to be uninitiated and effortless. I often attempt to demonstrate the notion of *wuwei* by leading my students in a brief set of "push-hands" exercises.

Wuzhi, as "no-knowledge," means the absence of a certain kind of knowledge, the sort dependent on ontological presence. Knowledge grounded in a denial of ontological presence involves the sort of acosmotic thinking that does not presuppose a single-ordered world and its intellectual accoutrements. It is, therefore, unprincipled knowing. Such knowing does not appeal to rules or principles determining the existence, meaning, or activity of a phenomenon. *Wuzhi* provides one with a sense of the particularity of a thing rather than what that thing is as a member of a class or an instance of a concept.

Wuzhi, or "knowing without principles," is tacit and, though inexpressible in literal terms, may be communicated though parabolic and imagistic language. The story alluded to at the very outset of this essay concerning the Confucian critic's challenge to Laozi's attempting to speak of the Way that rightfully cannot be spoken of indicates that he has missed the fact that one must approach parabolic language through *wuzhi*—that is, through a refusal to shape one's understanding by appeal to categories and principles of that which is to be known. Such parabolic language is distinctive in an acosmotic context since metaphor and imagery do not presuppose a literal ground. The parabolic language of the *Daode jing* is, from the beginning, a language of difference and particularity. It is this language that permits the communication of the results of *wuzhi*.

The best characterization of the term *wuyu* is "objectless desire." Since neither unprincipled knowing nor nonassertive action can in the strict sense objectify a world or any element in it, the desiring associated with the Daoist sensibility is objectless. Thus, *wuyu*, rather than involving the cessation of desire through possession and consummation, represents the achievement of deferential desire. Desire based on a mirroring understanding (*wuzhi*) and a nonassertive relationship (*wuwei*) is not shaped by the need to own, control, or consume, but simply to celebrate and to enjoy.

The Daoist problematic does not concern what is desired but the manner of the desiring. Objectless desire always allows for letting be and letting go. Enjoyment for the Daoist is realized not in spite of the fact that one might lose what is desired, but because of this fact. The world is a complex set of processes of transformation, never at rest. In Plato, the desire for knowledge (eros) is the only thing that can define both embodied and disembodied existence; it is the only desire that can be permanent, eternal. In Daoism, transient desire is the only desire that lets things be, that does not construe the world in a certain manner, that does not seek to render static a world of changing things.

The mirroring activity associated with the Daoist *wu*-forms is a form of activity that allows things to be themselves both in their transitoriness and their particularity. It is the things themselves as individual events and processes, and the orders construed from their particular perspectives, that are reflected in the mirroring process.

Summary

It has been my experience that the discussion of the *Daode jing* in an under-graduate class is remarkably beneficial in helping students gain insights into these and many other "uncommon assumptions" that highlight differences between Chinese and Western philosophical perspectives. By juxtaposing them in the way I've described, aspects of each tradition become clearer. Once students who have already been introduced to Western philosophy come to understand the cosmology implicit in the *Daode jing*, they can more easily recognize how Western cosmologies and ontologies are strategic choices rather than revelations of things as they are. At the same time, those students who are grappling with Chinese texts like the *Daode jing* can see its distinctiveness more clearly once they contrast it with Western ontological choices.

In closing I should note that the above notwithstanding, I certainly do recognize that the philosophical import of this work by no means exhausts its significance. Its poetic value, for example, is clearly as significant as its philosophical worth. Nonetheless, as a comparative philosopher of culture I have found the *Daode jing*—more than any other single work—to be well-nigh indispensable as an introduction to Chinese and Western thought.

NOTE

1. All citations are from *Tao Te Ching*, trans. by D.C. Lau (New York: Penguin Books, 1963).

Mysticism In the *Daode Jing*

Gary D. DeAngelis

Years ago, at another college, as I began a section of an Asian religions course on Daoism, one of my students stood up and announced rather irreverently that "talking about the *Dao* is total
bullshit and a waste of f——ing time." He then proceeded to pack
up his things and march out of the classroom, heading off, I presumed, into the existential void. While students sat in stunned dis-
belief I took this rather opportune moment to inform them that,
though undoubtedly apocryphal, nearly 2,500 years ago the great
sage Laozi enacted this exact same performance, albeit a bit more
eloquently, at the Western Gate of China, renouncing both society
and philosophical speculation as hopeless. Unlike the legendary
Laozi, this student did return at the next class session, and we went
on to explore and, in fact, talk about conceptions of the *Dao*.

That particular performance was so effective in jump-starting
that section of the course on Daoism that, in subsequent semes-
ters, I've considered paying a student to repeat it with, I hoped, the
same effect. I have refrained from following through on such a plan,
not wanting to violate the Daoist call for spontaneity, but I have
often recounted that story to new students; though undoubtedly
not having the same impact as the original performance, they generally have found it quite amusing. Having taught for over thirty
years I must admit to being rather shameless about reusing stories
or jokes that students still find amusing.

During my own career as a smug undergraduate, in reading the *Daode jing* for the first time I was struck by the fact that this supposed great Chinese sage claimed that one can never really define or even discuss the *Dao*, and yet he did discuss it. While others were enthralled by Laozi I was convinced (like my misinformed student) that I alone had unmasked this itinerant guru for the obvious charlatan that he was. Couldn't anyone see that after that classic opening refrain he would have been extremely wise to abide by his own maxim that "those who know don't say and those who don't know say"—a refrain that I continue to caution students against using on exams.

Now, considerably older and perhaps a bit wiser, I have come to appreciate the insight of the many Laozis of the *Daode jing*. The initial caveat in the opening lines is followed by subtle hints, suggestions, whispers, and allusions as to the nature of the *Dao*, which do provide glimpses for our rational mind to understand something about the *Dao*. If, in fact, the *Dao* is everything (as is claimed), it is, in part, rational mind. However, it is also true that these speculative glimpses are things *about* the *Dao*. To truly *know* the *Dao* it is strongly implied that one must go beyond intellect to intuition, where the knower, in a sense, becomes the known, that is, where one becomes the *Dao*.

What I would like to delineate in this essay is how I have explored and used the *Daode jing* as a mystical text over the years, primarily in the context of a course called "Comparative Mysticism," and how that particular perspective has helped both my students and me to better understand the nature, meaning, and basic principles of the *Daode jing* in whatever context it may be used. Unlike some of the other contributors to this volume, I am not a specialist in Chinese religions. My field is the comparative study of religions with a focus on Asian religions and a specific interest in sacred space, pilgrimage, and ritual. Although I have done fieldwork in China I do not read classical Chinese. So my use of the *Daode jing* has been dependent on the use of translations, which are identified at a later point in the essay.

I have used the *Daode jing* for the past twenty-six years, for the most part at small undergraduate colleges, in such courses as "Asian Religions," "Religions of China and Japan," and "Comparative Mysticism." My use of the text has changed over that time as both my understanding of it and my own scholarly interests have changed. In spite of the fact that I've been using this text solely with undergraduates and, for the most part, at the introductory level (presupposing little or no background in Chinese religions or culture), I am still committed to taking a scholarly approach, making them aware of both the complexity of this text and the necessity and value of examining it within its historical and cultural context. I have resisted the temptation and, at times, desire of students to oversimplify the text, take it out of context, and Westernize and romanticize it into what Norm Girardot refers to as "Pooh Bear Daoism." However, the challenge we continue to face, as both scholars and teachers of undergraduates, is how to walk that very fine line between maintaining the integrity of the text while effectively communicating its meaning to an audience of general readers.

I would agree wholeheartedly with numerous China scholars that the *Daode jing* reflects a particular school (used loosely) of thought, somewhat prevalent in fourth-century B.C.E. China, and that in order to make an attempt to understand the intended meaning of this text it is essential to understand not only Chinese culture and the Chinese religious worldview but also the cultural, religious, and political milieu of the late Zhou period. In addition, it would also be beneficial to have a sense of who was compiling this text and for whom it was being written. I think that this is true in reading any text from any culture. In a sense, the *Daode jing* reflects its period and culture and can provide us with a window into understanding classical China and perhaps something of the Chinese religious worldview as it has evolved over the past 2,500 years. It is important to note that although this is obviously a classical text, it continues to be widely read in China today.

There is undoubtedly inherent value in studying other cultures and worldviews in and of themselves. I would also argue that there is intrinsic value in discovering particular truths or insights in other cultures which may have a timeless and universal value and may help us to make sense out of life and understand something about the nature of our being and our place in the cosmos. Indeed, there is the danger of Westernizing a text like the *Daode jing* in order to make the foreign and exotic familiar and comfortable. I would also say, however, that, as scholars and teachers, we must be equally vigilant against being ruled by cultural relativism. Indeed, we want our students to have a true understanding of the Chinese worldview, but that does not mean that a classical text like the *Daode jing* does not contain basic principles that may inspire them in some ways, enlighten them in others, or may even be applied to their lives. They can be good scholars but also *moved* by what they discover without going native or surrendering their objectivity. They may be from a different culture and be shaped by different circumstances and forces, but ultimately they are of the same species and have the capacity to respond to certain universal truths. Why are the Japanese so enthralled with Shakespeare and the Chinese with Beethoven?

I am suggesting two distinct orientations or goals in interpreting and understanding the *Daode jing*: what it meant originally in its historical context and what it means to us now. However, these goals, as Michael LaFargue suggests, "are not by any means exclusive, and it is possible to combine them."[1]

The overwhelming majority of us using this text are not preparing students to become China scholars nor to fulfill some spiritual void in their lives. I would reaffirm, however, that we do have a scholarly obligation to use the text as honestly and truthfully as possible to capture its original meaning or intent, which, admittedly, will also be an interpretation based on what sources we choose. Our responsibility is to choose the sources wisely and judiciously and to provide a legitimate context for exploration.

Once again, what I would like to focus on is my use of the *Daode jing* as a mystical text and why I have used it this way. The particular course that I will be focusing on is called "Comparative Mysticism," which I have taught in numerous incarnations over the past twenty years. Initially, this course focused on the comparative study of the mystical dimensions, schools, beliefs, and practices in an assortment of different religious traditions. In its early incarnation the course was called "Saints and Mystics" and became affectionately known around campus as S&M. As my own work became more interdisciplinary and multidisciplinary over the years that shift was also reflected in the changing focus of this course. In its present incarnation it examines mysticism from philosophical, anthropological, psychological, religious, and scientific perspectives. I may vary the types of religious mysticism we look at, but more often than not it has been Sufism (Islamic mysticism) and Chinese mysticism (Daoism). I make it quite clear to students, through discussion and course readings, that there is a rich and complex history to both Islamic and Chinese mysticism and that while neither Ibn' Attar's *Conference of the Birds* nor the *Daode jing* are fully representative of either tradition, they do embody some basic principles from each.

For the purposes of this essay I am using the term mysticism to mean religious mysticism, but even then in a fairly general and inclusive way. While the term mysticism is used to cover a broad range of experiences among fairly diverse traditions, there has been general agreement among scholars of mysticism and phenomenologists of religion as to the nature of mystical experience and what characterizes mystical states.[2] The term generally covers a wide range of spiritual and religious experience in which one directly experiences that which is perceived to be ultimately real, for example, the transcendent, the sacred, the holy, the divine. This direct experience, which is usually identified as a state of union or oneness, is one that intuitively imparts knowledge of ultimate reality by virtue of the knower becoming the known. It is also conceived as a state of consciousness. Mystical experience has often been recognized as one of the more powerful and extraordinary aspects of human existence. It is not only a spiritual experience but is conceived by many traditions as the spiritual experience par excellence; it is not only a way of knowledge but a direct path to the knowledge of the really real; it is not only a state of consciousness but a consciousness, as Ninian Smart suggests, "where one acquires a fundamental insight into the nature of reality."[3] In addition, some have also claimed that it is the highest and most cognitive state of human existence.

If we look at certain qualities that generally characterize mystical states, the picture perhaps becomes clearer. Mystical experiences or states seem to be characterized by the experience of oneness or union, timelessness, transiency, loss of self, ineffability, transformation, passivity-receptiveness, and a noetic quality, that is, the gaining of knowledge. This general definition of mysticism should provide a sufficient frame of reference to consider the *Daode jing* as a mystical text. It has certainly been argued by Daoist mystics throughout the ages that one can know the *Dao* only by becoming the *Dao*. While that may or may not be true, I would suggest that examining this text from a mystical perspective can enable us to acquire a deeper understanding of its inner or essential meaning.

Although I personally consider the case for the *Daode jing* as a mystical text to be self-evident, I refer the reader to Harold Roth and Livia Kohn (China specialists and scholars of Daoism) for a scholarly deliberation of the mystical nature of the *Daode jing*.[4] In addition, for a consideration of the case against the *Daode jing* as a mystical text, see Mark Csikszentmihaly. I am certainly interested in this debate, but the intention of this essay is not to advance a scholarly argument on this issue but to discuss how and why I have used the *Daode jing* as a mystical text. I would add, parenthetically, that while there have been numerous insightful and interesting interpretations and commentaries related to the *Daode jing* since its inception, both within and outside of China, to the best of my knowledge there has yet to be produced an authoritative exegesis of this rather enigmatic text.

There are numerous texts, in translation, that are an equally important part of the early Chinese mystical tradition, such as *Zhuangzi, Liezi, Huainanzi,* and *Xisheng jing*. However, the *Daode jing* provides a fairly clear basis for a Daoist mystical philosophy of life, naturalistic and quietistic, which has been developed by different schools within China. It is important to note that although the *Daode jing* may not be the single foundation stone on which Chinese mysticism was built, its value and importance to the tradition is significant. Livia Kohn claims that there may be some question as to whether the *Daode jing* is obviously a mystical text, yet she does indicate that in the judgment of the later tradition the "*Daode jing* is a mystical text of the first import. Together with *Zhuangzi* it has shaped and influenced Chinese mysticism like no other text."[5] In addition, the text is accessible to students who lack an extensive background in Chinese religion and provides a mystic vision, characterized by certain basic principles and qualities, that can be found in mystical texts in general. This makes it ideal for both a study of mysticism and a comparison to other forms of mysticism. From a course-specific perspective, the *Daode jing* allows students, in their pursuit of the meaning of the *Dao*, to deal with issues of union, oneness, ineffability, timelessness, intuitive understanding, and egolessness. For a phenomenological study of mysticism it is a natural.

Using the *Daode jing* as a mystical text allows me additionally to raise larger epistemological and pedagogical issues, which, in one sense, are the raison d'être of this course. In other words, in pursuing the elusive *Dao* one comes face-to-face with basic issues of what it means to know, what is known, and how one comes to know. We, along with our students, are clearly immersed in an age of scientism fostered by thinkers like Descartes, Bacon, Hobbes, and Newton, among others, with an emphasis on scientific method and rational and analytical thinking. Although I am hardly antiempiricist or antirationalist, I do fear that in our headlong rush for certainty and intellectual credibility we have, in many areas of inquiry, allowed ourselves to be seduced by the promises of this limited worldview, where scientific knowledge is often considered the only acceptable kind of knowledge. That there can be other ways of knowing, for instance, intuitive reasoning or understanding or through direct experience of the known, that are perhaps equally valid and reliable is generally not recognized. Rationalism, in short, is inadequate for an understanding of some of the deeper and more elusive truths of life. In pursuing the scientific path we have forgotten how to use our intuitive faculties and our bodies as agents of knowing. Working with the *Daode jing* as a mystical text can serve as a type of Zen koan (enigmatic question or riddle), which may provoke a type of mental crisis, forcing one to go beyond the rational, analytical, ordering mind to intuition.

Ultimately, the significant issue for me becomes how the *Daode jing* can be used to force us to confront these larger epistemological issues. There is little argument among scholars that this extraordinary text is multilayered and can be read, legitimately, from a number of perspectives: as a philosophical text, a political statement, social commentary, a literary piece, and a mystical text. In my courses dealing with the Chinese religious worldview, where the emphasis is on looking at religion from a cultural perspective, we look at the *Daode jing* in both its cultural and historical milieux as well as from the aforementioned perspectives. While being aware of the cultural and historical context and the numerous ways that this text can be interpreted, students in the course on mysticism are obviously encouraged to read it as a mystical text. I would argue not only that the *Daode jing* can clearly be read as a mystical text but that, in fact, employing this perspective will greatly enhance other *ways* of reading and understanding the *Daode jing* and, again, serve to highlight certain epistemo-logical issues. Although, as previously noted, I consider the case for the *Daode jing* as a mystical text to be self-evident, I still expect students to make this case in the context of this course. Obviously they assume that it is a mystical text since it is being used in a course on mysticism. However, that does not preclude me from forcing them to establish that case, as they are required to do with texts from other traditions that are being used in the course. The two primary overarching issues that we deal with in this course are: What is the nature of ultimate reality? and How may one experience that reality? With the basic assumption that mysticism and mystical experience encompass those two issues, we work on establishing, through the use of numerous sources, what mysticism is and what generally characterizes mystical experiences or states. Our working definition tends to be fairly inclusive of many different types of mysticism and many different perspectives, including philosophical, anthropological, psychological, religious, and scientific. Although any model or definition has its obvious limitations, we work at developing a fairly comprehensive and flexible model that, while admittedly far-reaching, still has sufficient structure to allow for a workable schema.

At the point in the course where students are dealing with the *Daode jing*, they usually have a very good understanding of what generally constitutes mystical philosophy and what characterizes mystical experience. A particular piece that is extremely well suited for preparing students to deal with the *Daode jing* as a mystical text is Erich Neumann's essay "Mystical Man."[6] Neumann offers us a mystical anthropology in his basic claim that not only is man capable of mystical experience, but he is mystical by his very nature. In fact, Neumann argues that one does not become fully human, that is, realize one's full potential, until the outer self (individual self, ego) becomes fully united with the inner self (numen, numinous, transpersonal self, the creative void), which certainly could be conceived of as the *Dao*. Like Neumann's creative void, the *Dao* exists within each of us, whether discovered or not. This creative void and our mystical nature, whether realized or not, can be found in the early psychological source of original unity and lives in our psyche as the archetype of paradisal wholeness. For Neumann, one's journey through life is to recapture this lost wholeness (returning to the root, the *Dao*) in full consciousness and to see, in the transparency of the world, the numinous substratum (*Dao*) and that the human is an aspect of numinous existence.

With the preparatory background in place, students undertake both exegetical and hermeneutical analysis. I am fully aware of the limitations of this analysis for students at this level, but I am also convinced that this type of exploration will allow them to come to grips with some of the basic issues of the

Daode jing in a valuable way. In promoting a hermeneutical methodology I require students not only to think in these terms in preparation for class discussion but also to keep a journal in which they explore and wrestle with these ideas in some detail. The journal is effective preparation for class discussion because it forces students to go into much greater depth in exploring these ideas through interpretation, reflection, and critical analysis.

The beauty of the *Daode jing* as a mystical text is that it wastes no time hitting the reader right in the face with the critical epistemological issue, which, of course, becomes a significant pedagogical issue as well: How can you describe or talk about the *Dao* if it is ineffable? The *Dao* is quickly identified as the Ultimate, the First Principle, the Root of all existence, the Mother of all things, but also as the Nameless (*wuming*), the Ineffable, the Indescribable:

> As for the Way, the Way that can be spoken of is not the con-
> stant Way:
> As for names, the name that can be named is not the constant name.
> The nameless is the beginning of the ten thousand things;
> The named is the mother of the ten thousand things.
> Therefore, those constantly without desires, by this means will per-
> ceive its subtlety.
> Those constantly with desires, by this will see only that which they
> yearn for and seek.
> These two together emerge;
> They have different names yet they're called the same;
> That which is even more profound than the profound—
> The gateway of all subtleties.[7]

So we are initially made aware that there is, in fact, an ultimate reality, but it cannot be described. As students continue to search the text for the *Dao*, the issue of ineffability, common to mystical experience, becomes clear. In their pursuit of this elusive reality they discover within the text that the *Dao* is undifferentiated, the One, the source of the phenomenal world, change, everything that changes, transcendent, immanent, omnipresent, pervasive, and more (see *Daode jing* chapters 16, 25, 39, and 42).What they begin to perceive is that these are things *about* the *Dao*, that is, hints, suggestions, and allusions, but they are not *the Dao*. Whatever one can say about the *Dao* is not *the Dao*. Again, one is faced with one of the primary insights regarding mystical experience: that there is a certain transcendental truth that lies beyond words.

At this point the frustration and anxiety level among students is usually quite high due to their emotional and intellectual attachment to abstract ideas. They want absolutes! This is actually a very advantageous position for them to be in if they are patient enough to appreciate several things. First, when dealing with spiritual states and higher states of consciousness, language and abstract ideas are inherently limited. Second, if there is, in fact, a transcendent reality that incorporates all of existence and is a part of everything, including ourselves, there must be some way of apprehending that reality. Generally, their first conclusion is that there is an ultimate reality called *Dao* but that this reality can never be captured by words or concepts. This is obviously being claimed by the text itself.

After reading the *Daode jing* students turn to a number of secondary sources to further explore notions of the *Dao*. However, through their understanding of mysticism they know that now the challenge becomes one of discovering what the path to this reality is: How does one possibly come to know the *Dao*? While dismayed by the elusiveness of the *Dao* and the limitation of words in pursuing it, they do begin to sense, in pondering the *Dao*, that there is something there, just beyond their grasp—a kind of all-inclusive unity which the text suggests but which they can't quite apprehend. This sense of elusiveness is captured for them in their reading of the fourth-century c.e. poet T'ao Ch'ien:

> I gather chrysanthemums at the eastern hedgerow
> And silently gaze at the southern mountains.
> The mountain air is beautiful in the sunset,
> And the birds flocking together return home
> Among all of these things is a real meaning,
> Yet when I try to express it, I become lost in "no words."[8]

This particular poem usually strikes certain chords, stimulating them to draw analogies from experiences, particularly spiritual experiences, in their own lives, for instance, about love, nature, and the sacred. Reflection on these personal experiences allows them to bring the notion of ineffability more clearly into focus. At the same time they begin to appreciate the poetic structure and power of the *Daode jing*, that is, the value of symbolic language: metaphor, suggestiveness, images, ambiguity. This is a text that can't just be read and taken literally; it must be listened to, heard, and felt. Though we may not be able to fully apprehend the *Dao* through words or concepts, words can be used symbolically to suggest what cannot be stated and to engage the reader at a more existential or intuitive level. This experience begins to move them in the direction of intuition as a possible *way* of *knowing* or coming closer to the *Dao*.

After reading the *Daode jing* and the secondary sources we begin to discuss the Daoist notion of not thinking, in a rational sense, as a way of knowing and the Daoist fondness for paradox. To stimulate consideration and discussion of the value of not thinking I have them read a rather humorous piece, called "The Professor," which alludes to the limitations of thinking as we generally conceive it. The following excerpt captures its flavor:

> A few years ago I used to tell myself that I wanted to marry a cowboy. Why shouldn't an English professor say this to herself—living alone, fascinated by a brown landscape, spotting a cowboy in a pickup truck sometimes in her rearview mirror as she drives on the broad highways of the West Coast? In fact, I realize I would still like to marry a cowboy, though by now I'm living in the East and married already to someone who is not a cowboy...
>
> More important than the clothes a cowboy wore, and the way he wore them, was the fact that a cowboy probably wouldn't know much more than he had to. He would think about his work, and about his family, if he had one, and about having a good time, and not much else. I was tired of so much thinking, which was what I did most in those days. I did other things, but I went on thinking while I did them. I might feel something but I would think about what I was feeling at the same time. I even had to think about what I was thinking and wonder why I was thinking it. When I had the idea of marrying a cowboy I imagined that maybe a cowboy would help me stop thinking so much.[9]

This piece may not be heavily philosophical, but it does get them to consider how they generally attempt to know something, that is, to think about it, conceptualize it, and define it. When we discuss spiritual states or religious experience, however, they begin to realize the limits of rational and conceptual thinking and that there are additional powerful and profound ways of knowing at our disposal. Albert Einstein confessed, late in his life, that his deepest understanding of the universe did not come from his rational thought process but from his intuitive awareness.

As we continue to wrestle with the notion of the *Dao* being the One, students further appreciate the limitations of rational thought or thinking about the *Dao* as a process that is inherently dualistic. The mind objectifies the *Dao* by thinking about it, and thus the *Dao* loses its essential wholeness or oneness. Of course, if the *Dao* is everything, then it is also rational mind and subsequently can be apprehended, at least in part, by our rational thought processes. At this point they generally begin to realize, more fully, that indeed there are things that they have come to know in their lives intuitively as a result of direct experience, where there has been a sense of becoming the other, that is, the knower becoming the known. It is not necessary for them to become aware of the fact that they are the *Dao*, that is, have had a mystical experience, for them to come to the aforementioned realization. In a sense, their wrestling with this notion is like Zen koan practice, where the rational mind begins to sense its limitations. This raises some of the larger epistemological issues of how we come to know and the value of intuition.

One of the primary issues uncovered at this point, that they are quite familiar with in their study of mysticism and which is an essential part of the *Daode jing*, is the need to overcome the phenomenal self to acquire complete knowledge of the *Dao*. One needs to attain a state of selflessness and become the *Dao*. As Chang Chung-yuan suggests, "The awareness of the identification and inter-penetration of self and non-self is the key that unlocks the mystery of the *Dao*."[10] This need to overcome the limitations and restrictions of the ego is a persistent theme in mysticism universally. It is a theme that forces students to deal directly with notions of self and the relationship of self to some larger, and in this case ultimate, reality. In reading the *Daode jing* from any perspective, this is an issue that cannot be avoided. Once again, the larger epistemological issue comes to the fore: How does one come to know the *Dao*? As Livia Kohn points out, the main obstacles to truly knowing the *Dao* "are the senses and the intellect, which continuously boost a separate notion of ego through emotions and desires, classifications and conscious knowledge."[11]

At this point in our study students begin to understand that while the *Daode jing* presents them with a mystical vision of the Cosmos, and their place in it, it remains quite subtle and elusive regarding the path to this vision. In the realization of this mystical vision, one is directed to become the *Dao*, to be reunited, to return to the root from which one has come: "The thousands of things all around are active—I give my attention to Turning Back. Things growing wild as weeds, all turn back to the Root."[12] This idea of returning becomes an additional theme in the *Daode jing* that generally proves to be a rich and fruitful area of exploration and access for students. We explore this notion of *returning to the source* by focusing on the persistent universal human psychological urge to return to that from which we've come: God, the void, the universe, nature. As they contemplate what it means to return to the *Dao* this generally gets played out, by analogy, in a nostalgic longing to return to childhood, their hometown, or some spot in nature that they have been attracted to. They realize that these attempts to fulfill this urge of returning are ultimately unsatisfying because what they seek to return to is no longer the same—things change. They are not a return to the unchanging, the familiar, the source, the *Dao*.

Admittedly, the *Daode jing*, while offering some general guidelines to finding or becoming the *Dao*, is for the most part devoid of practical instructions.

Certainly the mystic path, as it is generally defined, can be found within the threads woven through this elusive text, from the necessity to overcome self and ego and the senses to ultimately attaining a state of union with the One. A further exploration of the later Daoist mystical sects points us toward more specific techniques that were, and continue to be, employed as methods to acquire what the *Daode jing* is calling for: becoming the *Dao*.

As part of the course we do have several sessions with a Qi Gong master and Daoist meditation instructor. The intent here is not to experience oneness with the *Dao* but to give students a sense of how one actually goes beyond intellect and abstract thinking to *know* the *Dao*. It is essential that they come to realize that in this pursuit of the *Dao* one must use one's whole being, that the body is also capable of knowing and experiencing this oneness, and that in the union of mind, body, and spirit is where the *Dao* lies.

Once again, I want to be clear that the mystic perspective is not *the* way to understand the *Daode jing*, but it is one way and, potentially, a very fruitful way. I am also fully aware of the reductionist argument from scholars like Steven Katz. However, being sensitive to the dangers of typologies—mystical vision, path, experience, states, and so on—I would still argue that if used prudently and flexibly they do have value. Does the *Daode jing* provide a mystical vision of the Cosmos and our place in it? I think so. I tend to agree with the *Laozi bianhua jing* (Scripture of the Transformations of Laozi) as interpreted by Livia Kohn, which describes

> a cosmological scheme . . . where the philosopher is no longer simply
> a human being; the *Dao* is no longer only a philosophical concept
> referring to the organic, inherent order of the world. In the merg-
> ing of both, philosopher and *Dao*, the cosmicization of humanity
> coincides with the humanization of the Universe. This coincidence,
> then, forms the mythological paradigm for the individual Daoist's
> aspirations to mystical oneness as well as for the communal practice
> of the *Dao*.[13]

By working through the text with an understanding of mysticism and what characterizes mystical states, students are able to reach these insights and conclusions by themselves. These qualities of oneness, intuition, selflessness, ineffability, and timelessness, so characteristic of mystical experience and philosophy, provide access into the meaning and power of the *Daode jing* and an appreciation of some of its claims and insights. These are not always easy concepts to deal with, but, along with an understanding of context, cultural and historical milieux, linguistic analysis, and so on, they can help us with meaning and understanding. I would argue, however, that if the mystical perspective is not employed, we are left with a rather lifeless and static philosophical tome representing something about a culture long gone.

It is important that we don't make the *Daode jing* what we want it to be. From my own experience in China, the *Daode jing* is still a widely read text that is vibrant, dynamic, and meaningful and continues to impact people's lives in a variety of ways. In part, the vital dynamic quality of the *Daode jing* can be understood by investigating and discovering the mystical dimension of this text, which provides access to what I've heard Michael LaFargue describe as "historical meanings for them and contemporary meanings for us."

NOTES

1. Michael LaFargue, "Recovering the Tao-te-ching's Original Meaning: Some Remarks on Historical Hermeneutics," in *Lao-tzu and the Tao-te-ching*, ed. Livia Kohn and Michael LaFargue (Albany: State University of New York Press, 1998), 255.

2. For a more detailed explication of mysticism, mystical experience, characteristics of mystical states, and the mystic path, consult Robert Elwood, *Mysticism and Religion* (Englewood Cliffs, N.J.: Prentice-Hall, 1980); F. C. Happold, *Mysticism: A Study and an Anthology* (Harmondsworth: Penguin, 1980); William James, *The Varieties of Religious Experience* (Cambridge, Mass.: Harvard University Press, 1985); Richard Woods, *Understanding Mysticism* (Garden City, N.Y.: Image Books, 1980); Steven Katz, ed., *Mysticism and Philosophical Analysis* (New York: Oxford University Press, 1978); Frits Staal, *Exploring Mysticism: A Methodological Essay* (Berkeley: University of California Press).

3. Ninian Smart, "Understanding Religious Experience," in Katz. *Mysticism and Philosophical Analysis*, 13.

4. Harold Roth, "The Laozi in the Context of Early Daoist Mystical Praxis," in *Religious and Philosophical Aspects of the Laozi*, ed. Mark Csikszentmihalyi and Philip J. Ivanhoe (Albany: State University of New York Press, 1999), 59–96; Livia Kohn, *Early Chinese Mysticism: Philosophy and Soteriology in the Taoist Tradition*. (Princeton: Princeton University Press, 1992).

5. Kohn, *Early Chinese Mysticism*, 44–45.

6. Erich Neumann, "Mystical Man," in *The Mystic Vision: Papers from the Eranos Yearbooks*, vol. 6, Bolingen Series, (Princeton: Princeton University Press, 1968), 375–415.

7. Robert G. Henricks, *Lao-Tzu Te-Tao-Ching: A New Translation Based on the Recently Discovered Ma-wang-tui Texts* (New York: Ballantine Books, 1989), 53.

8. Chang Chung-yuan, *Creativity and Taoism: A Study of Chinese Philosophy, Art and Poetry* (New York: Harper & Row, 1970), 53.

9. Lydia Davis, "The Professor," *Harpers'*, February 1992, 56–59.

10. Chang Chung-yuan, *Creativity and Taoism*, 20.

11. Kohn, *Early Chinese Mysticism*, 8.

12. Michael LaFargue, *The Tao of the Tao Te Ching* (Albany: State University of New York Press, 1992), 62.

13. Kohn, *Early Chinese Mysticism*, 44–45.

The *Daode Jing* in Practice

Eva Wong

The goal of this chapter is to present the teachings of the *Daode jing* from the perspective of practice. To the practitioner of the Daoist arts, the texts of Daoism are not just objects of intellectual inquiry but guidelines for practice. Almost all the texts of the Daoist canon (*Daozang*) were written by practitioners for practitioners. In the Daoist tradition, study and practice are inseparable: to study is to practice and to practice is to study. Understanding a text can help us practice its teachings; practicing its teachings can help us understand its meanings.

The *Daode jing* contains a wealth of knowledge and wisdom on subject matters as diverse as statecraft and politics, the nature of reality (the *Dao*), sagehood, and the arts of cultivating health and longevity. While much has been written about the *Daode jing*'s views on the first three topics, far less attention has been devoted to its approach on cultivating life. In this essay I highlight this aspect of the *Daode jing*'s teachings, discuss how understanding a text can help us practice its teachings, and show how practice can help us decipher meanings in a text.

The Art of Understanding a Text

Daoist texts, like most works from spiritual traditions, can be read and interpreted at multiple levels. The art of interpreting and deciphering hidden meanings in a text is called hermeneutics. It recognizes that a text has many levels of meaning and that the meaning carried in the semantics of the text is only its surface meaning. A deeper level of meaning is expressed in *how* the text was written, not just *what* was written. Even deeper levels of meaning are carried in the "intention" of a text, whose meaning can be grasped only if we listen to the language of the text and not just read its "words." To listen to a text, one needs to suspend judgment, quiet the critical mind, and become receptive to it. If we are willing to listen to and learn from a text, the text will open to us a world of meaning that is inaccessible to our analytical mind.

Many Daoist texts were written with the intention to encode several levels of meaning. The exoteric levels of meaning are carried in the superficial layers of the text, and the esoteric meanings are encoded in the deeper layers. Exoteric meaning can be grasped by the common or even casual reader, but esoteric meaning is meant for those initiated into the practice.

In the Daoist tradition, "safety" more than anything else was the motivation behind encoding multiple levels of meaning into a text. Some techniques are dangerous if they are practiced unsupervised or if the practitioner does not have the sufficient spiritual foundation. Most of the texts of Daoist internal alchemy written between the third and thirteenth centuries fall into this category.

Some Daoist texts, however, were not written with the "intention" of hiding secret meanings. But as Daoism became more a discipline of study than a practice, the number of practitioners dwindled, and meanings that were once known among a large community of practitioners became "hidden" or lost. I think this is why certain sections of the *Daode jing* (especially the parts concerned with the arts of health and longevity) have become esoteric. I do not believe that these sections of the text contain dangerous knowledge; it is more likely that they contain lost knowledge.

It is known that the *Daode jing* was written by more than one person. Its contents clearly fall into four separate categories: statecraft and politics, the nature of reality (the *Dao*), sagehood, and the arts of health and longevity. The parts of the text concerned with statecraft and politics are relatively easy to understand. The sections on the nature of the *Dao* contain more cryptic references. This is probably because anything that we can say about the *Dao* can only be indirect: "The way that can be spoken of is not the unchanging Way" (chapter 1). The parts of the text concerned with sagehood are easily decipherable if we listen to them with a receptive mind; most of them offer practical advice on daily living. The portions of the text that deal with the arts of health and longevity are considered to be the most esoteric and the most difficult to understand. Later in the chapter, I show that these esoteric passages of the *Daode jing* can easily be deciphered by "practice".

Deciphering the Meaning of a Text with Practice

From the hermeneutical point of view, the subsurface semantics (and pragmatics) of a text can be uncovered by deconstruction, but hidden meanings can be revealed only by listening to the language of a text. To these two methods of deciphering a text I would like to add the use of "practice". "Practice" can be a powerful tool for recovering meanings that cannot be accessed by semantics or pragmatics or by listening to the language. Listening to the *Daode jing* can help us understand its teachings, but practice can help us to recover its lost meanings.

Understanding the *Daode Jing* from the Perspective of Practice

The goal of Daoist practice is to maintain a healthy body and a clear mind, to be free from stress and anxiety, and to live a contented and long life. To this end, Daoists advocate cultivating the mind by emptying it of desire, cultivating the body by filling it with life energy, and adopting a lifestyle of simplicity and quietude. We shall consider the *Daode jing*'s teachings on each of these topics in turn.

The Daode jing *on Cultivating the Mind*

First we shall examine the *Daode jing*'s teachings on cultivating the mind by listening to the language of the text.

According to the *Daode jing*, desire is the cause of poor health, anxiety, mental anguish, and the inability to live a happy and contented life. Desire is attachment. The desire for material things comes from attachment to objects or things in the world; the desire to be important, to be recognized, to achieve, and to be in control comes from attachment to the self.

Anxiety arises as a result of attachment to material things. We are anxious to get what we don't have and anxious about losing what we have. Desire can blind us to the distinction between needs and wants. Consequently, many people end up spending more time and effort accumulating possessions than enjoying them. And the more possessions they have, the more afraid they are of losing them. The *Daode jing* (chapter 44) says, "If you have a lot of desire, you will probably be extravagant. The more you hoard, the more you will lose."

Attachment to material things can also affect the functioning of the senses. Instead of simply being things in the world, objects become attractive or unattractive (to the eyes), pleasant or unpleasant (to the ears), and pleasing or unpleasing (to the palate). When the senses become overstimulated, they become dull. When they become dull, they cease to function properly, and when they stop functioning, we become confused and disoriented. Moreover, if the senses are too preoccupied with objects of desire, they can no longer warn us of impending dangers. The *Daode jing* (chapter 12) says:

> The five colors can confuse your sight.
> The five sounds can dull your hearing.
> The five flavors can injure your sense of taste.
> Racing and hunting can drive you mad.
> Material goods that are hard to get will hinder your movement.

Excessive excitement can be detrimental to health. Activities that pump up the adrenaline (such as racing and hunting) may give us a temporary "high", but since excitement cannot last forever, a "high" is always followed by a "low". This cyclical swing between excitement and the return to normal levels of stimulation is harmful to both physical and mental health because it does not give the mind and the body sufficient time to adjust to two extreme states of functioning.

Desire is not just directed toward material things. We can also desire immaterial things, such as knowledge, fame, achievement, and power. According to the *Daode jing*, desire for knowledge can make thinking rigid and one-sided. This is because the pursuit of knowledge requires the mind to be oriented toward objects in the world, whether things, people, or ideas. If we place too much emphasis on knowing about the object-world, we will not be able to look inward and learn about ourselves. Chapter 33 of the *Daode jing* says:

> To understand others is to be clever.
> To understand yourself is to be enlightened.
> You can use force to conquer others.
> But you will need strength to conquer yourself.

Let us listen to the language in this passage more closely. First, the text contrasts "clever" (*zhi*) with "enlightened" (*ming*) to distinguish object-knowledge, which is associated with cleverness, from self-knowledge, which is associated with enlightenment. In Chinese, the word for cleverness, *"zhi,"* has connotations of "know-how" and "knowledge gained by trickery." In fact, *zhi* is used often with *"qu,"* as in *zhiqu* to mean using trickery and underhandedness to win. On the other hand, enlightenment is *"ming,"* which has the connotation of brightness. Thus, while cleverness can give us small gains and temporary knowledge, it is enlightenment (or self-knowledge) that can illuminate and guide us in our daily lives.

Second, the text contrasts "force" (*li*) with "strength" (*qiang*). *"Li"* has the connotation of brute force. *Li* has no intelligence and is incapable of admitting failure; it is like a bulldozer crashing against a wall. If the wall is weak, brute force will break it, but if the wall is strong, brute force will be ineffective. On the other hand, *qiang* has the connotation of inner strength. *Qiang* is intelligent; it recognizes its limits and is capable of accepting its own weakness. Thus, while force can give us temporary control of a situation, it is strength that allows us to evaluate the external situation, understand ourselves, and act accordingly.

A more subtle form of desire is the desire for self-importance. The desire for self-importance is associated with the desire to achieve and to be recognized. According to the *Daode jing*, the notion of "achievement" is created by us so that we can give importance to our actions. When insects procreate, flowers bloom, and water nourishes the soil, they do not consider their actions as "achievements". In contrast, humanity has transformed "action" into "achievement", and in doing so, we have given ourselves a false sense of self-respect as well as distanced ourselves from the natural way of things. Of self-importance, the *Daode jing* (chapter 24) says:

> Those who boast are not rooted.
> Those who inflate themselves will get nowhere.
> Those who display themselves do not shine.
> Those who publicize their actions accomplish nothing.
> Those who praise themselves do not last long.

The words "boast," "inflate," "display," "publicize," and "praise" describe different ways of distorting reality. To boast is to distort by adding personal opinions: the choice to emphasize particular actions is also the choice to omit others. To inflate is to distort by making something appear more important than it really is. To display is to distort by making one thing more prominent than others. To publicize is to distort by making one thing more obvious than others: the choice to make one thing known is also the choice to render certain things unknown. Finally, to praise is to distort by giving a favorable opinion: to praise oneself is to boast behind a veil of modesty.

The desire to achieve often leads people to do heroic and stupid things that can hurt or kill them. The *Daode jing* (chapter 73) says, "If you are brave and daring, you'll be killed. However, if you are brave and not daring, you'll survive."

Here the words "brave" (*yong*) and "daring" (*gan*) are used jointly to define the meaning of courage. The contrast is not between "brave" and "daring," but between "brave and daring" and "brave and not daring." "*Yong*" is a state of mind, and "*gan*" is a display of courage. Thus, to be "brave and daring" is to act *like* a hero with reckless disregard for consequences. We can think of *gan* as dumb courage. To be "brave and not daring" is to take the appropriate and necessary action after assessing the situation.

People who are brave and daring will usually find it hard to yield, because for them, to yield is to be cowardly. Thus, they would rather forfeit their lives than retreat. However, people who are brave and not daring will know when to yield, and in yielding, they will survive.

The desire to be in control makes people want to interfere, believing that they can make things happen or not happen. However, since we cannot control everything, to believe that we are in control only gives us a false sense of security, a security that is shattered when things do not turn out the way we expect them to. Thus, if we believe that we are in control, we will likely be sad, frustrated, irritated, and disappointed if things go wrong. However, if we accept that there are certain things that we cannot control, we will be better prepared when situations turn aversive.

Sometimes we can actually make things worse by trying to interfere and make them happen. Chapter 64 of the *Daode jing* says:

> Those who act on it will ruin it.
> Those who hold on to it will lose it.
> The sage does not act upon things,
> Therefore he does not ruin them.
> He does not hold on to things,
> Therefore he does not lose them.

In this passage we find the famous contrast between "action" (*wei*) and "non-action" (*wuwei*). "*Wei*" is the act of interfering. By acting upon something, we modify and transform it. On the other hand, *wuwei* is the act of not-interfering. By not-acting *on* something, we let it run its natural course and do not interfere with its natural tendencies. *Wuwei* does not mean "doing nothing"; rather, it means acting appropriately according to the natural way of things. If *wuwei* had meant doing nothing, then the text would have said "those who act," not "those who act on it." The *Daode jing* does not teach us to do nothing. Rather, it tells us to abstain from actions whose ends are to manipulate and to control.

To hold on to something is to be attached to it. In Chinese, the word for "hold" (*zhi*) also means to grasp, and to grasp means not to let go. If we cannot let go of things, ideas, and even relationships, we will always be anxious about gains and losses. There is a Chinese phrase that describes the meaning of "letting go" most aptly: "to be able to pick it up and to be able to put it down."

The *Daode jing* not only describes the causes of ill health, anxiety, and the inability to live a happy and contented life. It also teaches us how to overcome desire by cultivating a mind that is free of attachments. One way to cultivate the mind is to change our attitude toward ourselves and toward things in the world. In Daoist practice, decreasing self-importance, knowing our limits, learning to yield, practicing noninterference, and living a simple life are all part of the discipline called "taming the mind." Another way to cultivate the mind is to change it from being centered on itself to being centered on nothing. The practice of emptying the mind of thoughts through silence is part of the discipline called "stilling the mind." While the practice of "taming the mind" is typically integrated into everyday living and does not require formal supervision, the practice of "stilling the mind" requires rigorous training and formal instruction. Today, the techniques of "stilling the mind" are collectively known as "meditation."

In taming the mind, we must first dissolve the desire for material things. However, Daoism does not promote deprivation or even asceticism. Rather, it teaches us to live in moderation and understand the difference between wants and needs. The *Daode jing* (chapter 29) says, "The sage rejects the extreme, the extravagant, and the excessive." To be moderate is not to live in extremes; to live simply is not to be extravagant; and to live contently is not to indulge in excessiveness. If the *Daode jing* had favored asceticism, it would have endorsed hardship and told us to abandon all comforts in life.

Second, we need to minimize self-importance. This means doing things out of necessity and not for praise and recognition. In fact, we need to understand that "achievement" and "accomplishment" are the creations of a self-centered mind, and that in this world there are only appropriate and inappropriate actions. Pulling someone out of a burning house is not a heroic act or an achievement; it is the natural and appropriate thing to do given the situation. Of decreasing self-importance and self-centeredness, chapter 30 of the *Daode jing* says:

The sage produces results and does not brag about it.
He produces results and does not praise himself for it.
He produces results and does not boast about it.

He produces results because that's what he would do.
And he gets things done without using any force.

It is interesting to note that in the text, the word *"guo,"* which I have translated as "produces results," is used to describe the actions of the sage. *Guo's* original and literal meaning is "fruit." Therefore, *guo* means actions that yield fruits, results, or effects. The sage "produces results" with his actions and understands that it is the fruit of the action, not the actor, that is important.

Third, in taming the mind, we need to know our limits and not indulge in excesses. The *Daode jing* (chapter 44) says, "Know when to stop, and you will be around for a long time." All things have their limits. The key to health and longevity is in knowing when something is excessive, be it eating, drinking, walking, sitting, sleeping, or thinking. Excessive eating and drinking damage the bowels; excessive walking damages the tendons; excessive sitting and sleeping damage the bones; and excessive thinking tires the mind. If the activities in our daily life are balanced, then mind and body will be balanced and healthy.

Fourth, we need to let go of the desire to interfere and to be in control. Chapter 2 of the *Daode jing* says:

> The sage attends to the affairs of non-action and practices wordless teachings.
> The ten thousand things are set in motion but he is not their agent.
> He gives birth to them but does not hold on to them.
> He finishes his tasks but is not attached to them.
> He retires when the work is done.

If we understand that we are not the prime mover of events, and that many things are better off when they are left to run their natural course, we will be less prone to interfere or try to take control. The less we see ourselves as the center of things, the less we will be entangled in the affairs of others, and the less we will bring trouble and unnecessary worries into our lives.

Apart from changing attitudes and incorporating the changes into their daily lives, Daoist practitioners also use meditation to empty the mind of thoughts and desire. The passages that describe the techniques of "stilling the mind" (or meditation) are found in chapters 10 and 36. The meanings in these passages, I think, are best deciphered by "practice." There are three lines in chapter 10 that allude to three different forms of Daoist meditation. The first line reads, "In nourishing the soul—can you embrace the One and not let it leave?"

There is a form of Daoist meditation known as "Holding or Embracing the One." Holding or Embracing the One means keeping the undifferentiated energy of the *Dao* within. We are born with the primordial energy of the *Dao*, and this energy is kept within us by our spirit. However, desire and attachment to things in the world can lead the spirit away by drawing it toward the objects of desire. When the spirit departs, we can no longer keep the primordial energy within, and when the primordial energy leaves, we will become ill. A commentary on the *Daode jing* by Heshang Gong, believed to have been written in the Han dynasty (third century B.C.E. to third century C.E.), states, "If people can hold onto the spirit and unite it with the One, they will not die."

To keep the spirit within so that it can hold on to the primordial energy of the *Dao*, the practitioner first slows the thoughts and stills the mind until no mental activity is present. Physical stillness is recommended but not necessary; the mind can be still when one is walking. Once stillness is attained, the undifferentiated energy of the *Dao* can be held and gathered to nourish the body and clear the mind.

The second line reads, "In circulating the breath and making it soft—can you do it like that of an infant?" There is a form of Daoist meditation that uses techniques of circulating and regulating breath to cultivate physical health and mental clarity. Daoists believe that breath sustains life by circulating energy in the body. Thus, proper breathing can enhance health and longevity.

This passage refers to a form of breathing in Daoist practice that is known as "infant breathing." Infant breathing involves synchronizing abdominal movement with inhalation and exhalation. It is soft and slow and is never forced or controlled by conscious thoughts. The *Daode jing* (chapter 55) states, "If the mind were to control the breath, this would be forcing things." When we can breathe like an infant, energy in the body will be replenished and we will be rejuvenated.

Abdominal breathing itself is deep breathing. In this form of breathing, the air is allowed to sink into the belly before it is exhaled. Abdominal breathing requires much diaphragmatic action and the internal organs must be pliable enough to move out of the way when the diaphragm presses down during inhalation. Modern practitioners of the Daoist arts incorporate the techniques of circulating and regulating breath into a discipline called *qigong* (which literally means "the work of breath and energy"). Fetal or infant breathing is the most advanced stage of *qigong*, and it can be practiced only after many years of training.

The third line reads, "In cleaning the subtle mirror—can you make it spotless?"

There is a form of Daoist meditation that is designed to empty the mind of desire by stopping thoughts. The subtle mirror is the mind, which when cleaned (that is, emptied), can see through the illusions of desire. The image of the mind as a mirror and the metaphor of cleaning it are used also by the Chan (Zen) Buddhists (who were influenced by Daoism) to describe the process of stopping the thought processes and recovering the original empty mind.

Today, this form of Daoist meditation is practiced widely by members of the Complete Reality (*quanzhen*) School of Daoism, who believe that the mind must be emptied of thoughts and desire before the techniques of rejuvenating the body can be practiced.

Another form of meditation practiced by Daoists is "Internal Observation" (*dingguan* or *neiguan*). The principles behind this form of meditation are described in chapter 36 of the *Daode jing*:

> If you want to get rid of it, you must cooperate with it.
> If you wish to take something away from it, you must contribute to it.

Internal observation requires the practitioner to use the mind to subdue the mind. In this form of meditation, one observes the rise and fall of sensations, emotions, thoughts, and desires, becoming mindful that such phenomena are products of an active mind that is attached to desire. Internal observation encourages the use of "productive" mental activity (mindfulness) to conquer "wayward" mental activity. Productive mental activity is the mindful activity that analyzes the rise and fall of thoughts and sensations and eventually understands the futility of attachment. On the other hand, wayward mental activity is thinking that is directed toward objects of desire. To use productive mental activity to defeat wayward mental activity is what is meant by "getting rid of it by cooperating with it" and "taking it away by contributing to it."

The Daode jing *on Cultivating the Body*

Daoists believe that health and longevity are intimately linked to the level of energy in the body. When we were in our mother's womb, we were nourished by the primordial energy of the *Dao*. After we are born, the contact with that primordial energy is lost. From then on, any energy spent can no longer be replenished by this inexhaustible source. With growth, puberty, and maturity, energy continues to be spent as we think, desire, and have sex. The more we indulge in these activities, the faster the energy will dissipate. The faster the energy dissipates, the faster we will age. When the body does not have enough energy to heal its injuries or protect itself from diseases, we will become weak and ill. When the energy is completely spent, we will die.

Chapter 13 of the *Daode jing* says:

The reason why I have a problem
Is because I have a body.
If I had no body, then all my problems would go away.

Although *Daoists* believe that the body is the root of the problem of ill health, they do not believe that it is "evil" or "extraneous." The body is the source of the problem only because it is where desire originates. Daoists do not deny the body. If they had believed in the denial of the body, they would not have developed techniques to nourish it.

Desire damages health, because when energy is spent on satisfying wants, it cannot be used to nourish the body. The *Daode jing* (chapter 44) puts this choice between health and desire very bluntly:

Fame or your body, which do you want more?
Your Body or your wealth, which do you value more?

Energy can also dissipate through openings in the body. The mouth, for example, is an area of the body where energy can leak out. This is why the *Daode jing* (chapter 5) says, "Talk too much and you'll be exhausted." Speaking is an activity that can cause energy to escape from the body. This is because two major channels of energy in the body (the *du* and *ren* meridians) connect at the palate of the mouth. If we close the mouth, the channels are connected and energy is kept within the body. If we open the mouth, the two meridians are disconnected and an opening has been created for the energy to escape. Therefore, maintaining silence and speaking only when necessary can help us conserve energy.

One technique used by Daoists to cultivate health and longevity involves blocking the openings to prevent the energy from flowing out of the body. Consider this passage from chapter 52 of the *Daode jing*:

Block the holes and close the doors,
And you will not be labored all your life.
Open the holes and meddle in affairs,
And all your life you will never be saved.

Blocking the holes and closing the doors mean closing the orifices of the body so that energy does not leak out. The orifices are the mouth, the nostrils, the anus, and the sexual organs. (The ears are not considered orifices because the eardrum is a physical barrier.) If these openings are not blocked, energy will escape out of the body.

To prevent the leakage of energy, Daoists have developed techniques to block the four openings. To block the orifice at the mouth, we minimize speech and keep the tongue against the palate. To block the orifice at the nose, we soften the breath and breathe with the diaphragm. To block the orifice at the anus, we sit and sleep in postures designed to cover that opening. And to prevent the energy from escaping through the sexual organs, Daoists use special techniques to conserve and control the expenditure of energy during sexual intercourse. These techniques are called "bedchamber techniques" and are also recognized by the classics of traditional Chinese medicine such as *The Yellow Emperor's Classic of Internal Medicine (Huangdi neijing suwen)* and *The Spiritual Pivot (Lingshu)* as methods of conserving energy and cultivating health.

Another way to cultivate energy is to refine it. Chapter 10 of the *Daode jing* says:

> In circulating the breath and making it soft—can you do it like that of an infant?
>
> In opening and closing the celestial gates, can you become the female?

The circulation and regulation of breath can help us to cultivate and refine energy. Using the appropriate techniques, mundane breath (the air we inhale) can be transmuted and purified into primordial and pristine energy. Fetal and abdominal breathing (described earlier) are examples of how this process of transmutation can be accomplished.

In the transmutation of breath (*qi*) into energy (*qi*), the timing of the cycles of inhalation and exhalation is critical. During inhalation, the "valves" along the energy channels are opened to allow the outside air to enter. During exhalation, the "valves" along the energy channels are closed to keep the purified energy within while the impurities are expelled. The "valves" along the energy channels are called the "celestial gates" (*tianmen*), and the energy circuit inside the body is called the "celestial" or "royal" pathway (*huang Dao*). The more common name for this pathway is the Microcosmic Orbit (*xiaozhoutian*).

Energy spent is energy lost if it is not replenished. One way to replenish energy is to gather it from a source that has an inexhaustible supply. This source is referred to as the "valley spirit" and the "mysterious female." Chapter 6 of the *Daode jing* says:

> The valley spirit does not die.
> It is called the mysterious female.
> The gates of the mysterious female
> Are the roots of the sky and the earth.
> Lasting and existing forever,
> It cannot be exhausted.

The "valley spirit" refers to the exhaustible energy of the female that has the power to nourish and give birth. That is why it "does not die." Daoists call it the procreative or generative energy, and to be able to gather this energy is to renew life. Procreative energy in both men and women is considered "female" energy because, being liquid and formless, it is said to have a *"yin"* nature. It is referred to as the "mysterious female" because it is hidden and emerges only when aroused. The primordial energy of the *Dao*, which is the source of things, is manifested in the procreative energy that is present in all living things. This generative energy is called the "roots of the sky and earth" because both sky and earth are said to have been created from the copulation of the yin and yang components of the primordial energy of the *Dao*. Daoists believe that if we can arouse procreative energy and then draw it back into the body, we will be revitalized and rejuvenated. Chapter 55 describes a person who is filled with procreative energy:

> Although his bones are weak and his tendons soft,
> His grasp is firm.
> He does not understand the copulation of male and female,
> Yet his organ can be aroused.
> This is because his generative energy is at its height.
> He can scream all day and not become hoarse.
> This is because his harmony is at its height.

The Daode jing *on Lifestyle*

The techniques of cultivating the mind and body should be accompanied by a lifestyle that complements them. Otherwise, what is cultivated in meditation or *qigong* will be lost in daily living.

First, the *Daode jing* advises practitioners to live a simple contented life, to be moderate in all activities, and not to be involved with worldly affairs. Chapter 9 says:

> Even if your rooms are filled with gold and jade,
> You will not be able to protect them.
> Pride and arrogance invite disaster.
> When your work is done, you should retire.
> That is the way of Heaven.

If we do not have many possessions, we will not have to worry about losing them. If we are not famous, we will have less trouble in life. Famous people are scrutinized and investigated; on the other hand, unknown people are left to live a peaceful life. In a world where many are trapped by fame, fortune, approval, and greed, those who hide their skills are the ones who survive.

Second, the *Daode jing* recommends that practitioners live a quiet life. An overinquisitive mind and overactive body can be detrimental to health as well as be an obstacle to enlightenment. Knowledge is not equivalent to enlightenment. Whereas knowledge is involved with knowing about the world and is directed outward, enlightenment is insight into oneself and is directed inward. If we do not understand this difference, obsessive pursuit of knowledge can cost us insight into ourselves. Chapter 47 of the *Daode jing* says:

> You don't need to leave your home to know the world.
> You don't need to look out of your window to see the celestial way
> Because the farther you go, the less you'll know.
> Therefore the sage does not need to travel to know.
> He does not need to see to name.
> And he does not need to do to accomplish.

Finally, the *Daode jing* advises the practitioner to learn to accept the natural course of things. Accepting the way of things does not mean that we should believe in fate. Rather, it means that we should understand that we cannot control everything. If we try to make things happen or not happen, we will only bring trouble into our lives. Chapter 16 of the *Daode jing* says:

> To return to the roots is to be still.
> To be still is to accept your destiny.
> To accept your destiny is to know what is constant and unchanging.
> If you know what is constant, you are wise.
> If you don't know what is constant, your actions will bring you
>   misfortune.

The sage accepts the natural way of things because he understands the "constant." "Constant" (*chang*) means "unchanging," and to understand the "constant" is to understand both the changing and the unchanging aspects of the *Dao*. It is this ability to distinguish between that which *can* be changed and that which *cannot* be changed that allows the sage to embrace life and accept death.

Conclusions

For practitioners, the value of a text lies in its use. Can the *Daode jing* be used as a guide to living a healthy and long life? I believe the answer is "yes." For over two thousand years, the *Daode jing* has influenced the Chinese arts and sciences of cultivating health and longevity. Today, its teachings on cultivating mind and body can be found in the practice of Chinese medicine, meditation, *qi gong*, and martial arts. Do the teachings of the *Daode jing* work? I think this question is best answered by practice. From my experience, they do.

Imagine Teaching the *Daode Jing*!

Judith Berling, Geoffrey Foy, and John Thompson

The invitation to participate in this volume arrived while the three of us were working our way through the *Zhuangzi*. Zhuangzi has a way of challenging readers to imagine manifold viewpoints. Perhaps he inspired us. Although the three of us have different teaching backgrounds, we share a passion for teaching texts such as the *Daode jing*. We began a seriously playful conversation about teaching this text. We both expanded and honed our initial ideas as we learned from and with one another.

The three approaches we suggest represent three particular embodiments of the pedagogical strategies we explored. They have in common two basic moves: (1) an exercise in which students reflect and comment on their initial experience of and response to the text, and (2) an exercise to engage students with the text imaginatively, creatively, and constructively. The three particular approaches are complementary ways of implementing these principles. It is our hope that three options will inspire our readers to imagine creative approaches to teaching the *Daode jing* that will suit them and their students.

Letting the *Daode Jing* Teach

Most Chinese texts clearly situate themselves, providing not only an author but the date, place, and circumstances of their origins.

They fairly plead to be taught as the reflections of a specific person in a specific historical context. The *Daode jing* is an exception to this rule, its author shrouded in a dense mist of questionable traditions. Although we have some sense of the period in which the book was produced, the Old Master (Laozi) to whom it is attributed remains a figure of controversy and legend; the more one pursues his historical origins, the more one is convinced that the party or parties behind this remarkable book chose to remain obscure. The hiddenness of the author coincides well with the teachings of the book: avoiding fame, unlearning, and leading by nondoing. I seek to honor the text by letting it teach itself, as far as possible. That is, I teach the text by allowing the students to learn from it for themselves.

The *Daode jing* is difficult to teach satisfactorily in a lecture mode, but it offers wonderful possibilities for student engagement and reflection. A careful setup by an instructor to give the students a feel for the text and its interlocutors and then to highlight central themes and images can yield very successful self-learning experiences for students, alone and in small groups.

Some contextualization is required to engage students fruitfully with the text. Situating the *Daode jing* is best accomplished if the text is taught in a course or a unit that deals with classical Chinese thought. In that case, the context of late Zhou China will already have been introduced, with its lively debate over the foundation of a strong and stable government. Those vying for positions as political advisors competed by offering "better ideas." Prevailing wisdom held that the sine qua nons of a strong state were keen understanding of political and military institutions, crafty political scheming, skilled negotiation, and strong legal and military strategies.[1] The other classical philosophical and religious positions, which came to define Chinese cultural discourse, all arose in contradistinction to the prevailing view. The *Daode jing* was one of those countervailing voices. It was also a counter to the opposition voice of the early Confucians, who argued for reestablishment of civic virtues and rituals of propriety as the key to establishing a strong stable society.

If these broader themes have already been introduced, then the *Daode jing*, in responding to that context, will virtually speak for itself. If not, then I create an exercise to identify the rhetorical opponents of the book. In what follows I assume that the *Daode jing* is being taught in isolation, although recognizing that such isolation is the exception, not the general rule.

In my experience, teaching the *Daode jing* requires at least two or three class sessions. This is because the book requires some getting used to by the students. Moreover, it takes time for students to move from passive responses (What is this book like/about?) to more constructive responses (How would nonaction work in my life?).

The first assignment is a get-acquainted reading. Students read the book from beginning to end, reflecting on the following questions: How would you characterize the book? What was it like to read? Did you perceive any threads of continuity? What response(s) did the book draw from you? Who were the targets of criticism in the book? I facilitate responses to this last question by highlighting a few chapters for special comment. Given these chapters, what would you say is the primary target of this book's teaching? What errors is it trying to address?[2]

Subsequent assignments build on the first. I take the poetic language and the suggestive imagery of the book as its teaching device and group chapters along such themes and images (*Dao*, water, the uncarved block, the female, the infant; nondoing, the power and virtue of *Dao* [*de*], the *Daoist* ruler/sage/ master).[3] The first five pertain to the nature and movements of *Dao*, the second three to human activity based on the *Dao*. There is, of course, considerable overlap between these two groupings. I ask students to read and think about the themes and images offered in these grouped chapters. Each student is asked to select a theme (a group of chapters) and write a brief reflection paper (one to three pages long). That paper is used as the basis of small group discussions in the next class period. Each group becomes expert on a theme or image in the *Daode jing*. The small groups report back their reflections to the larger class, thereby becoming teachers of the book. If time allows, the two subgroups (images of *Dao* and humans modeling themselves on the *Dao*) can be separate class sessions.

Although the experience of inviting class members to become interpreters and teachers of the *Daode jing* is the primary goal of my teaching strategy, I also include an exercise for constructive reflection focused on nondoing or the ruler/sage who leads and teaches by nonaction. My experience is that undergraduates who have spent a little time with this text begin to ask very challenging and probing questions, questions that are not easy to answer. The difficulty of the questions posed has led me to lead a plenary discussion on these questions; as a teacher, I can acknowledge the profound challenge of questions raised and help the class negotiate the difficult path of addressing them. Shortly after several undergraduates had died in drinking and driving accidents, one class asked whether a Daoist would let a friend drive drunk. Is there any way to intervene without violating the premises of nonaction? Another asked, "What would a Daoist do if his or her child were being threatened with bodily harm?"

These are extremely difficult questions. If the *Daode jing* is taught in a unit on classical Chinese thought, the teacher has the option (or escape route) of asking the class whether Confucians would have a more satisfying response to such dilemmas. This question raises the important issue of the relationship of Confucianism and Daoism. Although Westerners tend to construct these two streams of thought as competing and exclusive, the Chinese viewed them as complementary options. If the *Daode jing* is taught in isolation, I lead the class to the best possible Daoist response to such difficult moral conundrums. My classes have delighted me with their ability, after just two or three sessions with the *Daode jing*, to raise and wrestle collectively with difficult Daoist moral questions. I have been more successful with this text than with any other at engaging undergraduates not only in interpretation, but also in constructive response.

The *Daode jing* is genuinely a paradoxical text. On the one hand, it is difficult because it is hard to pin down historically and to summarize as a clear-cut position. On the other hand, its poetic language and richly suggestive images invite interpretation and reflection, drawing readers into the vision of the text, inviting them to try on an alternative approach to life. True to its own philosophy, the *Daode jing* teaches itself with some prior setup by the teacher.

Gender and the *Daode Jing*

The *Daode jing* can also be taught by using gender as a framework of exploration. There are several ways of conceptualizing gender as a teaching framework. I discuss one of them here.

I begin with the language and meaning of polarity as represented in the dialectic of *yin* and *yang*, the cosmic principles that produce and sustain creation in its harmony. This *yin-yang* polarity is basic to understanding the cosmic dimensions of the *Dao*. One way we witness the existence of the *Dao* is through the activity of *yin* and *yang* as manifested in polar opposites, such as being/ nonbeing, action/nonaction, luminous/shadowy, hot/cold, up/down, right/ left, male/female. A class session directly or indirectly dealing with the last relationship (male/female) presents a viable approach to the text by engaging students in a familiar issue: women's and men's experience in culture. Granted, gender is a culturally conditioned construct and its representations in culture are enigmatic. Nevertheless, its ambiguity is the very characteristic that lends itself to be a useful heuristic. As Caroline Walker Bynum suggests in her introduction to *Gender and Religion*, gender-related symbols are "polysemic"; they possess a variety of meanings that concurrently engender manifold questions. With this perspective in mind, students not only investigate issues concerning the text itself, but they also examine issues concerning the context of the text and their own interpretations of it. The matter of students' interpretations deserves more attention here.

Because gender is used in the *Daode jing* as a manifestation of the *Dao* (i.e., by way of polar opposites, as well as anthropomorphic imagery), the door is open for students to apply their culturally gendered ideologies to the text as they analyze and discern the meaning of specific words and phrases. However, as they do this they will discover a conflict: the way the text understands gender challenges or subverts the students' culturally embedded assumptions. It goes without saying that the Chinese commentators themselves entertain differing opinions of how to interpret certain chapters.[4] Consequently, as the students learn about gender through the voice of the text, they are invited to reexamine their own conceptions of gender. The *Daode jing*, then, offers a new model for thinking about gender. Rigid gender categories (e.g., males are this, women are that) are questioned as students consider how to adapt the *yin* and *yang* dynamic to their cultural experiences. In this exercise the text is engaged on several different levels. The two most relevant here are the text within its own boundaries as a classic and the text offering formulations of gender that students can engage.

Two particular translations of the *Daode jing* offer some assistance for utilizing gender as a pedagogical tool: Stephen Mitchell's *Tao Te Ching* and Ellen M. Chen's *The Tao Te Ching: A New Translation with Commentary.* Mitchell's translation incorporates inclusive language throughout. For example, Mitchell translates the phrase *shenren* as "master," but when the text excludes the phrase and yet still implies it, Mitchell alternates the pronouns "he" and "she." The result is that his translation differs from many other translations in not using English pronouns to reinforce male-dominated language.[5] The significance of such a maneuver is revealed in the kinds of queries developed by the students as they read this type of translation. Students may ask whether the inclusive language makes a difference in understanding the main ideas of the classic, or if Mitchell's choices reflect a contemporary interpretation. Likewise, students may ponder whether a female *shenren* would interpret the manifestations of the *Dao* differently from a male *shenren*. Although such questions are difficult to answer, the investigations themselves are worthwhile.

Chen's translation is a useful accompaniment to Mitchell's. Whereas Mitchell's rendition is accessible to novice students due to its fashionable and simple format, Chen's exposition offers a detailed analysis along with a more precise translation. Like Mitchell, Chen is cognizant of gendered and nongendered language in the text and is helpful in elucidating its significance for both the meaning of the text and the context of the document. This becomes most apparent when Chen deals with two particular fertility symbols for *Dao, gushen* (Valley Spirit) and *xuan pin* (Dark Mare), in chapter 6 of the *Daode jing* and the two dynamic principles of *yin* and *yang* in chapter 42.[6] In both cases Chen discusses the meaning and function of gender-related language and symbols as she translates the chapters.

My conceptual model for using gender as a teaching framework for the *Daode jing* can be implemented in different ways. Let me briefly suggest two, both of which assume a class of upper-division undergraduates.

The first proposal is to cover the *Daode jing* in one class session with two external assignments, one a preparation for the session and the other a follow-up. For the preliminary assignment, students read introductory material to the *Daode jing* which covers appropriate historical background, including date and authorship, cultural context, and compilation and redaction.[7] Students then read Mitchell's translation once through to acquire a general impression of the text. Students then reread the text while keeping in mind some focus questions: What is gender? How is gender manifested in the text? It would be useful to specify some chapters for student reflection, starting with 6 and 42. What is the significance of gender-related language or symbols for the meaning of the text? When the author mentions the Master, does the term refer to a male or a female? Would the meaning of the text change at all if the master was either sex? How would a male master view the *Dao* versus a female master? How do Western or contemporary ideas or manifestations of gender affect your reading of the text?

The class session is focused around a discussion. I briefly introduce the text, summarizing key points in the introductory material and eliciting students' initial reactions to their first general reading of the text. Students break into groups of mixed genders and discuss the above questions in relation to specified chapters. They then reassemble and summarize what they learned in the small groups. At this point, I provide additional material and commentary for parts of the text that need further explanation (e.g., Chen's analysis of chapters 6 and 42). As a postscript, students write a one- to two-page reflection paper on a particular chapter of the *Daode jing* that they believe best exemplifies the *Daode jing*'s presentation of gender. As the students write their papers they are expected to keep in mind the questions mentioned above and the general themes of the text.

If time permits, I suggest a three-session unit, developed as follows. A general discussion of gender and religion focuses on cultural differences and similarities, primarily between Eastern and Western cultures, to introduce the basic questions concerning gender and religion and what kind of method would be employed when reading the *Daode jing*. I introduce the text, including its general themes. (By this session students would have read the text and be ready to give preliminary responses.) We discuss gender-related imagery in the classic and its significance for the meaning of the text, utilizing group sessions on gender issues described above, with the same follow-up exercise.

The purpose of both formats is to provide students with a framework to engage a classic Chinese text in a fresh way. Although gender is a familiar issue in the 1990s, the issues are raised in a fresh way by a classic like the *Daode jing*, separated both culturally and temporally from the lives of today's students. Not only did the cultural constructions of gender in the late Zhou period affect the author's development of a philosophy or religious ideology, but the cultural construction of gender in our times also affects readers of the text. The *Daode jing* offers an excellent opportunity to explore both gender issues and issues of cross-cultural understanding.

The *Daode Jing*: An Exercise in How Interpretations Change

I admit I've been stumped about how to teach the *Daode jing*, mainly because after years of reading it, I still don't know what the text is about! It occurs to me, however, that this insight provides an important clue: maybe a class reading of the *Daode jing* could be a series of attempts to explore what the text is about. This may initially be very unsettling for students, but it would be fun. It's not often that in the midst of our normally staid academic pursuits we actually allow ourselves to play with what strikes our fancy. Recently when I taught the text, a student who had never read the book before told me that her son thought that if more people read it, soon we'd find there would be no need for seminaries. I laughingly agreed. The *Daode jing* is a *real* book, unlike so much of what we find in the self-help, psychology, or religion sections of the average bookstore. It deserves as many readings as we can give it.

What follows is a practical proposal for teaching the *Daode jing* in a course on Chinese religions and philosophies. The premise of my pedagogical strategy is quite different from the first two in this essay, both of which allowed for the possibility that the text was taught in a course not about China. I have designed this to cover four class sessions. I then suggest books I have found helpful in understanding the text. After outlining each session I briefly explain my thinking and reasons for recommending the works I list, hoping thereby to make my approach accessible to teachers who are not specialists in Chinese culture.

Let me be very clear at the outset that I do not intend this particular format to be ironclad and hope that it can be adapted to suit various contexts (classes in East Asian religions, world philosophy, classical Chinese, even a graduate seminar on textual interpretation). My aim is for students and instructors to engage with the text, not necessarily to come up with a final, agreed-upon reading. To this end I have fallen back on having students write short reflection papers to stimulate their thinking and questions, preparing them for discussion. There is, I think, little danger here of using up all of our ideas. After all, the *Dao* is the Way of Heaven and Earth—which would seem to rule out the possibility of us mere mortals ever exhausting it.

Class 1: Introduction
Preparation: Read whole text. Write one-page reaction paper: "What is this text about?"
Class Lecture and Discussion: Short history of text; who Laozi is; importance of text in Chinese history.

This is the basic "just the facts, ma'am" session, aimed at conveying a sense of the *Daode jing*, when it probably was written, who the mysterious author Laozi may have been. At the very least an introductory course should convey this information to give students some sort of initial overview and orientation, even at the risk of oversimplification. There are, of course, numerous sources for much of this information.

A. C. Graham's good discussion in *Disputers of the Tao* and D. C. Lau's introduction to his translation have both proved helpful.[8] In addition, Herrlee Creel's classic essay "What Is Taoism?" and Wing-tsit Chan's "Influences of Taoist Classics on Chinese Philosophy" provide useful discussions of the complexity of the *Daode jing* and its relationship to traditional Chinese culture.[9]

Class 2: Religious Daoism
Preparation: Read selections from John Lagerwey's *Taoist Ritual in Chinese Society and History* (chapters 4, 10) and Kristofer Schipper's *The Taoist Body* (chapters 5,8).
Exercise: Sit quietly for 5–10 minutes, counting your breaths.
Reread chapters 4, 9, 10, 12, 19, 20, 28, 37, 42, 43, 50, 54, 61.[10]
Write one-page reaction paper: "What is this text about?"
Class Lecture and Discussion: rise of sects; formation of orders; rituals; self-cultivation.

Although the dichotomy between so-called religious and philosophical Daoism is often overemphasized (usually to the detriment of the former, *pace* Creel), I think it can be a useful way of getting at different aspects of this amorphous beast we call Daoism. To this end, both Lagerwey and Schipper show how complex Daoism as a practicing cult is. Students need to realize that the *Daode jing* is truly scripture (like the Bible and the Qur'an) and that it is used in actual worship services and as a guide to personal spiritual cultivation. The text takes on new depth when we see it as part of a living tradition, as opposed to just the musings of long-dead thinkers.

Class 3: Philosophical Daoism
Preparation: Read selections from Benjamin I. Schwartz's *The World of Thought in Ancient China* (first section of chapter 6), Robert Cummings Neville's *Behind the Masks of God* (chapter 4).
Reread chapters 1, 2, 14, 18, 19, 25, 32, 34, 39, 40, 42, 52, 70, 81.
Write one-page reaction paper: "What is this text about?"
Class Lecture and Discussion: philosophical Daoism, Wang Bi and the "Dark Learning."

Until quite recently most of the Western academic literature focused on the philosophical aspects of the *Daode jing* (this is understandable, as it is a fascinating topic), and this will probably be the aspect most readily accessible to first-time readers. The *Daode jing* certainly articulates one of the main currents of Chinese thought and, together with the Confucian philosophy found in the *Analects* and the *Mencius*, remains essential for understanding East Asian civilization. Indeed, to see how the teachings of the *Daode jing* serve as a critical response to the more regimented and hierarchical aspects of mainstream Confucian learning (although technically, the Confucian and Daoist strains of Chinese thought have never existed separately from one another) can prevent a reading of this text from sliding into mushy New Age feel-goodism. Schwartz is excellent here, and Neville opens the discussion out into the greater context of world philosophy. I chose to emphasize the role of Wang Bi (and the other Neo-Daoists) for two reasons: first, because Wang's commentary has been so influential in Chinese and Western readings of the *Daode jing* (almost all but the most recent translations are from his redaction), and second because the role of Neo-Daoism[11] in the history of Chinese thought has often been overlooked. Chinese Buddhism, for example, is virtually impossible to understand without some knowledge of the "Dark Learning."

Class 4: Is there a text in this class?
Preparation: Choice of assignments:
(1) Visit an Asian Art museum,[12] taking the text with you. Pause between various works and reread chapters 2, 6, 11, 14, 16, 21, 22, 25, 41, 45, 47, 81.
(2) Go on a strenuous day hike (no matter what the weather). Leave the umbrella at home even if it's raining, but take the text with you.

At some rest point, stop and reread chapters 2, 5, 6, 7, 8, 16, 23, 32, 34, 37, 41, 51, 55, 73, 77.

(3) Visit a New Age bookstore, and take note of titles relating to Daoism. Read sections from one of them (e.g., *The Tao of Pooh*). Reread chapters 24, 28, 33, 37, 38, 41, 43, 45, 48, 53, 63, 66, 68.

Write a one-page reaction paper: "What is this text about?"

Class Discussion: "What is this text about?"

This session will probably be the most interesting. The idea came to me initially while reading through the lavishly illustrated translation of the *Daode jing* by Man-Ho Kwok, Martin Palmer, and Jay Ramsay and recalling my experiences of hiking in the high Sierra. As for New Age bookstores, the Bay Area (and most of the United States) is crawling with them. They love to focus on Asian and Native American themes, and the *Tao of Pooh* is a perennial best seller.

It may be useful in this final discussion for students to look over all four of their reflection papers, perhaps even exchange them, to see whether there is any sort of consensus. Who knows—perhaps there really *is* a text in this class! Or it may be that there are many competing and complementary texts here. A question I leave open is whether we contemporary readers of the *Daode jing* can agree that all our readings are somewhat right (and somewhat wrong as well) and rest comfortably with this (or not!). The teacher adopting this approach will have to decide to what extent she or he will affirm and accept diverse ideas of "what this text is about," or whether she or he wishes to offer, or develop from within class conversations, some critical principles by which to establish some boundaries or limits. This may entail a class discussion on principles of interpretation and where the meaning of a text resides (or how it is construed and constructed).[13]

I never know what to expect from this series of exercises, but I'm fairly certain that students (and instructors) will come away surprised at just how much readings of the text vary from context to context. I know that in engaging in these exercises myself I found that I came away with a different take on the text each time. This brings up an important point I would like to stress: the instructor should do the same preparation for each class as the students do. If reading the *Daode jing* is to be more than just the dry recapitulation of what others have said, then it requires our engagement each and every time we take it up. In the humanities we are trying to encourage critical and reflective thinking, a willingness to try new things, and the ability to appreciate different perspectives. The *Daode jing* gives us the perfect opportunity to do this in a classroom situation. It is one of those few books for which we are all students with much to learn. As Wing-tsit Chan rightly notes, "You may not like it, or you'll like it a lot because it's boldly vigorous, provocative, and stimulating."[14] After having read the text many times in various translations over the years, I swear the book changes from day to day depending on my mood, the weather, and just how many deadlines are pressing in on me at the time! Perhaps I should end on that note. Or better yet, let me end by asking one question: Is it just me who's muddled?

NOTES

1. Frederick W. Mote, *The Intellectual Foundations of Ancient China.* 2nd ed. (New York: McGraw-Hill, 1989).

2. As noted above, if the *Daode jing* is being taught in the context of classical Chinese thought and religion, the question can be framed as responses to positions already discussed in previous sessions.

3. Differences in terminology follow differences of various translations. I particularly recommend those of Stephen Mitchell, *Tao Te Ching* (New York: Harper Perennial, 1992), and D. C. Lau, *Lau Tzu Tao Te Ching* (New York: Penguin Books, 1963), both of which are affordable paperback editions. I encourage teachers to design their own groupings of chapters. The chapters selected in each grouping will shape the issues and questions raised by students in discussion. Teachers need to think strategically about how the chapters they choose will function in this respect, including or highlighting those deemed most promising and de-emphasizing or even excluding chapters that may raise distractions or confusions. Which groupings work will also depend on the translation(s) used.

4. Ellen Chen, *The Tao Te Ching: A New Translation with Commentary* (New York: Paragon House, 1989), 44–47, 157–159.

5. The Chinese language does not require a pronoun to indicate second and subsequent references, and thus gender is linguistically indeterminate.

6. Chen, *The Tao Te Ching,* 60–71, 157–160.

7. Ibid., 3–48.

8. A. C. Graham, *Disputers of the Tao: Philosophical Argument in Ancient China* (LaSalle, Ill.: Open Court Press, 1989), 215–235; D. C. Lau, introduction to *Lau Tzu Tao Te Ching.*

9. Herrlee Creel, "What Is Taoism?" (1956), in *What Is Taoism? And Other Studies in Chinese Cultural History* (Chicago: University of Chicago Press, 1970); Wing-tsit Chan, "Influences of Taoist Classics on Chinese Philosophy," in *Literature of Belief: Sacred Scripture and Religious Experience* (Provo, Ut.: Religious Studies Center, Brigham Young University, 1981).

10. Because this model explores a variety of forms of Daoism and interpretations of the *Daode jing* with which the nonspecialist may not be familiar, I specify the chapters I consider relevant to each session to give readers a concrete idea of which motifs of the text inform which session.

11. *Xuanxue* (dark learning) was the reigning intellectual movement in the third to fifth centuries c.e.

12. For those teaching in institutions where such a museum is unavailable, the exercise could be to browse in one of a range of books on Chinese art.

13. A useful resource for this exercise is the title essay from Stanley Fish, *Is There a Text in This Class? The Authority of Interpretive Communities* (Cambridge, Mass.: Harvard University Press, 1980).

14. Wing-tsit Chan, "Influence of Taoist Classics," 142.

PART II

Recent Scholarship and Teaching the *Daode Jing*

My Way: Teaching the *Daode Jing* at the Beginning of a New Millenium

Norman J. Girardot

The Dao that can be Dao'ed is not the Dao.

> —*Laozi/Daode jing*, chapter 1

That was Zen. This is Dao!

> —Bumper sticker observed on an aging Volvo

Dao Now

Daoism is as Daoism does. Or, as the diarrheal "Forrest Gump and Pooh Bear Going-with-the-Flow School of Daoist Studies" declares, "Daoism, like shit and a box of chocolates, just happens!" Doesn't the excremental vision of the *Zhuangzi* remind us that the Dao is in both the high and low of the world, in the piss and shit as well as in the mountains and valleys? And doesn't that overweight slacker, Steve, tell us in the "Tao of Steve" that Daoism is, after all is said and undone, the most perfect and natural way to pick up chicks? Isn't this crappy lesson, then, the pointless point of it all?[1] Shouldn't we recognize that, during these meandering MTV days at the start of the third millennium, the teaching of the Dao may indeed be reduced to a boldly tasteless T-shirt slogan about guru guano; Bruce Lee's warbling falsetto scream of kung-fu revenge; the amazingly obscure lyrics from a song by the deadhead wannabe band known as Phish; the rhythmically choreographed violence of a John Woo and Jackie

Chan film or (most transcendentally of all) Ang Lee's *Crouching Tiger, Hidden Dragon*; the muddled message of a particularly puerile Pooh parable; the pretty pastel poems on the side of environmentally friendly herbal tea boxes; the earthy blue-collar mysteries of the *Tao of Elvis*; or (finally and most important) a single pithy text like the ancient *Laozi-Daode jing*, a.k.a. the "Bible-Book of the Wiggy Way and Its Pulsating Power"?

Along with feng shui kits at Wal-Mart, the *I Ching* on CD-ROM, and McDonald's in Beijing, should we not ask why, in this apocalyptically frightened post-9/11world, there were not more Enron executives who studied the *Zhuangzi* along with their tattered copies of Sunzi's *Art of War*? After all, do not the darkly ironic teachings of the *Daode jing*, the most provocatively enigmatic of all world scriptures, tell us that "the Dao that can be Dao'ed is not the Dao"? Isn't Daoism clearly the religion of choice for a postmodern 9/11 age when all systems of representation have been so completely depleted and deconstructed, so thoroughly destroyed as were the twin towers of the World Trade Center? Doesn't the Old Boy himself, Laozi, teach us that all meaning resides in the pregnant void of ground zero, within the gaping mouth of language and laughter that, with freely running saliva, opens and releases the body? Doesn't the holy *Book of the Way and Its Power*, the "gate of all mysteries," assure us that knowing derives not from the eyes and brain, but from the instinctual rumbles of the belly? Thus Daoists, like Nietzscheans, have always preferred existence to essence, tumbling turds to the totalizing shine of Shinola. Finally, is it not the saving grace of Daoism to be one of the very few world religions to cling firmly to a sense of humor about the profane *and* the sacred, the pissy-prissy and the pure, the ridiculous and the sublime, the historical tradition of Daoism and the ineffable Dao itself? Weren't the early Daoists, mumbling the Mandelbrot-mantra of hun-hun-dun-dun, the ones who saw into the silly-serious heart of a sacred cucurbitic chaos? Zhuangzi, in his Chinese Frank Zappa persona as an Andy Kaufman "Foreign Man" or seedy Elvis impersonator, put it best: "Now I have just said something, but I'm not sure if I've really said something or nothing at all!² Tank you berry much." Laozi has left the building.

Yes, it sometimes seems that the Way is *that* way, whether spelled with a *t* or a *d*. Moreover, I dare say that many teachers of the Dao in North American colleges and universities during this past quarter century have had to contend with student wayfarers much too certain of the method and destination of their Daoist journeys. Too certain, for example, that a close reading of Stephen Mitchell's "new English version" of the *Daode jing*, along with a well-thumbed copy of Benjamin Hoff's *The Tao of Pooh* and repeated exposure to Kevin Smith's Silent Bob opus on director's cut DVDs, give them everything they need to know about going fully with the flow. And if in the course of their travels they've done a little sitting meditation, Taiji or Gongfu on the side, so much the better—so much transpires, it seems, that is just plain "self-so" (*ziran*). Shit happens. Such is the Business of Isness. So also I suspect that numerous contemporary practitioners of the Dao outside of the academy have encountered many Western students with an overly romanticized appreciation of the nature and history of Daoism.

There is, in fact, a growing number of knowledgeable and articulate practicing Daoists teaching and writing about the tradition these days in North America who impressively combine extensive academic and experiential understandings of the tradition.[3] But whether academically or practically oriented, or possessing some real combination of mental and bodily learning, all teachers today must contend with an often aggressively predetermined climate of opinion about the how of the Dao. How now? Dao Now! To be religiously hip these days is to know that "Zen was then; Dao is Now!" Or, as suggested by a recently observed bumper sticker on an aging Volvo mysteriously parked by my house in Bethlehem, Pennsylvania: "That was Zen. This is Dao!" While the Beatles, the Maharishi, Ken Kesey's merry pranksters, and D. T. Suzuki's Bent Zen defined an earlier precybernetic age of pop-enlightenment, it's now the age of the Cremaster Cycle, "Reality TV," *Jackass the Movie*, *Kill Bill*, and Daoism—Dao-Lite if you will.

Despite these shortcomings in the state of Daoist learning in North America, it is partially comforting to know that there are some active students of the Dao in the West these days. Unfortunately, in the ancient Central Kingdom of its origins and efflorescence, Daoism has been culturally and politically compromised during much of the modern period—even to the point of its near extinction in the land of its birth. Imperiously condemned by Protestant missionaries in the nineteenth century, stridently spurned by the Chinese literati and Manchu court throughout the Qing dynasty, and violently emasculated during the Chinese communist cultural revolution, Daoism has encountered the ebb without any flow.[4] There are some hopeful signs that in post-Mao and post-Tiananmen China the serious study and appreciation of the age-old Chinese religious heritage is being revived, but it is still the case that, whatever the Orientalistic distortions of the tradition in the West, the torch of Daoist book learning in the twentieth century has mostly been kept burning outside of China itself. Thus we have the haunting situation of Chinese students traveling to Paris, Kyoto, Berkeley, Boston, and Bloomington to rediscover and study the discursive ways of the Dao in the world today.

There is reason to be encouraged by recent developments in the native Chinese and worldwide appreciation of the Daoist tradition, which was, until quite recently, the least understood of the major world religions. But for the time being I would like to emphasize the problem of earnest American students of the Dao too often relying on a whole set of questionable assumptions about what an Asian "mystic" tradition like Daoism must be like. Speaking personally from the background of a thirty-year teaching career that embraces Notre Dame University, Oberlin College, and Lehigh University, I have received too many course papers consisting of a title page and a final bibliography framing fifteen absolutely blank pages. At times a vague twinge of conscience would generate an attached note quoting the *Daode jing* about "those who know, do not speak," and pleading with me to be "Daoist" enough to realize how perfectly and preciously the paper conveyed the inner *wuwei* emptiness of the assignment! Woe to the teacher of Daoism when confronting the presumptions of the Dao-Wow crowd.

Some students these days are indignantly resistant even to the possibility that there may be more to the Daoist tradition than a single short text, some whimsical Pooh Bear commentary, some vague Dao-Zen affinities, and a few basic Taiji movements. They have already been duly warned of the excessively clever and rational procedures of various owlish and poorly dressed university professors who only seek to complicate the simplest thing of all: that Daoism, in its essentially Zennish, Gumpian, Poohish, and New Age way, speaks intuitively and organically about politically correct self-cultivation, "buns of steel" physical rejuvenation, the spiritual "joy" of sex with green tea-flavored condoms, sects without guilt, a prescient proto-feminism and manifest penis power, the satisfactions of a cleansing bowel movement, and an acutely green (if not chartreuse) environmental awareness. Among the upper-middle-class students at many expensive private colleges and universities, there is also the implicit addendum that it is possible to accomplish all of this while driving a Saab, Lexus SUV, or aging Volvo station wagon. And please note that the Office of Homeland Security has just declared that we are now on a Magenta Alert status. All of this is rather surprising since traditional Chinese civilization had no conception at all of Enlightenment-style ideals of personal authenticity, American commercialized individualism, Thoreauian "back to nature" mysticism, Emersonian pragmatism, bourgeois feminism, or trendy principles of vegan and Gaian ecology. But never mind, say some self-styled Telluride Daoists and BMW Buddhists, that's what Daoism is really all about. He who knows does not speak! And those who speak may be university professors!

Pop-Daoism, or Dao-Lite, of this kind—like the earlier Kerouac stream-of-consciousness Zen of the '50s, the Suzuki-Wattsian "fundamental" Zen of the '60s and '70s, and the "engaged" Zen-Tibetan Buddhism of the '80s and '90s—seems to suggest that knowledge and religious experience are completely independent of cultural context, social history, and linear textuality.[5]

There's only a cybernetic immediacy and a frenetic now—oh wow! Speed kills, but within the Matrix or the Fight Club of life it is the Keanu Reeves–Siddhartha–Brad Pitt–Richard Gere–Dalai Lama who saves. Dao Now. Dao Wow. And *De*, by the way, is pronounced like a second tone "DUH." Or, as the Discordian Religion of Bob would say, it's the chaotic flicker of superficial information that dictates the fractal patterns of human life. Along with T-shirt and bumper sticker slogans, everything has been reduced to digitized and prepackaged pellets of "information." It's the frenzied bombardment of Quentin Tarantino images and digital *I-Ching*–yin-yang–on-off factoids that fleetingly stimulate and temporarily focus one's attention amid the "booming and buzzing confusion" of the void (the perfect simulacrum of the traditional Chinese concern for the leaping-bleeping "monkey mind"). There's no meaning, no interpretation, no real imagination—only the sentimental omnipresence of the Home Shopping Network and the Office of Homeland Security. Cultural garbage in, colonic garbage out. Where is Monty Python when we need them? The eerily apocalyptic implication of this real and imagined terror is that, unlike the hopelessly combative religions of the Abramic tradition, Daoism becomes the perfect inheritor of the mystic mantel of ironic Zennish pluck and Dalai Lama smiling nonviolence. Cheshire Cat shit-eating grins abound! Thus it seems that Pooh Bear Pop-Daoism, Planet Hollywood Tibetan-style Buddhism, flannel-shirt-ecologically-sensitive Zen, and Barbra Streisand botox-injected Kabbala become the preferred religions and theme restaurants of the twenty-first century.[6] Heaven's Gate opens; crop circles are found in Roswell, New Delhi, and Shanghai; and within the hallowed space of ground zero a black monolith appears replete with myriad tiny American flags, Nike slashes, and yin-yang emblems. Shitty stuff happens.

The Way Trodden

So Zen was then and now it's Dao. Whatever. But that's really too much of a wimpishly relativistic and blithely Daoistic answer to give to serious seekers of the Way. More pointedly and neoconservatively, let me just say no. No, hardly anything that popularly parades as Daoism and the mesmerizing message or mental massage of the *Daode jing* has much relation to the historical Daoist tradition or, for that matter, to the amazingly malleable text attributed to the wizened and pointy-headed Chinese Yoda known as the Old Boy. It's not that I think Mitchell's Zennish pseudo-translation of the *Laozi*, Hoff's New Age Pooh Bear Dao, or Kevin Smith's Silent Bob are intrinsically evil.[7] They assuredly are not, and I have used both Mitchell's and Hoff's works in the classroom. When employed strategically and contextually, they constitute an effective way to begin and end a course on Daoism. First, before the long hard journey into the murky byways of the tradition, these works give temporary comfort and confidence to the wayfarers. Besides being appealingly well written and broadly accessible, they accomplish this by articulating prevailing sentimental expectations and desires about the tradition. But it is exactly this consciousness raising about our cultural preconceptions concerning the text and the tradition that helps to set up and significantly problematize the meaning of "Daoism" in both Chinese and Western cultural history. Contrary to Pooh Bear Daoism, the *Laozi* never announced that the Disney World secret of the cosmos is that "life is fun." Nor was the actual Daoism of Chinese tradition intrinsically nontheistic, nonritualistic, or nonclerical. Indeed, the Daoism of Chinese history, like Buddhism for that matter, was never a tradition that focused exclusively on the individualistic practice of meditation or the "idiot savant" purity of Pooh Bear intuition.

I regularly begin my current writing-intensive seminar on the Daoist tradition at Lehigh University with an initial short evaluative essay on the "life is fun" Daoism as presented by the *Tao of Pooh* and as contextualized by Nathan Sivin's brilliantly vexing article "On the Word 'Taoist' as a Source of Perplexity."[8] I conclude the course with an assignment that requires my students to write a final brief reflective paper on the accuracy of the Hoffian vision of Daoism in light of the course's semester-long struggle with pooh-perplexing issues of comparative interpretation, Daoist history, and other, much more obscure and awkwardly off-putting Daoist texts. More than anything else, it is my hope that, by the end of the term, my students will continue to dance with the Dao as portrayed by Hoff and Mitchell (a disciplined tango rather than the formless abandon of a mosh pit), but that they will also have learned critically to appreciate the stubborn historical, cultural-social, and religious otherness of the tradition. The slippery truth is that it is extremely difficult to know how easy knowing the Dao really is. One must suffer to experience the transmutation of new knowledge. Shit happens, but only after ingestion, mastication, digestion, and colonic absorption. After all, both Chinese and Western alchemists agree that the secret formula of creative knowing is always *solve et coagula*. That is, all things must be dissolved down to a state of utter confusion so that real knowledge can congeal and emerge—so that there may be, as Coleridge once said about the alchemy of translation, a "transparent defecation" of meaning.

I do not want to sound smugly superior regarding Hoff's *Tao of Pooh*, Mitchell's *Daode jing*, the Dao of Steve, Silent Frigging Bob, the *Idiot's Guide to Daoism*, or other works of this ilk. Hoff and Mitchell, in particular, beautifully convey much that is in keeping with the early texts, if not some essentialized or purely mystical "Daoism." We must always keep in mind that, even with the wealth of pioneering Daoist scholarship and new translations now becoming available, many well-intentioned, and more philologically and technically sophisticated, studies by sinologists and scholars of comparative religions fail miserably at communicating either the letter or the spirit (thought and practice, myth and ritual, head and belly) of the Daoist tradition to a general audience. I must also say that, despite my various caveats, I truly appreciate the often marvelously foolish productions of American popular culture. A strong case can be made that an Americanized pop-Daoism, along with the more seriously acculturated Daoism of practicing resident masters, legitimately represents an aspect of the latter-day diasporic history of the tradition, as well as the progressive global unfolding of the Dao. I confess to sentimental attachments to some of these ideas, but I also believe in my owlish heart of hearts that we need to know where something came from and how it has discursively walked down its own cultural path. We need to take these first baby steps before, in a heroic act of interpretive license and mixing metaphors, we plunge headlong into the ambiguous waters of Daoism's contemporary cross-cultural transformations.

During my long teaching career, the study of Daoism has become one of the most exciting and revolutionary areas in sinology and in the overall comparative history of world religions. In this sense, my real grievance is not so much with the inevitable sway of popular conceptions about Daoism on students and teachers, but rather with the realization that so few of these dramatic new findings have made much of an impact on the general academic or public awareness of the tradition. This is truly unfortunate because it is already abundantly clear that Daoism as the "indigenous national religion" of China had a textual and social history as richly complex and fascinating as anything seen in European Christian history. Hoff and Mitchell cannot be blamed for this oversight. Rather, we are the ones largely at fault. That is, we (the professional *teachers* of Chinese tradition and the comparative history of religions) are the ones who have failed to imaginatively synthesize and effectively communicate the findings of specialized scholarship.

To some degree this state of affairs is understandable since it has only been within the past two decades that significant new translations and research findings have become widely disseminated. We are also starting to get some helpful synthetic treatments and textual anthologies appropriate for use in an undergraduate classroom.[9] For the first time, also, several state-of-the-art classroom introductions to the overall Daoist tradition have appeared.[10] However, it remains to be seen whether these introductory works will do for Daoism what Laurence Thompson's groundbreaking undergraduate textbook accomplished for Chinese religions more than thirty years ago.[11] The field of Daoist studies is expanding so rapidly (and, most significantly and thankfully, the field is on the verge of passing back into the hands of native Chinese scholars versed in the latest Western research and methodological perspectives, especially the academic study of comparative religions) that it is becoming increasingly difficult for any single scholar and/or teacher to keep up with all of the latest developments. In the meantime, we are too often left with only yesteryear's Beatnik *Daode jing* and miscellaneous mystical leftovers. In this respect, an earlier generation's Zennish approach to Daoism and the Old Boy's text has only been transposed today into Poohish terms. So shall the twain meet and merge in the blur of popular sentiment. In the end, and despite all evidence to the contrary, we (the people, both students and teachers) tend to prefer the familiarity of the Disney version to the alien peculiarities of the real thing. But that does seem to be the Way of the World.

So Daoism is as Daoism does. But such a saying only has meaning in the course of time and with a little help from its intertextual friends. Daoism, or rather the discursively constructed meaning of Daoism and important textual artifacts like the *Daode jing*, has a complex cultural history. But even more pertinent to our concerns here is that the *teaching* of elusive and intrinsically foreign Chinese productions like the *Daode jing* and Daoism also has a significant cultural history that should not be ignored.[12] Both text and tradition in the contemporary Western academy are embedded in a pedagogical phantasmagoria of shifting cultural shapes, mythologies of political correctness, shadows of academic careerism, changing student expectations, institutional transformations, and the ritual actions of the prevailing civic religion of corporate capitalism.

There is, then, no single, original, fundamental, or pure Daoism that is somehow "defined" by the *Daode jing*. And there is no single, original, fundamental, or pure way to teach the Way to American students. A sinuously insinuating path has been staked out over the past quarter century, however, and it should be our mission, should we as teachers of the Dao decide to accept it, to walk resolutely down this discursive path while watching over both shoulders and protecting our hindquarters. This is a ritual perambulation that requires that we pay equal attention to where we have come from and to the sporadic markers and clearings that blaze the trail ahead. I will, therefore, proceed autobiographically in the pages that follow with an eye to sketching out some of my own struggle with the artless art of teaching such a mesmerizing text and such a little-known tradition. This will involve a descriptive appraisal of the three primary phases of my career that roughly correspond to the cultural history of the '70s, '80s, and '90s. The Dao that can be trodden is not the Dao, but it nevertheless may be revealing (if not amusing and embarrassing) for me to retrace some of the stumbling steps I have taken along the way.

On the Way in the 1970s

I am not exactly sure when I first taught a course on Daoism and the *Daode jing*. I think it was in the spring of 1972, during my second semester of teaching at Notre Dame University in South Bend, Indiana. It was at about that time that I offered an undergraduate course devoted solely to the Daoist tradition—or, more accurately, a class that began with the *Daode jing* and went on to Burton Watson's *Chuang Tzu*, selections from A. C. Graham's *Lieh Tzu*, James Ware's quirky *Pao P'u Tzu/Nei P'ien*, and various messy purple mimeographed copies of Ch'en Kuo-fu and Tenny Davis's renditions of "outer" and "inner" al-chemical texts. Background readings for this course in the 1970s included Holmes Welch's *Taoism, The Parting of the Way*, which is a popularly written and still helpful guide to the *Daode jing* (the second half of the book on the "Taoist Church" is now hopelessly outdated), and Max Kaltenmark's *Lao Tzu and Taoism*, which covered both the *Zhuangzi* as well as the *Daode jing* and introduced students to the important French school of Daoist studies (it also dealt intelligently with the "Daoist Religion," albeit in an extremely truncated way). In addition to these works, I often assigned various selections from Jo-seph Needham's monumental *Science and Civilisation in China*, the Bellagio conference on Daoist studies, and (after 1974) the new macropedia edition of the *Encyclopedia Britannica*. I must also confess that, at times throughout the 1970s, I used such secondary materials as John Blofeld's *The Secret and Sub-lime: Taoist Mysteries and Magic*, Fritjof Capra's *The Tao of Physics*, and the Richard Wilhelm and C. G. Jung version of the *Secret of the Golden Flower*. These works were not only titillating crowd pleasers, but also played into my lingering graduate school fascination with alchemical "mysteries."

With regard to the *Daode jing* during much of the 1970s, I primarily used the Wing-Tsit Chan (*The Way of Lao Tzu*, 1963) or the Gia-fu Feng and Jane English translation (*Tao Te Ching*, 1972), supplemented or replaced by Arthur Waley's "mystical" version (*The Way and Its Power*, 1958) and D. C. Lau's neo-Confucian rendition (*Lao Tzu, Tao Te Ching*, 1963). This became a pattern in my teaching of the text that persists down to the present day—that is, an insistence that, since most of my undergraduate students had no command of the Chinese language (although over the years at Oberlin and Lehigh I have had a number of students who majored in Asian studies and knew modern, if not classical, Chinese), it was crucial to come to grips with the intertextual and cross-cultural multiplicity of translations, readings, and interpretations of such an ancient and ironically terse text. This was a text that was already in its received form a composite and redacted document. Furthermore, the allusive "Laozi" helped to raise several premodern and postmodern issues of authorship and the locus of intentional meaning. Given my own background and training as a historian of religions and a fresh-from-graduate-school assistant professor, I am sure that at this time in the 1970s I mainly focused on methodological issues concerning the philosophical and/or religious nature of the text and attempted to frame the discussion and reading of the text with interpretive quasi-Eliadian structures of myth, symbol, and shamanism.[13] Let me only say that over the years, while using multiple translations, I have moved away from such prescriptive tactics to a more open-ended interrogative approach that emphasizes the importance of multiple questions, multiple readings, and multiple meanings of the text—especially, to borrow from Michael LaFargue and reader response theory, the interplay of a latter-day scriptural "meaning for us" and the historical "meaning for them" interpretations.

From these beginnings down to the present, I have taught some kind of specialized course on Daoism almost every other year of my career (as well as a regular survey course on the religions of China, an offering that regularly assigns the *Daode jing*). These have mostly been small-enrollment, seminar-style undergraduate courses, but I have also taught Daoism as a graduate course in the history of religions at Notre Dame and at Lehigh have mounted one (never to be repeated) mega-enrollment and multimedia Daoist extravaganza ("The Daoist Phantasmagoria," given in the spring of 1995; on this course, see below). It is noteworthy that, in keeping with my methodological bent in the 1970s and as a way to combat various pious fictions about "Daoism," I spent considerable time tilting at windmills concerning the assumed two, and utterly distinct, forms of Daoism (the so-called *daojia* "philosophical" and *daojiao* "religious" forms). Thus throughout most of the 1970s, the dominant scholarly and popular construct of Daoism was that it was an interesting, but relatively obscure and certainly minor, sinological subject which, according to both native Chinese and Western scholarly opinion, rather neatly divided itself into an early classical, elite, or philosophical phase and a later ritualistic, superstitious, popular, or religious tradition.[14]

Not surprisingly, the philosophical power and scriptural authority of the early tradition were mostly defined by the gloriously evocative verses found in the *Daode jing*, one of the very few "Daoist" texts then readily available in multiple English translations. The foundational significance of the text seemed ratified by the simple fact that there were so many translations. It was often said that the *Daode jing* was second only to the Christian Bible in the ranking of the most frequently translated sacred books in world literature. Whether or not this judgment is truly accurate is largely beside the point. The more important fact is that there were at that time dozens of English translations of the *Daode jing*, a handful of which were decent scholarly versions in an affordable paperback format.[15] Almost nothing else of the vast Daoist literature was easily available for classroom use. This situation reinforced the too easy assumption that Laozi's little work was certainly the crucial source for fathoming the "original" spiritual "essence" of East Asian culture. Moreover, given its five-thousand-Chinese-character brevity and poetic fluidity, it was a text that naturally lent itself to multiple translations and to quasi-plagiarized renditions of previous translations. So it was that "Daoism" at this time, and in keeping with a tradition canonized by the great Scottish missionary translator James Legge in the 1890s, was primarily a matter of what was alluded to in the *Daode jing*, along with some parabolic adumbration from the other early texts attributed to the shadowy sages known as Zhuangzi and Liezi. The incredible riches of the *Daozang*, or the so-called Daoist canon, were still known to only a very few scholars working primarily in Paris, Japan, and Taiwan.

Also directly relevant to the general understanding of Daoism in the early 1970s was—amid the ongoing Vietnam war, Richard Nixon's opening of Maoist China, and the beginning of the Watergate affair—the heightened fascination with direct religious experience and a flirtation with non-Western religions, especially forms of Hinduism and Buddhism that seemed to be fundamentally "mystical" in nature. Given the literary and cultural influence of the beatnik and hippie generations in the '50s and '60s, the one Asian religion (aside from the Beatles' temporary infatuation with the Maharishi Yogi and transcendental meditation) that epitomized these concerns for experiential "highs," methods of spiritual self-cultivation, and immediate personal enlightenment was the kind of Japanese Zen Buddhism promulgated in North America by charismatic cultural entrepreneurs like Jack Kerouac, Alan Watts, Gary Snyder, and D. T. Suzuki. Associated with these trends, and something that had semi–cult status among some faculty and students at Notre Dame in the 1970s (and in many other academic and intellectual circles at that time), was the romantic passion for the archetypal dream psychology of Carl Jung. Coming under the esoteric Jungian spell at this time were also the best-selling English translations of Richard Wilhelm's German versions of the ancient Chinese *Book of Changes* and the crypto-Daoist *Secret of the Golden Flower*.[16] Finally, it is worth noting that the works by comparative religion scholars like Joseph Campbell and Mircea Eliade were fashionable and were often identified with a pervasive counterculture-Jungian-Zennish-Shamanistic myth of individualistic spirituality. Whatever was popularly (or, for that matter, scholastically) known about Daoism at this time was largely subsumed under the more overarching categories and hip sensibility of Zennish mysticism. Thus it was often intimated that the unique Protestant "genius" of Zen had something to do with the Chinese transmogrification of a corrupt ritualistic Buddhism. Moreover, the crucial agent of this reformation was (in some inchoate fashion) the pure "philosophical-mystical" Daoism of the *Daode jing* and the bluntly scatological and humorous spirit of the *Zhuangzi*.[17]

All of these factors led to a situation in the 1970s where the eclectic study of world religions (or, still in those innocent times, the "religions of man")— as well as things like mysticism, tribal religions, new religions, altered states of consciousness, shamanism, and occult traditions like alchemy—were extremely popular subjects for undergraduate course offerings. Furthermore, the cultural and academic climate was such that, in response to the growing demand, new nontheological departments of religion (or religious studies) were being created at many colleges and universities. As a personal exemplification of these developments I should point out that my arrival at Notre Dame in the fall of 1971, after graduate studies at the University of Chicago and Chinese language study in Taiwan, depended entirely on the decision of the Theology Department to establish for the first time a regular position in the comparative history of non-Christian religions.

Even though Daoism was still largely understood in canonical, philosophical, Zennish, shamanistic, and mystical terms linked with the *Daode jing*, there were signs that there was something seriously wrong with this perspective concerning the Daoist tradition in particular and Chinese religions in general. It was almost as if the sinological Orientalists woke up one day from several hundred years of dogmatic philological slumber and discovered that China actually had religious traditions that were critical to an understanding of the larger civilization (beyond the orthodox "great tradition" of the Ruist or Confucian scholar-bureaucrats). The trigger for this scholarly *satori* was in many respects the interdisciplinary revolution in the study of Daoism that started to manifest itself in the late 1960s. There were earlier indications of an impending reformation of the mostly unimaginative, nonmythological, and irreligious "classical" narration of Chinese tradition—for instance, the work of French masters like Henri Maspero, Marcel Granet, Rolf Stein, and Max Kaltenmark; the maverick studies of the Chinese American scholar C. K. Yang in the sociology of religion; and the iconoclastic interpretations of the Cambridge polymath and historian of traditional Chinese science Joseph Needham—but it was not until the pioneering First International Daoist Conference in Bellagio Italy in 1967 and the work of Kristofer Schipper that the axis of sinological understanding really started to shift (Schipper's work being significantly furthered by a bevy of other sibilated scholarly *s*'s: Edward Schafer, Michel Strickmann, Michael Saso, Anna Seidel, along with Isabelle Robinet). Equally significant in this regard was that the groundbreaking papers from the conference were published in Mircea Eliade's *History of Religions* journal, an event that, along with the creation of the interdisciplinary Society for the Study of Chinese Religions at an American Academy of Religions meeting in Washington, DC, in 1974 (led by Laurence Thompson and Daniel Overmyer), signaled the collapse of the traditional sinological aversion to most interdisciplinary interlopers and comparative approaches.

The revelatory nature of these new perspectives was that they immediately and radically challenged the artificially dichotomized understanding of Daoism as comprised of a philosophical tradition largely defined by the *Daode jing* and a later, mostly degenerate and superstitious, Church religion of rituals, "priests," and "popes." After the Ma-wang-tui archaeological discoveries in 1973, it was also gradually becoming evident that the text we thought we knew so well had, in its earliest extant form, turned into a Han-period Huang-Lao political treatise known as the *Te Dao Ching*. Whatever the interesting implications of these developments, it was basically evident that very little could be taken for granted about this text or the tradition. This was exhilarating but also bewildering, since the simple mystical purity of the *Daode jing* was in the process of being absorbed into the labyrinthine literary and religious caverns of the *Daozang*.[18] And the recognition of the *Daozang* as the defining textual and intertextual body for Daoism, along with the newfound appreciation of the living sectarian tradition in Taiwan by scholarly participant-observers like Kristofer Schipper and Michael Saso, meant that we were forced to contend with a vast universe of meaning in the past and present that was almost totally unexplored. Furthermore, the highly esoteric vocabulary of Daoist texts associated with the visionary Shangqing/Highest Purity and liturgical Lingbao/Numinous Treasure traditions seemed hopelessly arcane and off-putting. But this condition of bafflement was understandable given the fact that the decipherment of the technicalities of Daoist literature was just beginning. The state of Daoist studies at this time was roughly the way Buddhist studies were some one hundred years earlier.

I do not want to rehearse any more of this scholarly history here, but it is terribly important for a younger generation of students, teachers, and scholars, whether sinologically or comparatively inclined, to remember what it was like just twenty or thirty years ago. If one was a sinologist at that time, there was really not very much worth studying with respect to Chinese religion or Daoism. If one was a comparative scholar, China also seemed singularly impoverished when contrasted with the lush religious riches of the Indian subcontinent and the Indo-European tradition. Both sinology and the comparative history of religions were peculiarly insulated disciplines in relation to the emergence of the human sciences and the professionalization of academic life in the late nineteenth and early twentieth centuries—themes that I have written about in my recent book on sinological Orientalism and comparativism.[18] By the mid-1970s, however, there were portents in the air that the Kingdom of Dao, and the classical and scriptural centrality of the *Daode jing*, were not as they had been imagined for centuries by loyal Chinese scholar-bureaucrats, clever Catholic priests, righteous evangelical Protestant missionaries, furtive sinological Orientalists, hesitant comparative scholars, and romantic popularizers of the "mysteries of the East." The '60s and '70s were a significant turning point in the meager history of the Western understanding of Daoism and the tantalizing text attributed to Laozi. We are only now at the end of the century, and at the threshold of a new millennium, starting to assimilate and understand the implications of the revolution in Chinese studies and the comparative history of Chinese religions associated with these developments in Daoist studies.

Part of the Way in the 1980s

By 1979–80, I had left Notre Dame to move on to Oberlin College in Ohio and then to take up a more permanent residency at Lehigh University in Bethlehem, Pennsylvania. The times had changed and I had changed. No doubt, my teaching had also changed. I was battle hardened in the petty political ways of academe by this time, yet strangely enough I found myself ensconced in the position of chair to the Lehigh Religion Studies Department, then the smallest departmental unit in a university known more for engineering and Lee Iacocca than Laozi. I will not bore you with a description of my activities as the tiny administrative poobah of the minuscule Religion Department, except to say that, contrary to almost everyone's expectation, the department grew and prospered. This is a result that I would like to attribute to my *wuwei*-ish style as chief executive, but probably had more to do with the trickle-down effect of Reaganomics in higher education during the go-go 1980s. Despite these successes, my ten-year tenure as a low-level academic functionary only served to drive home the *Daode jing*'s central admonition that one should, at all cost, avoid the temptations of administrative rank and power, no matter how trivial one's pond of operations. I had no difficulty therefore in returning to the ragged ranks of the teaching faculty at the end of the decade. I also welcomed the opportunity to reactivate my yearly schedule of teaching a course focused on Daoism, an offering that had become irregular during my bureaucratic years.

Some of the interconnected changes in the cultural and academic environment as they relate to the Dao during the decade of the 1980s are suggested by the odd fact that Ronald Reagan seemed to have discovered the Dao at this time. Thus Reagan, as the president of the United States and as the wizened Hollywood avatar of the brave new entrepreneurial age of conservative politics and corporate "Death Star" triumphalism, once actually quoted the *Daode jing*'s hoary laissez-faire proverb (chapter 60) "Ruling a big country is like cooking a small fish."[20] One rather doubts that Reagan himself spent much time perusing the ancient Daoist classics, but it is interesting to see that the presidential handlers and speech writers had appropriated Laozi's little antinomian text for their own ideological ends. It might be said that such an apparently foreign and erudite reference in the body of a popular political speech by America's *Bedtime for Bonzo* president demonstrates the increased sophistication of the general public. It could also be said that inasmuch as Reagan was our first Chauncy Gardener or Forrest Gump president, it was inevitable that he would discover, with or without a Teleprompter, the simplistic recommendations of this most simple of scriptures.

It is most likely that Reagan's scripted use of this Chinese text shows the developing concern in the 1980s for manipulating, massaging, and spinning a political message in relation to the lowest common denominators of popular culture. This episode consequently appears to be a sad commentary on the increasingly popular but impoverished and tabloidized status of the *Daode jing* in American cultural discourse. This ancient Chinese and Daoist "mystical" work had now become a Poor Ronald's Neo-Con Almanac of vaguely "universal" political and practical maxims. Most of all, these hauntingly enigmatic verses seemed to hint at a fundamental "practicality" of purpose, something along the lines suggested by the American tradition of transcendentalist pragmatism and the continuing popularity of Robert Pirsig's *Zen and the Art of Motorcycle Maintenance* (first published in 1974). Laozi's little text was basically viewed as a specimen of the "gems of world wisdom" tradition of literature handy for lending some unusual yet homespun gravitas to after-dinner speeches or presidential addresses. So also was Benjamin Hoff, the exact political opposite of Reagan, writing in this same sappy vein of pop appropriation when he produced his winsome Poohification of Laozi, a work first published in 1982, but not achieving an amazing long-term best-seller status until the late 1980s and early 1990s.[21] It seems, in other words, that it does not make much difference what the *Daode jing* or Daoism actually says. Rather, we are dealing with a text and a tradition that have become impressively exotic and infinitely flexible templates for totally different, and often contradictory, points of view.

I present here only a composite picture of my teaching of Daoism and the *Daode jing* during the 1980s. This was an evolving enterprise that was affected by various factors, not the least of which were the changing cultural and political situation alluded to above, my own small participation in the promulgation and proliferation of the new revolutionary Daoist scholarship, some wrenching involvement with Holmes Welch at the time of his suicide, and the final preparation of my own early interpretive contribution to the study of the *Laozi* and *Zhuangzi* (along with some analysis of the *Liezi* and *Huainanzi*), my *Myth and Meaning in Early Taoism*.[22] One of the most important elements in this mixture was that my Lehigh students of the 1980s were a different breed from the ones I had been teaching at Notre Dame and Oberlin in the 1970s. Although in my 1960s' soul I was at first prepared to bemoan the increased vocationalism and commodified careerism of students in the 1980s, as well as the heightened conservative political climate (and Lehigh University was a conspicuously conservative institution), I have subsequently come to appreciate the fact that it forced instructors of such intrinsically artsy and noncommercial topics as religion and Daoism to work harder at making a case for the humanistic, cultural, and practical significance of such subjects. This was actually not as difficult as it might at first seem because the 1980s were also the years of the Japanese economic ascendancy, a situation that, in tandem with the decline of American heavy industry and manufacturing, allowed for much anxious discussion about the secrets of the Japanese success. Pedagogically, it made good strategic sense to promote a discussion that asked basic questions about the continuing role of religion in contemporary Asian culture—especially to consider the sometimes silly and pandering questions about the role of some kind of Corporate Confucianism or Samurai Zen in the Asian economic miracle. Thus various books appeared during this period that championed the idea of a "Zen of Management" or, by extrapolation, the mysteries of the "Dao Jones Averages" (e.g., Bennett Goodspeed's *The Tao Jones Averages*, 1983) and the appearance of Daoists on Wall Street (e.g., David Payne's *Confessions of a Taoist on Wall Street*, 1984). In the Reaganomics sense, the *Daode jing* was now discovered to be a guide for cooking a small fish and for "whole-brained investing."[23] As ridiculous as many of these works were, it can be said that the progressive commodification and co-optation of such improbable materials as the ancient Daoist texts dialectically tended to provoke a return to some of the more anarchistic implications of the early Daoist vision. Amid the creeping corporate sameness, there was an increasing tendency to go back to some of the recalcitrant foreignness of Daoism. In this way, there was a continuing discovery of the uncolonized islands of the Daoist imagination, Zhuangzi's villages "of not even anything," and, even more exotically, the internalized cosmic kingdoms of the Highest Purity tradition.

A significant sign of my more experimental and experiential approach to these matters is indicated by the fact that during the 1980s I had started to grow my own Daoist calabash gourds in my backyard in Bethlehem, Pennsylvania. Although my neighbors became increasingly nervous as my backyard was overwhelmed by dozens of large, creeping, and oddly shaped *Little Shop of Horrors* gourds, I felt that I had finally been brave enough to go my own way in the cultivation of my academic and teaching career. From these fecund cucurbitic years in the 1980s down to the present, it has been my habit to start my courses on Daoism by bringing one of my large, lacquered, bipartite, and hollow calabashes into the classroom on the first day. As the spirit so moves me, this will either lead to some meditation on the symbolically "embodied" Dao in front of the class or to a minilecture on the strange cosmogonic ontology of gourds, *hun-tun*, Won-ton soup, and chaos in Daoist tradition.

Finding My Way in the 1990s

During the 1990s, I felt a growing appreciation for the nature and role of performative ritual in teaching and knowing. It may seem strange to say that this awareness has been a latter-day development for me, particularly because the history of world civilization knows no tradition so replete with ritual practice as that of the Chinese. But this obtuseness is not necessarily a matter of my own special failings since the neglect of the study of ritual has been a quite general problem in sinological and comparative studies of Chinese religious tradition. The fact that so little descriptive and interpretive scholarship has been devoted to the role of ritual throughout all aspects of Chinese tradition is truly an incredible state of affairs. Far more attention has been devoted to attempts to reconstitute the shards of Chinese mythology as the crucial key for understanding the tradition (and I have, admittedly and unapologetically, contributed to this genre of scholarship). There are all sorts of interesting and peculiar reasons for the prestige of mythology over ritual in the emergence of Western academic discourse concerning religion.

As revealing as it would be, this is not, however, the time or place to go into this legacy. It is better simply to observe along with Schipper and Lagerwey that even a work like the *Daode jing*, which seems at first glance to give support to the notion of Daoism's, if not Confucianism's, special mystical antipathy to ritual, actually suggests something much more interestingly pragmatic and corporally behavioral about practicing the Dao. Again, it is premature here to do more than say that it may be fruitful to approach the *Daode jing* with a more balanced appreciation of the imaginative and ritually practical aspects of "returning to the Dao" in the text—thinking also of this text's relation to the later, more manifestly liturgical sectarian traditions. This newfound awareness of the broad ritual implications of the "Daoist body" has special relevance for dealing with the apparently unbridgeable chasm between the mythic and ritual dimensions of Daoism, between the individual and communal aspects of the tradition, between the spirit and body, between the universal and regional, urban and rural geographic bodies, and between the early, apparently individualistic and mystical texts and the later, more manifestly social and liturgical Daoist sectarian traditions.[24]

One magnificently silly manifestation of these ideas linking Daoism, ritual, teaching, and performance—as well as my increasing fascination with the interestingly strange relation between satirical humor and religion in the raw—was my experimentation with a new, more participatory and liturgical way of teaching about the spirit of the Daoist tradition. Earlier explorations of these issues as related to teaching resulted in a quasi-shamanistic classroom project that involved the infamous levitation of the Lehigh business school building using the special spiritual "mojo" of Australian bullroarers and the *Tao of Elvis*, but my first attempt to design an entire course devoted to Daoism along these lines came in the spring of 1995 (after a long retreat in the wilderness to finish the writing of a long book manuscript) when I taught a course called "The Daoist Phantasmagoria." In some ways, I suppose this sounds like I had sold my soul to the seductively foolish forces of Pooh Bear Daoism. But it was really my intention to use the "Dao of Pooh"—along with a whole host of popular assumptions about the mystical, individualistic *Daode jing*—as a counterfoil to the ritualistic and performative point of the course.

For much of the first part of the course, my students and I engaged in many traditional academic exercises: books to read, classroom discussions, papers to be written, and multiple quizzes and exams. During the last month and a half of the course, the students and I collectively designed and executed a campuswide ritual event known as Dao Day. This involved an eclectic assortment of carnivalesque activities, culminating in a ritual procession through the campus, a communal meal, and an actual Daoist spring ceremony performed by Master Hsuan Yuan, a Lungmen Daoist priest from the North Pole Gold temple in New York City—ably assisted, I should note, by a student dressed resplendently in a Disney Pooh Bear costume. The climax of these joyfully peculiar events came at the conclusion of Master Hsuan Yuan's ritual performance, when a gigantic papier-mâché Cosmic Egg/Gourd/Lump started to quake and, amid sound, smoke, and light, split open. Gloriously emerging from the embryonic shards came the Old Boy himself—Laozi in this case being played by a diminutive but athletic Korean American student dressed in sagely drag and wearing the enigmatic "Dao Socks of Mystery." After several cartwheels and back flips, the Old Boy proceeded to lecture the assembled multitude with the five thousand characters of the *Daode jing*—an oration delivered entirely in Korean! So at the end of the day, it was clear that the Dao that can be spoken is certainly *not* the Dao. But as Laozi once said: "Small people can only laugh when encountering the Dao for the first time." Ritually and communally speaking, we had all on that day surely released the spirit of the Dao at Lehigh University.

Even more important for me personally and for my teaching than the "Daoist Phantasmagoria" was the dawning realization over the years that I had found my own disciplined rite of "one pointedness." There were times, in other words, when I had entered into the empty abyss of the gourd and experienced, to borrow from Mihaly Csikszentmihalyi, a flowing state when I was no longer thinking or acting. I am alluding here to my own regular practice of the disciplined rituals of embodied language. I mean, of course, the path of writing which in the early 1990s, after a two-year period of intense full-time devotion to the writing of an impossibly long manuscript coming at the culmination of many years of painful preparation (that is, *The Victorian Translation of China*, which finally appeared in 2002 after more than fifteen years of work), led to my own small transformative epiphany of bodily, intellectual, and spiritual alchemy. *Solve et coagula*.

It was the ritual discipline, the struggle, the pain, the difficulty of working with the "flesh of language," the deep "fetal breathing" of periodic inspiration, and the gradual development of a habitual, and always imperfect, art of writing (no matter what the subject) that led me to a further conviction about teaching Daoism and the *Daode jing*.[25] The Dao that can be Dao'ed is not the Dao, but at the same time, the "invariant" or Great Dao will only be reached through the assiduous work of grappling with the Dao's embodied forms. It was my realization, therefore, that out of a spirit of Dao'ed timeliness and situational, or *ying*-ing, responsiveness to my own immediate pedagogical circumstances, the better way to teach the ritually pragmatic art of the Dao to students was to build on our shared academic and personal struggles with the practice and experience of writing. It is in this sense that my commitment to teaching the *Daode jing* and Daoism as part of a writing-intensive seminar became obsessional.

This newfound passion for the revelatory linkages of writing–ritual–meditational experience–alchemical transformation has led to the incorporation of various supplementary course materials on these themes (such as a reading Lu Ji's "The Art of Writing"/*Wen Fu*, Csikszentmihalyi's *Flow*, and selections from Steven Nachmanovitch's *Free Play*).[26] But most of all, I stress the discipline of regular short free-form reflective writing assignments and the central role of the ongoing rituals of revision in dealing with the mysteries of the interactions of style and content, form and thought, in the Dao-ing of a more formal essay. Along with this commitment to the disciplined rites of writing as a way to creep up on the Invariant Way, I also had the good fortune at this time of discovering a work that, as a necessary complement to my emphasis on the Dao of Writing, masterfully taught a kind of Dao of Reading as associated with the *Daode jing*. I refer here to my use of, and enthusiasm for, Michael LaFargue's new (1992) translation and commentary on the *Laozi* entitled *The Dao of the Daode jing*. There are several aspects to this work that make it, in my estimation, one of the best ways to read, understand, and teach the *Daode jing*. It is curiously revealing that part of the success of LaFargue's approach to the text seems to derive from the fact that he was working as an outsider to the conventional sinological tradition of translation and analysis. LaFargue therefore shows us that an application of biblical methods of hermeneutics gives serious students a practical method for working through the literary forms of the text to some informed interpretive judgments, while keeping in balance the text's historical "meanings for them" and its contemporary "meanings for us."[27]

My Way after the Turn of the Century

The "Daoist Phantasmagoria" and Dao Day are behind me now, never to be done again. Such unconventional exercises in the "deep play" of ritual are too personally exhausting and too publicly frightening to sustain. But life goes on and my quasi-ritualized teaching of Daoism and the *Daode jing* continues, although in a somewhat less frantic way. What gives me heart to go forward is the feeling that I am finally learning, after some thirty years of effort, how to teach this text and the Daoist tradition. Not that these feelings themselves will not, in time, change, since that is the nature of the Dao and its power. Along with experimental courses on American visionary folk art and something deeply disturbing called "Jesus, Buddha, Mao, and Elvis," I want very much to teach a semester-long course devoted to Daoism and that other important American New Age religion of salvational environmentalism, interests that have been sparked by my involvement in a recent conference at Harvard University and the publication of a book entitled *Daoism and Ecology, Ways within a Cosmic Landscape.* Related to these concerns is my desire to also de-velop a new course exclusively devoted to the emergence of a full-fledged "American Daoism": embryonic developments that draw upon the Poohish Daoism discussed here but also more significantly refer to various Daoist groups in North America and the beguiling neo-Daoist writings of the novelist Ursula Le Guin. In this respect it is worth noting that there is an important new resource for reflecting on, and teaching about, the Western appropriation of Daoism: J. J. Clarke's engaging overview of the Western romance with Daoism entitled *The Tao of the West: Western Transformations of Taoist Thought.*[28]

In the meantime, I am encouraged that my regular writing-intensive Daoist seminar still displays some strong *qi*. The last time I taught the course, I had one of the most invigorating and rewarding seminars of my teaching career. Not only was I blessed with a diverse lot of bright and energetic students, but (for whatever subtle alchemical reasons) the discussions and student pa-pers were also unusually interesting and stimulating. Even better was that the course seemed to engender some healthy appreciation for the Dao of Reading and Writing, as well as some recognition of the importance of the kind of foolish ritual behavior elicited during the events of Dao Day. The culminating oral presentations and papers that grew out of this seminar were wonderfully eclectic and creative, covering such topics as the political philosophy in the *Daode jing*, the Tao of the *Matrix* films, a hip-hop rap composition based on chapter 2 of the *Zhuangzi*, the relation between mathematical chaos theory and some themes in the early Daoist texts, and finally (and always a crowd pleaser) Daoist sexual alchemy. Moreover, I did not receive any seminar papers that attempted the strategy of unadulterated emptiness or transparent defecation. Shit didn't happen! For that I am thankful. So goes the Dao.

NOTES

1. Along with Elvis Presley, spam, and pornography, one of the more ubiquitous subjects on the Internet (and on T-shirts) is the comparative listing of different world religions that begins with the taken-for-granted association of Daoism and the slogan "Shit happens." This cow pat of popular American urban legend most dramatically surfaced in the hugely successful film *Forrest Gump*. We may only speculate that this quasi-proverbial saying probably stems from some half-remembered appreciation of the famous "piss and shit" passage in the *Zhuangzi*. The passage is found in chapter 22, which in Burton Watson's translation is as follows:

> Master Tung-kuo asked Chuang Tzu, "This thing called the Way—where does it exist?" Chuang Tzu said, "There's no place it doesn't exist." "Come," said Master Tung-kuo, "you must be more specific!" "It is in the ant." "As low a thing as that?" "It is in the panic grass." "But that's lower still!" "It is in the

tiles and shards." "How can it be so low?" "It is in the piss and shit!" Master Tung-kuo made no reply.

Burton Watson, trans., *The Complete Works of Chuang Tzu* (New York: Columbia University Press, 1968), 240–241.

2. See the *Zhuangzi*, chapter 2.

3. On some of the contemporary Daoist practitioners in North America, see Solala Towler, *A Gathering of Cranes: Bring the Dao to the West* (Eugene, Oreg.: Abode of the Eternal Dao, 1996). On Saso, see his *The Teachings of Master Chuang* (New Haven: Yale University Press, 1978); and on Schipper, see N. J. Girardot, "Kristopher Schipper and the Resurrection of the Daoist Body," in *The Taoist Body*, by Kristofer Schipper (Berkeley: University of California Press, 1993).

4. On the recent history of Daoism, see, among other works, K. Schipper, "The History of Daoist Studies in Europe," in *Europe Studies China: Papers from an International Conference on the History of European Sinology*, ed. Ming Wilson and John Cayley (London: Han-Shan Tang Books, 1995), 467–491; Anna Seidel, "Chronicle of Daoist Studies in the West," *Cahiers d'Extreme-Asie* 5(1990): 223–347; and N. J. Girardot, "Chinese Religion: History of Study," in *Encyclopedia of Religions* 3 (1987): 312–323 and "Finding the Way: James Legge and the Victorian Invention of Taoism," *Religion* 29 (1999): 107–121.

5. See, for example, Philip Zaleski's review of the reprinted work by Alan Watts, *Zen and the Beat Way* (Boston: Charles E. Tuttle, 1997) in the *New York Times Book Review*, September 9, 1997, 46. As Zaleski correctly notes:

> Our knowledge of Asian religions has come a long way since the 60's, and it's obvious now that in many ways Watts got his facts about as wrong as is humanly possible. His gaffes make one gasp: that Eastern religions "do not involve belief," that they offer no ethical codes, that "what they are concerned with is not ideas," that they contain little worship, that their rites are not "very essential." In lieu of the dazzling reality of these faiths, with their elaborate rituals, complex devotions and strenuous discipline, Watts creates a fantastic theme park, where wise old sages down bottles of sake, spin out haiku and whack one another with sticks in displays of crazy wisdom.

See also the defense of Watts's "fundamental Buddhism" in the letter by Sergei Heurlin, *New York Times Book Review*, October 12, 1997, 4. For scholarly discussions of these issues, see the works by Donald Lopez, especially *Curators of the Buddha: The Study of Buddhism under Colonialism* (Chicago: University of Chicago Press, 1995) and *Prisoners of Shangri-la: Tibetan Buddhism and the West* (Chicago: University of Chicago Press, 1998).

6. Even a recent "Gospel of Elvis" alludes to Daoism. See Louie Ludwig, *The Gospel of Elvis: The Testament and Apocrypha of the Greater Themes of "The King"* (Arlington, Texas: Summit, 1994). Most egregiously, see David Rosen's *The Tao of Elvis* (New York: Harvest, 2002).

7. Most problematic is Mitchell's presumption that his experience with Zen meditation gave him some unique and seamless insight into the inner "perennial

philosophy" embedded in the ancient Daoist text. It should also be noted that it is not always the philologically sophisticated sinological scholar that is able to produce a good translation. This is demonstrated by the infamous "Philological Notes on Chapter One of the *Lao Tzu*" by the formidable sinologist, Peter A. Boodberg, in *Harvard Journal of Asiatic Studies* 20 (1959): 598–618. For all of his erudition, Boodberg managed to produce a "translation" that amounted to almost total gibberish.

8. See N. Sivin, "On the Word 'Taoist' as a Source of Perplexity: With Special Reference to the Relations of Science and Religion in Traditional China," *History of Religions* 17 (1978): 303–330. See also Russell Kirkland's acerbic "The Taoism of the Western Imagination and the Daoism of China: De-Colonizing the Exotic Teachings of the East, unpublished lecture, University of Tennessee, 1997.

See also Steven Bradbury, "The American Conquest of Philosophical Daoism," in *Translation East and West: A Cross-Cultural Approach*, ed. Cornelia N. Moore and Lucy Lower (Honolulu: University of Hawaii, College of Languages, 1992), 29–41.

9. See, for example, Livia Kohn's *The Daoist Experience: An Anthology* (Albany: State University of New York Press, 1993); Eva Wong's *Shambhala Guide to Daoism* (Boston: Shambhala, 1997); and Steven Bokenkamp's *Early Daoist Scriptures* (Berkeley: University of California Press, 1997). On the scholarship surrounding the *Daode jing*, see Livia Kohn and Michael LaFargue, eds., *Lao Tzu and the Tao-te-ching* (Albany: State University of New York Press, 1998).

10. See James Miller's *Daoism: A Short Introduction* (Oxford: Oneworld, 2002); Livia Kohn's *Daoism and Chinese Culture* (Cambridge, Mass.: Three Pines Press, 2001); and the forthcoming work by Russell Kirkland, *Taoism: The Enduring Tradition* (New York: Routledge).

11. The first edition of Thompson's *Chinese Religion: An Introduction* appeared in 1969. For a discussion of the pedagogical and cultural significance of this book, see N. J. Girardot, " 'Very Small Books about Very Large Subjects': A Prefatory Appreciation of the Enduring Legacy of Laurence G. Thompson's *Chinese Religion. An Introduction*," *Journal of Chinese Religions* 20 (fall 1992): 9–15.

12. Some of these issues as they relate to the nineteenth century are treated in my *The Victorian Translation of China: James Legge's Oriental Pilgrimage* (Berkeley: University of California Press, 2002).

13. Concerning my association with Eliade and my growing estrangement from him in the 1980s, see my "Whispers and Smiles: Nostalgic Reflections on Mircea Eliade's Significance for the Study of Religion," in *Changing Religious Worlds: The Meaning and End of Mircea Eliade*, ed. Bryan Rennie (Albany: State University of New York Press, 2000), 143–164.

14. See my discussion of these issues in "Part of the Way: Four Studies on Taoism," *History of Religions* 11 (1972): 319–337.

15. On the multiple translations of the *Daode jing*, see Knut Walf, *Westliche Taoismus-Bibliographie: Western Bibliography of Taoism* (Essen, Germany: Verlag Die Blaue Eule, 1992).

16. On the Jungian cult, see Richard Noll, *The Aryan Christ: The Secret Life of Carl Jung* (New York: Random House, 1997); and especially J. J. Clarke's *Jung and Eastern Thought: A Dialogue with the Orient* (London: Routledge, 1994).

17. On the liberal Protestant paradigm (and its accompanying anti-Catholicism) as applied to Daoism and other Chinese religions, see my *Victorian Translation of China*. See also Gregory Schopen, "Archaeology and Protestant Presuppositions in the Study of Indian Buddhism," *History of Religions* 31 (1991): 1–23.

18. The daunting nature of this situation is suggested by Isabelle Robinet's evocative description of the amazingly heterogeneous *Daozang*:

> The existing Daoist canon . . . , which was first issued in 1442, contains more than a thousand works. It simultaneously gathers together works by philos-ophers like Lao-tzu and Chuang-tzu; pharmacopoeial treatises; the oldest Chinese medical treatise; hagiographies; immense ritual texts laced with magic; imaginary geographies; dietetic and hygienic recipes; anthologies and hymns; speculations on the diagrams of the *I ching*; meditation techniques; alchemical texts; and moral tracts. One finds both the best and the worst within the canon. But it is exactly this state of affairs that constitutes its richness.

Isabelle Robinet, *Daoist Meditation: The Mao-shan Tradition of Great Purity*, trans. Julian Pas and N. J. Girardot (Albany: State University of New York Press, 1993).

19. See Girardot, *The Victorian Translation of China*.

20. I no longer have the exact reference for Reagan's use of the *Daode jing*. I think it may have been mentioned in an article in the *New York Times* describing the amazing six-figure advance given to Stephen Mitchell for his rendition of the *Daode jing*.

21. See Patricia Leigh Brown's "Peace Is a Bookshelf Away: Benjamin Hoff's Pooh-as-Daoist Joins a Genre That Combines Self-help with Spiritual Discovery," *New York Times*, November 19, 1992.

22. *Myth and Meaning* was first published by the University of California Press in 1983, with a corrected paperback printing in 1988 (the connection with chaos theory was discussed in my preface to the paperback edition).

23. Such is the subtitle of Goodspeed's *Dao Jones Averages*, a work that is replete with the secret stock market wisdom of the amazingly adaptable *Daode jing*.

24. See Schipper's suggestive discussion of some of these matters in *The Taoist Body*, 183–216; see also John Lagerwey, *Daoist Ritual in Chinese Society and History* (New York: Macmillan, 1987), ix–xvi, 241–290. For some of the problems associated with the use of the category of mysticism, see the general discussion in the *Harper-Collins Dictionary of Religion* (San Francisco: HarperSanFrancisco, 1995), 747–749.

25. I borrow the phrase "the flesh of language" from David Abram's meditation on the ecology of language, *The Spell of the Sensuous: Perception and Language in a More-Than-Human World* (New York: Vintage Books, 1996), 73.

26. For Lu Ji's essay, see Tony Barstone and Chou Ping, trans., *The Art of Writing: Teachings of the Chinese Masters* (Boston: Shambhala, 1996). See also Stephen

Nachmanovitch, *Free Play: The Power of Improvisation in Life and the Arts* (New York: G. P. Putnam's Sons, 1990) and Mihaly Csikszentmihalyi's *Flow: The Psychology of Optimal Experience* (New York: Harper & Row, 1990).

27. For LaFargue's hermeneutical method as applied to the *Daode jing*, see *The Dao of the Daode jing: A Translation and Commentary* (Albany: State University of New York Press, 1992), 190–213 ("Hermeneutics: A Reasoned Approach to Interpreting the *Daode jing*"). The literary forms include what LaFargue calls "polemic aphorisms" and "self-cultivation sayings." In his discussion of the "origin sayings" (a subset of the self-cultivation sayings), LaFargue suggests that some scholars (hinting at my *Myth and Meaning*) misconstrue these passages as instructions about cosmogonic and metaphysical theories which are then used by Daoists to "build the rest of their thought and their approach to practical problems" (207). Let me take this opportunity to say that my point of view about the cosmogonic implications of some of the passages and images in the *Daode jing* is not so far removed from LaFargue's idea that these passages are basically "celebratory" in nature—that is, that these passages celebrate "the existentially 'foundational' character of Dao as concretely experienced in the self-cultivation practice of the ideal Laoist" (208). It is worth mentioning that another excellent recent translation is Stephen Addiss and Stanley Lombardo, *Daode jing Lao-Tzu* (Indianapolis: Hackett, 1993). In the past few years, numerous other translations (good and otherwise) have appeared. Moreover, there is also the recent excitement of the discovery of the oldest extant version of the *Daode jing*, the so-called Guodian text. See, for example, *The Guodian Laozi: Proceedings of the International Conference, Dartmouth College, May 1998*, Early China Special Monograph Series, No. 5, edited by Sarah Allan and Crispin Williams. For a translation of the text, see Robert Henricks, *Lao Tzu's Tao Te Ching* (New York: Columbia University Press, 2000).

28. See also the critical appraisal of Clarke's work in the symposium "The Tao of the West: Western Transformations of Taoist Thought," in *Religious Studies Review* 28 (2002): 303–338 (commentary by N. Girardot, Julia Hardy, Russell Kirkland, Elijah Siegler, James Miller, Jonathan Herman, Jeffrey Dippmann, Louis Komjathy, and J. J. Clarke).

The Reception of Laozi

Livia Kohn

In teaching Daoism, one of the key texts that is usually discussed early in the class is the *Daode jing*, also known as the *Laozi* after its alleged author. The text, which in its standard version consists of eighty-one chapters and is divided into two parts, is highly philosophical and inspiring and has been translated into English numerous times. As likely as not, students are already familiar with it and may even own one or the other translation. From reading it—and from popular citations and adaptations made of it, such as the famous *Tao of Pooh*—students in close imitation of mainstream America have gained the idea that Daoism is all about going along with the flow, living in harmony with nature, acting by not acting, cultivating quietude and spontaneity, and generally being a nonachieving, nature-loving kind of person. It typically comes as somewhat of a shock to them to learn that there are some serious historical realities in the background of the book, that not everyone reads it in the same, Americanized way, that translations differ considerably in wording and outlook, and that there is an entire two-thousand-year-long religious tradition called Daoism, in which the text has played an important and often devotional role, being used both in communal ritual and in personal cultivation.

The first reception of Laozi, therefore, that our students tend to be already familiar with is the reception of the text *Laozi* as scripture, that is, as something of eternal value that can and must be adapted to one's own particular circumstances and interpreted accordingly. As

Michael LaFargue has described it, this reception focuses on the idea that the text has something important to say to the present-day reader.[1] The main problem to be overcome, then, is the apparent cultural distance between this reader and the ancient writing, the best way of bringing the text into the modern world and making it into a document addressing questions of most interest today. A given interpretation is most successful if it allows the reader to find in the text something stimulating, moving, or inspiring. While this approach is perfectly valid and should be discussed in the classroom, we as educators also have the task to inform students about the historical realities surrounding the text. At this point three different topics emerge as central to the discussion: the concrete, textual unfolding of the work; the historical reality surrounding its conception; and the text's role in the later religious tradition.

First, the concrete, textual history of the work includes a discussion of the three major editions of the work. Among them is most prominently the so-called standard edition, also known as the transmitted edition. Handed down by Chinese copyists over the ages, it is at the root of almost all translations of the text. It goes back to the third century C.E., to the erudite Wang Bi (226–249), who edited the text and wrote a commentary on it that Chinese since then have considered inspired. It has shaped the reception of the text's worldview until today.

A somewhat earlier edition is called the Mawangdui version, named after a place in southern China (Hunan) where a tomb was excavated in 1973 that dated from 168 B.C.E. It contained an undisturbed coffin surrounded by numerous artifacts and several manuscripts written on silk, mostly dealing with cosmology and longevity techniques, such as gymnastics and sexual practices. Among them were two copies of the *Daode jing*. The Mawangdui version differs little from the transmitted edition: there are some character variants that have helped clarify some interpretive points, and the two parts are in reversed order; that is, the text begins with the section on *De*, then adds the section on *Dao*. The manuscripts are important because they show that the *Daode jing* existed in its complete form in the early Han dynasty, and that it was considered essential enough to be placed in someone's grave.[2]

Yet another important edition of the *Daode jing* was discovered in 1993 in a place called Guodian (Hubei). Written on bamboo slips and dated to about 300 B.C.E., the find presents a collection of various philosophical works of the time, including fragments of Confucian and other texts. Among them are thirty-three passages that can be matched with thirty-one chapters of the *Daode jing*, but with lines in different places and considerable variation in characters. Generally, they are concerned with self-cultivation and its application to questions of rulership and the pacification of the state. Polemical attacks against Confucian virtues, such as those describing them as useless or even harmful (chapters 18–19), are not found; instead negative attitudes and emotions are criticized. The Guodian find of this so-called Bamboo Laozi tells us that in the late fourth century B.C.E. the text existed in rudimentary form and consisted of a collection of sayings not yet edited into a coherent presentation. Another text found at Guodian, the *Taiyi sheng shui* (Great Unity Creates Water), gives further insights into the growing and possibly even "Daoist" cosmology of the time, as does a contemporaneous work on self-cultivation, the "Inward Training" (*Neiye*) chapter of the *Guanzi*. It appears that, gradually, a set of ideas and practices was growing that would eventually develop into something specifically and more religiously Daoist.[3]

In describing and discussing the textual history, instructors must make it clear that the *Daode jing* was not naturally standardized, but that the standard version evolved over time, from a rudimentary form found at Guodian through the first fairly complete texts at Mawangdui to the standard edition of Wang Bi in the third century C.E., which did not arise until six centuries after the text's first conception. This standardization, moreover, depended on what the Chinese of that age considered valuable and relevant. Prior to Wang Bi—and less so but still even after him[4]—the *Daode jing* was a text in flux, consisting of miscellaneous sayings in various stages of coherent collation that were changed, rearranged, and reinterpreted many times. Especially the new Guodian find is of importance here, because it shows the context of the work as part of the educational repertoire of a southern crown prince, used—at least as much as we can tell so far—together with philosophical works of other schools to give the next ruler the best possible education for his future responsibilities.[5]

Another topic is the historical reality surrounding the text's creation, the environment of Warring States China, as well as the wider perspective of world history. In this context it is helpful to students to point out that both the person and the text *Laozi* arose around 500 B.C.E. in a period of great change not only in China but the world over. The German philosopher Karl Jaspers called this period the "axial age" in his seminal work *The Origin and Goal of History*. The term refers to the fact that at this time in many different cultures new thinkers and religious leaders arose who, for the first time, placed great emphasis on the individual as opposed to the community of the clan or tribe. Examples include the Buddha in India, Zoroaster in Persia, Socrates in ancient Greece, and Confucius in China. The ideas proposed by these thinkers and religious leaders had a strong and pervasive impact on the thinking of humanity in general, contributing significantly to our thinking even today.

Students should understand that no document arises in a historical vacuum. They need to see how China at this time was undergoing tremendous economic and political changes. The arrival of iron-age technology, and with it better ploughshares, wagon axles, and weapons, had caused an increase in food production and massive population growth, as well as greater mobility and wealth among the people. This in turn led to a heightened hunger for power among local lords, who began to wage wars in order to expand their lands and increase their influence, setting large infantry armies against each other. While the central king of the Zhou dynasty (1122–221 B.C.E.) was still officially in charge of the entire country, there were in fact many independent states in a more or less constant state of conflict. The period is thus appropriately named the Warring States (*zhanguo*). It was a time of unrest and transition which left many people yearning for the peace and stability of old, and ended only with the violent conquest of all other states and the establishment of the Chinese empire by the Qin dynasty in 221 B.C.E.

Most Chinese philosophers of the Warring States, in accordance with the situation they faced, were concerned with the proper "way" or "method" (*dao*) leading to the recovery of the harmony and social manageability of an earlier, golden age. The word *dao* was accordingly not limited to one specific school but arose as a generic term used by all philosophers, so generic, in fact, that A. C. Graham entitled his work on early Chinese philosophy *Disputers of the Dao*. The works of the ancient Chinese philosophers can thus be described as characterized by a strong backward focus and feudalistic vision. Although Western scholars usually characterize them as "philosophers," they always placed a strong emphasis on the practical dimensions of their teachings, both in regard to the individual's social behavior and to his or her personal self-cultivation. In fact, at the core of most ancient Chinese thought are practices of social discipline and the transformation of individuals and communities. Followers often congregated in small, almost sectarian groups rather than in what we think of as philosophical schools.[6]

This phase of the discussion of the text also lends itself most opportunely to an introduction of the basic history and doctrines of Confucianism as a comparative backdrop. It can be emphasized here that, while the quest for harmony and political stability was equally at the root of philosophers' efforts, early Confucians focused predominantly on the idea of ritual formality or etiquette (*li*), the proper behavior in all social situations. This social formality was to be observed on all three levels of life: in family and society, in government, and in religious ritual. It meant the guidance toward proper behavior among people of different rank and status, defined through the five relationships of ruler-minister, father-son, husband-wife, elder-younger brother, and friend-friend. In each case, there was a senior and a junior, and each had obligations toward the other, expressed in the so-called Confucian virtues.[7]

This social focus and emphasis on set behavior patterns, then, can be contrasted effectively with the doctrines of *ziran* and *wuwei* in the *Daode jing*.

An aspect students should be made aware of is the role of the text in the later religious tradition, and especially its importance in Daoist ritual. As early as the first century B.C.E., the *Daode jing* was considered a sacred text that should be recited to the greater benefit of self and state. By the second century C.E., it was the central text of the Celestial Masters, who recited it regularly both as a devotional exercise and for its magical effect. To ensure the proper efficacy of this recitation, practitioners had to be morally pure. Accordingly, the Celestial Masters also used it as the inspiration for certain behavioral rules. These rules are connected with the *Xianger* commentary to the *Daode jing*, a text that survives among the manuscripts found at Dunhuang. Attributed to Zhang Lu, third Celestial Master and grandson of the founder Zhang Daoling, who lived in the early third century, it describes the contemporaneous interpretation of the text. The precepts listed here are of two kinds: a group of nine precepts providing general rules of behavior based on the philosophy of the *Daode jing*, and a group of twenty-seven precepts, which present a mixture of general rules, behavioral regulations, and temporal taboos.[8]

In the fifth century, recitation of the *Daode jing* was widely practiced among Daoist schools and linked closely with the attainment of immortality. As such, it appears in the *Wenshi neizhuan* (Inner Biography of the Master at the Beginning of the Scripture), a sixth-century hagiography of Laozi that tells of his transmission of the *Daode jing* to Yin Xi, the Guardian of the Pass—a tale symptomatic for the idealized relationship between master and disciple in the religion. At first Laozi rejects Yin Xi's demand to join him on his further travels, saying:

> In order to follow me, you first have to attain the Dao. But your many impurities are not eradicated yet, so how can you follow me on my distant wanderings? For the present, recite the "Text in Two Sections" [the *Daode jing*] ten thousand times. Then your Dao will be perfected and you can follow me on my distant wanderings.[9]

Yin Xi did as he was ordered and recited the *Daode jing* ten thousand times over a period of three years. As a result, he "gained eternal life and the state of no death." According to another source, he "attained inner sincerity in his essence and pervasion in his meditation so that he could pervade the mystery," as the *Xisheng jing* (Scripture of Western Ascension, DZ 726) states (1.11ab).

That this practice and its effect was not merely part of mythology is evidenced in the *Zhen'gao* (Declarations of the Perfected, DZ 1016), a record of Daoist teachings and practices dated to around the year 500. According to this, a certain Old Lord instructed three members of the Zhou family, the father and two sons, to recite the *Daode jing*. The father and elder brother succeeded in reciting the text ten thousand times and flew off as celestials. The younger brother, however, reached only 9,733 times and did not attain immortality (5.6a).

In addition, the *Daode jing* also stood at the center of a ritualized meditation. According to a fifth-century text that survived in Duhuang and served as a preface to the text, the *Daode zhenjing xujue* (Introductory Explanations to the *Daode jing*), Laozi gave detailed instructions on how to properly venerate the scripture. Adepts should purify themselves thoroughly and enter a special meditation chamber, where they burn incense, straighten their robes, bow to the ten directions, and actively visualize Laozi and his major assistants.

Only in the venerable presence of these divine personages is the *Daode jing* to be opened. Its recitation must further be preceded by a formal prayer, by which the adept calls upon the Lord of the Niwan Palace, the central representative of the gods and resident in the central palace of the head, to descend. As the divinity approaches, the room undergoes mysterious changes: a radiance as of seven jewels spreads, doors and windows open spontaneously. A link of light to the higher spheres is thus established, through which the practitioner floats up and away into the purple empyrean. Finding himself among the stars, he has the sun and moon at his sides and approaches the divine immortals to gain immortality for himself—and not only for himself but also for his ancestors of seven generations.

After this invocation, when the adept has placed himself firmly among the celestials, he proceeds with the ritual. The text says:

> Finish the recitation, then clap your teeth and swallow your saliva thirty-six times. Visualize the green dragon to your left, the white tiger to your right, the red bird in front of you, and the dark warrior at your back.
>
> Your feet stand between the eight trigrams, the divine turtle and the thirty-six masters bow to you. In front, you see the seventeen stars, while your five inner organs give forth the five energies and a network pattern streams across your body.
>
> On three sides you are joined by an attendant, each having a retinue of a thousand carriages and ten thousand horsemen. Eight thousand jade maidens and jade lads of heaven and earth stand guard for you. (sect. 5)

Clapping one's teeth and swallowing saliva are part of the standard Daoist meditation ritual, symbolic forms of announcing one's communication with the deities. The adept is instructed to place himself in the cosmic center by seeing himself surrounded by the four mythical animals of the four directions, representing constellations in the sky, and placing his feet firmly on the eight trigrams of the *Yijing* (Book of Changes). Everyone bows to him, and he is fully established among the stars; his body has become a pure constellation of light and energy patterns. Then he sees himself supported by attendants, one on each side and behind him, who in turn, as in an imperial procession, are joined by thousands of followers and servants. Now that the celestial position of the meditator at the center of the cosmos is firmly established, he can recite the *Daode jing* in its truest environment and to its greatest effect.[10]

Over the following centuries, the *Daode jing* continued to be actively used both in meditation and liturgy and played an important role in the formal ordination of priests, representing a level of advanced lay followers who were preparing to leave the householder's life but had not yet done so. Their progress was divided into two stages. First, he or she—women being treated as equals in the priestly system—learned basic meditation and recitation techniques, worshipped Laozi and Yin Xi as their major patriarchs, and observed ten precepts that included five basic rules against killing, stealing, lying, sexual misconduct, and intoxication, together with a set of guidelines to help practitioners to live in harmony with their families and their communities, striving for the liberation and salvation of all beings.

Second, they took additional precepts and received more detailed instructions on the *Daode jing*, undergoing an ordination ceremony that named them *Gaoxuan fashi* or Preceptors of Eminent Mystery and bestowed upon them a variety of exegetical, devotional, and technical materials linked with the text. These included early commentaries on the *Daode jing*, technical interpretations of the text, philosophical and mystical exegeses, practical manuals on *Daode jing* meditation and ritual, and formal hagiographies of Laozi and Yin Xi.[11] The importance of the *Daode jing* as a sacred scripture in priestly and monastic ordination continues to the present day. It is one of the texts chanted at religious services in the Complete Perfection (Quanzhen) school, handed to ordinands at the time of first initiation together with a set of ten precepts and certain guidelines for self-cultivation. The *Daode jing* as much as the figure of Laozi have inspired seekers of self-cultivation, and numerous meditation techniques through history as well as Qigong methods of recent years have appeared in their name.[12]

Discussing these topics with students and placing the text in its larger historical and ritual context will inevitably lead into the reception of Laozi the person, a figure typically thought of as a contemporary of Confucius. Based on an account of his person in the *Shiji*, he is typically described as a learned and somewhat reclusive official at the Zhou court, where he served as an archivist. His first call to fame came when Confucius, eager to expand his knowledge of the ancient rites, went to the Zhou capital to consult him. Lao Dan, instead of imparting his wisdom, put Confucius down, advising him to forget all about things to cram into his head and instead to let go of everything and follow the natural way. Confucius, stunned for several days, finally emerged with the verdict that he had met many impressive people in his day but none like Lao Dan, who was "truly like a dragon," free from all constraints and powerfully soaring in the sky. Laozi's second call to fame came when he decided to emigrate because nothing much good was going to come of the Zhou dynasty anymore. Stopped by the Guardian of the Pass, he was compelled to spell out his ideas and thus, under some duress, wrote the *Daode jing*.

As A. C. Graham has shown, this image is largely legendary, the figure Laozi being originally a Confucian creation, used to show the master's humility and eagerness to learn. The hoary master was then taken over by the growing "Daoist" school when it needed a respectable founder in the fourth century B.C.E. Presented to the conquering Qin rulers as a powerful political thinker of unusual longevity in the third century B.C.E., Laozi was then removed from the scene by the story of his western emigration, which conveniently also accounted for the compilation of the *Daode jing*. Under the Han, finally, when the close connection to the Qin turned problematic, Laozi's birthplace was located at Bozhou (Henan) near the Han rulers' homeland of Pei, and he was linked with the Li clan, a family of loyal Han retainers.[13]

While Laozi the man remains shrouded in the mists of early history and legend, Laozi the god has been a significant and dominant figure in the religion from the Han dynasty to the present day. In the Han dynasty, he was divinized through adoption by three separate groups:

1. The magical practitioners (*fangshi*) or individual seekers of immortality, who saw in him the patriarch of their arts and idealized him as an immortal.

2. The political elite, that is, the imperial family and court officials, who found in Laozi the personification of the Dao and worshiped him as a representative of their ideal of cosmic and political unity alongside the Yellow Emperor (Huangdi) and the Buddha and engraved inscriptions to this effect.

3. Popular, millenarian cults, who identified Laozi as the god who manifested himself through the ages and would save the world yet again and bring about the age of Great Peace (Taiping). Called Venerable Lord (Laojun) or Yellow Venerable Lord (Huanglao jun), this

deified Laozi was like the personification of cosmic harmony worshipped by the court but equipped with tremendous revolutionary
power. As a messiah, he could overturn the present and reorganize the
world, leading the faithful to a new state of heavenly bliss in this very
life on earth.

Through this adaptation of Laozi as a deity of these various groups, his
biography changed into a hagiography, the mythical life of a cosmic saint. He
was described as fully identical with the Dao, the creator of the entire world, and
the ever newly appearing savior of the world, the so-called teacher of dynasties.
His birth on this earth as Laozi was embellished by increasing his time in the
womb to eighty-one years and giving him the physiognomy of a sage. His life
after his western emigration was also elaborated, so that he was either said to
have wandered west and converted the barbarians to his teaching, which duly
became known as Buddhism, or believed to have ascended back to heaven and
returned variously to reveal the different Daoist teachings in China.

The result is a highly complex Laozi myth, which describes his supernatural existence in six distinct parts or phases:

1. Laozi as the Dao creates the universe (creation).
2. Laozi descends as the teacher of dynasties (transformations).
3. Laozi is born on earth and serves as an archivist under the Zhou
   (birth).
4. Laozi emigrates and transmits the *Daode jing* to Yin Xi (transmission).
5. Laozi and Yin Xi go west and convert the barbarians to Buddhism
   (conversion).
6. Laozi ascends to heaven and comes back again to give revelations to
   Chinese seekers, founding Daoist schools (revelations).

This fully developed myth appears first in the fifth century, then is further
elaborated in more extensive details until a high point is reached during the
Song dynasty, when three major hagiographies appear that each encompass
many chapters in the Daoist canon and include and systematize all previous
information on the god.[14] Aside from these, there were also many shorter
works of Laozi. He is further mentioned in countless passages in Daoist texts,
and large numbers of scriptures are claimed to go back to his revelations. To
the present day, he plays an active role in the Daoist religion as the sponsor of
new methods of Qigong and a key deity of both major Daoist schools, the
Celestial Masters and Complete Perfection.

To bring these intricate and complex historical facts to our students is not
an easy task. Students often resist the debunking of their ideas and reject the

religious dimensions of a text and a figure that they have learned to associate with personal philosophy and a spontaneous way of life. It is important, therefore, to make it clear from the beginning of the class that Daoism is first and foremost a religion and that, while philosophical ideas bandied about in its name have their place in this religion, they are far from dominant in it. Even the early texts, interpreted largely as philosophical documents in academia, are, as Harold Roth has shown convincingly, based on meditative and cultivation experiences and come from a distinctly religious context. To make the adjustment to this new view easier for students, it helps greatly to introduce comparative perspectives into the discussion.

For example, the phenomenon of mysticism is very helpful in placing the scriptural reception of the *Daode jing*, because it makes it clear that mystics of whatever tradition, like practicing Daoists, are primarily religious practitioners whose ideas are secondary to their experiences. In addition, Daoist seekers aim to undergo a transformation from ordinary life and perception to a more spiritual dimension in a threefold progress, which can be matched with the spiritual progress outlined in other traditions. Daoist transformation as understood from reading the *Laozi* and *Zhuangzi*, then, begins first with the embrace of simplicity, both physical and mental, with the goal of "seeing things as equal" and "having no one-sided feelings." This involves a withdrawal from ordinary sensory experience and a refocusing of one's goals, a tendency to "diminish and again diminish" (*Daode jing*), as opposed to the urge to accumulate things and grow bigger and better all the time.

Once the mind is emptied of worldly concerns, it is, in a second step, opened up to perceive the intricacies of Dao, filled anew with a more cosmic, flowing, and universal perspective. It comes to accept all things equally, to stand alone among the multitude, to appear stupid and simple where everyone else is bright and complex. This new vision in turn leads, third, to a complete letting go of all personality, to a merging with the "Great Thoroughfare" of the Dao, the attainment of nonaction in all aspects of life and thought, the realization of perfect happiness and free and easy wandering. These three stages of withdrawal, openness, and merging with the Dao can then be compared, but of course never equalized, with the three mystical stages outlined by Evelyn Underhill on the basis of Christian writings: the purgative, where one eliminates old ideas and attachments; the illuminative, where one is filled with a new vision and complete focus on God; and the unitive, where one finds mystical union with the deity and enters a completely new life.[15] They can, moreover, be linked to other religions and their visions of spiritual attainment.

Then again, a discussion of the controversy surrounding the historical Jesus and his role in later Christianity may help to place the idea of Laozi as a legendary figure and as a god into a wider and more familiar context. Here it may be pointed out that certain classical motifs of the hero myth appear in both figures' hagiographies, for example, the virgin birth, the rejection by the establishment, the fight for their ideals, and the stylization as king over a vast empire (in Laozi's case, after his emigration).[16] Both figures, in addition, have become models for the believers of the religions that grew in their wake, giving people guidance and representing the ideals of the religion. The historical Jesus is often quite as unfathomable as the historical Laozi, and the veneration as savior has caused both figures to be stylized as immensely supernatural.

If students are not familiar with the debates surrounding the historical Jesus, the figure of Santa Claus might be a useful means of clarifying the legendary and divine status of Laozi. Most certainly, students are familiar with the common image of Santa Claus as a white-haired, chubby, and cheerful old man who makes toys galore, then rides around in a wondrous sled drawn by reindeer (some with red noses), and drops his gifts into the chimneys and stockings on Christmas morning. No student, I am sure, would assert that he is a fully real, historical figure, yet they all realize that Santa Claus is important in our culture today. It can be pointed out in class that there was in fact a historical person at the origin of our Santa Claus story, namely Saint Nicholas, a wealthy man from Asia Minor who gave away all his wealth to the poor, especially favoring children, and died a saint—his ascension day of December 6 becoming a holy day in the Catholic Church. The story we know grew over the centuries on the basis of the historical facts, reaching a culminating point in the nineteenth century. Yet most people are totally unaware of them, and what is important for them is not the man, but the saint: the religiously stylized figure who represents more an idea than a real life.

On another note, teachers of Daoism profit greatly from firmly establishing the idea that no religion ever is a unified and fully integrated entity. Just as there are many different forms of Buddhism, Islam, Judaism, and Christianity; as all major religious traditions of the world have undergone serious schisms in their history; as they all are expressed in a multitude of forms, including mysticism, doctrine, philosophy, ritual, ordination hierarchies, and popular practices (even superstition)—so Daoism is a multifaceted tradition that has continued to reinvent itself ever since its first inception in the Warring States. It is unreasonable and unrealistic to demand of a Chinese tradition what no Western or other religion can deliver, and to pass judgment if it fails to do so. It is equally meaningless and even detrimental to understand modern Daoism or Daoism in the United States as a deviant and declined form of the tradition, when all we see here is just another way in which the tradition reinvents itself right under our eyes. On the contrary, encouraging students to actively seek out and engage themselves with these modern forms will increase their practical understanding of the religion and open their eyes to its historical forms, while also aiding their appreciation of its religious unfolding and growth in general.

In fact, the practical and contemporary dimension of Daoism can be regarded as another important teaching tool. Students tend to relish hands-on experiences and have a great deal more empathy for ideas and practices active in the here and now than those important in China fifteen hundred years ago. Showing the historical, scriptural, and devotional dimensions of Laozi the text and the personage together with their contemporary transformation offers the opportunity to teach Daoism in a way that is both academically sound and practically relevant to our students.

To sum up, the multiplicity of views and interpretations attached to both *Laozi* the book and Laozi the personage is a positive phenomenon that can greatly enrich the teaching experience of Daoism for both students and teacher. There is no single *Daode jing*; there is no single figure Laozi. Rather than looking for unity, we should realize that it is exactly this multifaceted richness of the text and the personage that attracts us to them and that makes them model cases for the study of Daoism and, by extension, of religion in general. Sharing this attraction and fascination with our students in an atmosphere free from prejudice and preconception will increase their critical awareness of both Daoism and the phenomenon of religion in their academic study, in contemporary society, and in their own lives. This is what makes teaching Daoism so rewarding.

NOTES

1. See Michael LaFargue, "Recovering the *Tao-te-ching*'s Original Meaning: Some Remarks on Historical Hermeneutics," in *Lao-tzu and the Tao-te-ching*, ed. Livia Kohn and Michael LaFargue (Albany: State University of New York Press, 1998), 255–276.

2. The Mawangdui manuscripts are translated in Robert Henricks, *Lao-Tzu: Te-Tao ching* (New York: Ballantine, 1989). He also has an article on the division of the chapters: "A Note on the Question of Chapter Divisions in the Ma-wang-tui Manuscripts of *Lao-tzu*," *Early China* 4 (1978/79), 449–57.

3. For a translation of the Guodian text, see Robert G. Henricks, *Lau Tzu's Tao Te Ching: A Translation of the Startling New Documents Found at Guodian* (New York: Columbia University Press, 2000). For an initial study of the documents, consult Sarah Allan and Crispin Williams, eds., *The Guodian Laozi* (Berkeley: Institute of East Asian Studies, 2000).

4. The most recent rearrangement of the *Daode jing* into new sections and divisions is found in Michael LaFargue, *Tao and Method: A Reasoned Approach to the Tao Te Ching* (Albany: State University of New York Press, 1994). For a translation of

Wang Bi's work, see Paul J. Lin, *A Translation of Lao-tzu's Tao-te-ching and Wang Pi's Commentary* (Ann Arbor: University of Michigan, Center for Chinese Studies Publications, 1977). A thorough discussion is found in Alan Chan, *Two Visions of the Way: A Study of the Wang Pi and the Ho-shang-kung Commentaries on the Laozi* (Albany: State University of New York Press, 1991).

5. To demonstrate the variety of interpretations and the versatility of the text even in later centuries, students may be referred to Isabelle Robinet, "Later Commentaries: Textual Polysemy and Syncretistic Interpretations," in Kohn and LaFargue, *Lao-tzu and the Tao-te-ching*, 119–42.

6. For a broader account of the *Daode jing* in the philosophical and political climate of Zhou-dynasty China, see A. C. Graham, *Disputers of the Tao: Philosophical Argument in Ancient China* (La Salle, Ill.: Open Court, 1989); Benjamin Schwartz, *The World of Thought in Ancient China* (Cambridge, Mass.: Harvard University Press, 1985).

7. A good discussion of the early Confucian school that also pays attention to social context and ritual realities is found in Robert Eno, *The Confucian Creation of Heaven: Philosophy and the Defense of Ritual Mastery* (Albany: State University of New York Press, 1990).

8. On the precepts and the *Xianger* commentary, see Stephen R. Bokenkamp, "Traces of Early Celestial Master Physiological Practice in the *Xiang'er* Commentary," *Taoist Resources* 4, no. 2 (1993): 37–52. He also has a complete translation of this text in his *Early Daoist Scriptures* (Berkeley: University of California Press, 1997).

9. This text is cited in the encyclopedia *Sandong zhunang* (A Bag of Pearls from the Three Caverns, DZ 1139, 9.10b). The materials are also discussed in some detail in my *God of the Dao: Lord Lao in History and Myth* (Ann Arbor: University of Michigan, Center for Chinese Studies, 1998).

10. For more details on the ritual uses of the *Daode jing*, see Livia Kohn, "The Tao-te-ching in Ritual," in Kohn and LaFargue, *Lao-tzu and the Tao-te-ching*, 143–161.

11. For an overview of Daoist ordination in the Middle Ages, see Charles Benn, "Daoist Ordination and *Zhai* Rituals," in *Daoism Handbook*, ed. Livia Kohn, (Leiden: E. Brill, 2000), 309–338. For a detailed discussion of the main forms of ordination practiced in the Tang, many of which focus on the ten precepts and the *Daode jing*, see Kristofer M. Schipper, "Taoist Ordination Ranks in the Tunhuang Manuscripts," in *Religion und Philosophie in Ostasien: Festschrift für Hans Steininger*, ed. G. Naundorf, K. H. Pohl, and H. H. Schmidt, (Würzburg, Germany: Königshausen and Neumann, 1985), 127–148. A more recent discussion of the precepts and ordination in Daoism is forthcoming in my *Daoist Precepts* (Cambridge, Mass.: Three Pines Press, 2004).

12. On the contemporary rules and practices of ordination in Complete Perfection Daoism, see Livia Kohn, "Monastic Rules in Quanzhen Daoism: As Collected by Heinrich Hackmann," *Monumenta Serica* 51 (2003).

13. See A. C. Graham, "The Origins of the Legend of Lao Tan," in *Studies in Chinese Philosophy and Philosophical Literature*, ed. A. C. Graham (Albany: State University of New York Press, 1990), 111–124.

14. For a detailed study of the development of Laozi in history, from the beginnings to the 1990s, as well as an analysis of his myth in the *Youlong zhuan*, one of the key Song dynasty hagiographies, see Kohn, *God of the Dao*.

15. See Evelyn Underhill, *Mysticism* (London: Methuen, 1911).

16. The understanding of Laozi as hero is discussed in more detail in Kohn, *God of the Dao*. For more on the hero myth, see Robert A. Segal, ed., *In Quest of the Hero* (Princeton: Princeton University Press, 1990).

Hermeneutics and Pedagogy: Methodological Issues in Teaching the *Daode Jing*

Russell Kirkland

Naturally, there are many ways of teaching the *Daode jing*. My own approaches have shifted in several ways over the years, and will doubtless continue to do so. In addition, I continue to teach the text in different ways to different audiences, adjusting to the level and focus of the participants of each course. So I recognize no definitive way to teach the text. Nonetheless, I maintain that there are better and worse approaches, and that it is necessary (1) to base one's approach soundly upon the facts, and (2) to adjust it in accordance with the evolution of the field. What follows, therefore, examines the hermeneutical and pedagogical implications of a variety of methodological issues.[1]

I should note first of all that my approach is, in many regards, contrarian. That is, I never settle for teaching students to understand the *Daode jing* along traditional lines. For the most part, our textbooks do a credible job of explaining traditional concepts of the text's content (the sage, *wuwei*, etc.). And at any course level, I ensure that my students are duly exposed to such inherited "mainstream" lenses. But those lenses are warped by Confucian bias and an abundance of Western misconceptions, mostly born of a desire to find in the *Daode jing* a utopian antidote to an array of perceived deficiencies in Western culture.[2]

My primary thrust is generally to stimulate critical thought about such mainstream interpretations. My justifications for doing so reside, in the first instance, in my assumption that a primary facet of liberal education is to stimulate critical examination of inherited models of understanding. But in this case, our culturally constructed model of the educator as Socratic gadfly is, at least in my own mind, supported by a comparable Zhuangzian thrust. Of course, using a Zhuangzian method to elucidate the *Daode jing* is, on a theoretical level, somewhat arbitrary, but doing so provides me with, at the very least, the pleasant illusion that my predilection for shocking my students with untraditional perspectives can be justified in "Daoist" terms. I should also acknowledge my former colleague Lee Yearley for convincing me that we are not entirely unjustified in reading Zhuangzi in terms that are, to some degree, postmodern. That is, I have come to the position, presumably Zhuangzian if not Socratic, that there is no position that can simply be assumed to be valid, and that it is proper to question every assumption, no matter how well-accepted it might be. For these reasons, my lenses for studying and teaching the *Daode jing* are constantly being removed and reexamined, and sometimes replaced by other lenses that for some intelligible reason seem preferable, if not necessarily demonstrably correct. Such a reflexive deconstructionism (to appropriate a term from part of my own culture) is often appreciated by advanced students, and, if presented in terms of delicious Zhuangzian parables rather than postmodernist jargon, is tolerated even by students at the most introductory level.

In essence, my approach to teaching the *Daode jing* is, in various ways, to challenge students to grapple with an array of hermeneutical issues. I challenge them to question whatever they read or hear about the *Daode jing*, even from their knowledgeable and conscientious instructor. Many college students, particularly at the introductory level, have rarely been exposed to critical thought, much less expected to perform it themselves: they have been taught to assume that "truth" is known, and that their job is simply to accept what they are given (by their textbooks and by their instructors) and to commit it to memory. Naturally, the conscientious educator must (whether by Socratic or Zhuangzian imperatives) challenge students to consider truth as not necessarily known and to stimulate them to reconsider all that they learn from others. In other words, in teaching students the *Daode jing*, I teach them to ponder the viability of the "radical" new perspectives that I present to them while, in the final analysis, thinking for themselves. This model is quite alien to the mind-set of Qing dynasty Confucianism and its parallels in Christian catechism and its various secular analogues. To the shock and consternation of many students, I, like Zhuangzi, challenge my students to imagine that what they read in their books about the *Daode jing* might be unreliable, and that it is not just permissible, but actually necessary, for them to reflect on their own response to the material.

For these reasons, I frustrate some students by requiring them to read the *Daode jing* in translations that are stark and minimalist, translations like those of D. C. Lau or Robert Henricks.[3] Students are sometimes frustrated by such translations because these translations tell them only what the text says, not what it means. Most students would be happier with one of the many translations (or pseudo-translations) that presume to explain the meaning of each passage. What I challenge students to understand is that such explanations are really a window not into the text itself, but merely into the mind of the translator. Such windows provide false comfort indeed, for whether any of us like it or not, the text of the *Daode jing*—in the original Chinese—is stark, murky, and remarkably polyvocal. My goal, therefore, is to give students an experience of the text that is, to the greatest extent possible, comparable to the frustrating experience of reading the original text.

Before my students read the text for the first time, I often urge them to think about their experience of reading it and to ask themselves the following questions:

- What kind of text is this?
- How is this text affecting me?
- How is this text supposed to affect the reader?
- Who is "the reader" supposed to be?
- Why is the text in the form that it is in?
- How is the form of the text related to the message(s) that it intends to convey?

In sum, I challenge students to set aside all that the text has generally been read to mean and to do something radical and original: to read it for themselves and to allow their own experience of the text to help inform their interpretive efforts. My assumption is not that students can find its "true meaning" within themselves, or even by themselves. I assume, rather, that because they have a starting point somewhere in a knowable cultural setting, one in which many of us grew up ourselves, the educator can identify and work to dislodge identifiable cultural illusions and stimulate students to react creatively to the facts of the text and its proper historical context.

Interpretation through Exegesis

Once, in a 1988 course at Oberlin College, I gave my students a stark, "literal" new translation of several intriguing *Daode jing* chapters (5, 6, 26, 35, and 56, in the traditional numbering), along with a colleague's explanation of the exegetical process, as formulated and practiced in the field of biblical studies. I then tasked students to choose one of those passages and perform an exegesis of it, as follows:

1. *Carefully* think through the following questions:

What point is the writer trying to make in this passage? How is he trying to make it?[4]

What is the structure of the passage? How does the writer present his point? What does the structure of the passage communicate? Is the passage a coherent unity? Does it have "seams"? What conclusion can one draw from these facts?

What type of language is used in the passage? If symbolic language is used, how is it used? What are the symbols, images, metaphors? Why are those symbols used as they are? If the writer uses devices such as imperatives or interrogatives, why?

Can one discern different levels of meaning in the passage? If so, how was the writer using those different levels of meaning to help communicate his point?

Are there specific key terms on which the writer relies to communicate his point? If so, what do those terms mean here, in this context? Is there any evidence that the writer means for other associations to carry over from other passages?

Can one identify a particular audience for the passage? What does the writer assume from his audience? Does he assume certain common knowledge, certain viewpoints, certain experiences? What is the "world of discourse"?

2. With these questions in mind, select one of the specified chapters of the *Daode jing* with which you feel that you can work most productively. Use *all* of the "authorized translations." Analyze the chapter exegetically, and outline the results. It is not necessary to attempt to determine specific answers to all of the questions raised above: "Let the text set the agenda" (or, to employ idiomatic aphorisms: "Hit the ball where it is pitched," and "Take what the defense gives you."). Synthesize the results of your analysis, and present your synthesis in a brief paper of one to two double-spaced pages.

In the Oberlin course, this assignment worked well: students took one of the assigned passages and analyzed it as a text, interpreting it on its own terms. In so doing, they disregarded not only everything outside the text of the *Daode jing*—a radical move in itself—but everything outside of the specific passage in front of them. For instance, in performing exegesis, it is illicit to assume that a symbolic reference to "the mysterious female" in *Daode jing* 6 can necessarily be interpreted in terms of other passages in which images of "the feminine" or "the Mother" appear. And of course, it is illicit to assume that such a phrase can be interpreted in terms of maternal images found in other texts, other ages, or other cultures.

This assignment illustrates my rejection of certain "traditional" models for interpreting the *Daode jing*. For instance, I reject altogether the common assumption that the *Daode jing* represents the thought of an ancient Chinese school of philosophy, which is today widely, though incorrectly, called Daoism. Historically, there was, in fact, no such thing: the conflation of the thought-content of the *Daode jing* with the thought-content of the *Zhuangzi*, and subsequent reification of the overlap into a coherent school of thought, is a common but insidious fallacy.[5] Critical scholars have for decades generally agreed that there was actually no "philosopher" named Laozi.[6] And they have generally agreed that the text that we call the *Daode jing* was actually the result of a complex process of accretion and reinterpretation, which probably began in an oral tradition and took its final form sometime in the early third century B.C.E. Recent research furthermore suggests that the form of the *Daode jing*, as well as some of its ideas, were modeled on those of the germinal fourth-century B.C.E. text called the *Nei ye*, "Inner Cultivation."[7]

In any event, if the *Daode jing* was not, as is generally agreed, the product of a single mind, it logically follows that passage A and passage B may share a given idea fully, incompletely, or not at all. I therefore teach my students that some passages of the *Daode jing* are likely more closely related than others, and that we will find in it a plethora of inexplicable "inconsistencies" unless we acknowledge the plurality of layers and voices that are embodied in it.

Elsewhere, I have argued that the multivocality of the *Daode jing* might best be explained by seeing the text as having been composed in layers. In my classes, I give students a "Historical Outline of Taoism," which summarizes that explanation as follows:

The *Daode jing* ["Laozi"] (early third century B.C.E.)
Origins:
(1) Ideas from anonymous people (not intellectuals) of sixth through fourth century B.C.E., probably including local elders ("laozi"), possibly including women; possible origins in the land of Chu.
(2) Teachings about meditative practices and ambient spiritual realities influenced by the tradition that produced the *Nei ye*.

Transmitted orally for generations, shifting and expanding in content; committed to writing in the early third century B.C.E. by an unknown intellectual, who converted the content to a sociopolitical program in response to the concerns of the intellectual elite of the political centers of his day. Eventually attributed to a character called "Laozi," who was actually a pious fiction.

Contents:

1. Early layers: Emphasis on natural simplicity, harmony, "feminine" behaviors.

   Ideal: The *Dao* ("Way")—the source and natural order of things.

   Thesis: One should act through Nonaction (*wuwei*).

Education is unnecessary, and can be destructive of natural simplicity.

2. Later layers: Emphasis on sagely government; rejection of Confucian moralism.

   Human ideal: The "Sage" *(sheng ren)*—one who is like the *Dao*.

   Government: If the sage–ruler holds to the *Dao*, the world will be orderly.[8]

Naturally, this analysis, though based on textual and historical research, is an expression of my own interpretive vision, a vision that is continually evolving as I, and the field, mature.

This exegetical approach to the text results from my early training in biblical criticism, as well as my later sinological training as a philologist and historian. It is a radically particularistic approach. But it is also, to a substantial degree, an approach that grapples meaningfully with the hermeneutical issues that reveal themselves as our interpretive movements slowly work their way free from patterns inherited from earlier, less reflective eras.

Lofting "The Torch of Doubt" to Illumine a Colonialistic Cave

In earlier generations, interpreters (in this case, Western, Chinese, and Japanese interpreters) went about their task on the basis of assumptions rooted securely in their own traditions. When Westerners encountered the religious and intellectual traditions of Asia, they went about making sense of those traditions by comparing and contrasting what they saw in them with what they "knew" from their own tradition. For instance, throughout the colonial age, Europeans understood the concept of "scripture," and, after the Renaissance and Reformation, many of them rejected the assumption that the individual can interpret scripture only under the guidance of sacral authority. In the European tradition, such authority had been devoted to seeing that members of the human community conform their lives to a revealed truth that, by its nature, transcends all individuals' interpretive abilities. But by the time Westerners reached China and began attempting to make sense of it, the individualistic humanism that surrounded Protestantism had awarded the interpreter with the real or imagined ability to make sense of the world for himself.[9] Chinese traditions, including the *Daode jing*, therefore came to be interpreted according to a variety of Western agendas, and any historical or textual facts that could not be made to fit into the interpreter's agenda were simply ignored or explained away. The extreme of that thrust continues today, as hundreds of Westerners continue to assume that they are entitled to decide for themselves what the *Daode jing* says, ignoring not only two thousand years of Chinese interpreters, but even the text itself, thereby reducing it to epiphenomenality.

I attempt to induce productive shock in my students by teaching them these facts and urging them not to colonize the *Daode jing*. This text, I teach them, was never written for *us*. The naïve assumption that any ancient author or composer considered his thoughts applicable to modern or postmodern lives is patently ludicrous, though saying so is contrary to modernist norms.

Lofting Zhuangzi's "torch of doubt," I challenge students to question the assumption that we today, Asian or Western, can really understand the *Daode jing* at all. Adducing Zhuangzi as our hermeneutical sherpa, I challenge students, for instance, to ask themselves how we know that the *Daode jing* is really a work of "philosophy."[10] If the text be, as traditional interpretations have supposed, an exposition of a great mind's analysis of the nature of life, why did such a percipient person not expound his views in a more orderly and comprehensible manner?[11] The evidence of the text, unsystematic in any perceptible sense, demonstrates either that its composer had no philosophical positions or that, as some analysts today suggest, he was too stupid to understand or explain his own philosophy.[12]

Holding up my hermeneutical torch of doubt in other corners of our cave, I challenge students, more generally, to ponder the alienity of ancient China, a culture fairly devoid of modern or postmodern minds. In this corner, for instance, I challenge them to ask themselves how we know that the *Daode jing* represents, as many have claimed, a work of "mysticism."[13] In that corner, my torch of doubt reveals that the *Daode jing* may have provocative references to "the female," but that an interpreter who reads it as a text of late twentieth-century feminism has to ignore a great many uncomfortable textual and historical realities.[14] The *Daode jing*, I teach, was not written to help us with our own lives: it is a text from an alien culture, in a distant age, and studying it means exploring an alien world—not ourselves.

The common assumption that the *Daode jing* ought to be interpreted as a text applicable to our own lives actually reflects our lingering Judeo-Christian faith in the eternal relevance of scripture. Having rejected Church as interpreter of Scripture, then the validity of the Bible itself, many moderns have searched for a replacement—for a classic text that can be appropriated and reinterpreted as a Bible for the non-Christian modern believer. Following the lead of early sinologists, decades of Westerners have ripped the *Daode jing* from its moorings in Chinese culture and society, and re-created it in their own idealized image, resulting in a plethora of "Daos" perfectly suited to the tastes and prejudices of modern and postmodern minds.[15]

I attempt to convince students to take seriously two radical and, for many, highly uncomfortable assertions:

1. That the *Daode jing* is, contrary to popular belief, actually Chinese, that is, a product of a specific social, historical, and cultural context of which we, student and teacher alike, are not—and logically cannot be—a part.[16]

2. That both that context itself, and this textual product of it, deserve to be understood and respected in their own right, not for what they can do for us.[17]

By this process, I encourage respect for other cultures, justify the necessity of sound textual and historical research, and challenge students to examine their own unexamined assumptions about how we are, and are not, entitled to relate to other cultures.

Accepted Truth: The Confucians Are Always Right

Holding aloft Zhuangzi's torch, I warn students to question other common models for interpreting the *Daode jing*. For instance, I challenge the widely accepted "Great Books" model for studying "Great Civilizations."[18] To date, the West's acceptance of the *Daode jing* as a Great Book has been based on the text's usefulness to Confucians in their wildly successful effort to preclude any form of respect for Daoism among Western observers. So successful were the Confucians of the nineteenth and twentieth century (including highly Westernized Confucians like Fung Yu-lan and Wing-tsit Chan) that to this very day there are only a handful of educators—in Asia or the West—who teach the *Daode jing* as it is, or has been, taught by people who operate in its living tradition: Daoists.

Like their Confucian informers, Western sinologists (with the singular exception of Henri Maspero, whose singularity earned him the contempt of the more mainstream H. G. Creel) have generally dismissed the Daoist tradition as it has existed in Chinese society of premodern and modern times.[19] For instance, until thirty years ago, there was hardly a Western sinologist who could even name a Daoist religious thinker of the past fifteen hundred years. Yet, the *Daozang*—the immense corpus of Daoist literature that has been in Western libraries since the 1930s—is replete with writings by such thinkers. The *Daozang* represents, in fact, the Great Books of the Daoists. But because Western sinology trusted Confucians as its "native informants," and because modern Confucians (unlike their medieval predecessors) rudely dismissed every product of the Daoist religious tradition, the Western Daoist canon was quickly limited to two texts—the *Daode jing* and *Zhuangzi*—which represent the range and complexity of Daoist thought to about the same extent as the Gospel of John represents the range and complexity of Christian thought. While it is true that it is difficult to imagine Christianity without that gospel, it is also true that Christian beliefs and practices can hardly be understood by reading that text alone: centuries of practitioners reinterpreted the Christian message to fit their own age and their own lives and developed different ways of understanding and living the Christian life. Imagine a teacher from a non-Christian culture handing her or his students a translation of the Gospel of John (a "translation," moreover, made by someone who had never bothered to learn Greek) and telling them that all the rest of what Christians call Christianity is merely "moribund superstition": by doing so, that teacher would be dismissing not only the lives and faith of two thousand years of Christian men and women, but also the theological subtleties of hundreds of thoughtful people who had labored to explain Christian faith in ways that make sense to intelligent minds of every age and culture. Yet, today's courses—even in many of our most elite universities—entirely dismiss the lives and practices of two thousand years of Daoist men and women, as well as the dozens of extant texts by thoughtful men and women who labored to explain Daoist principles and practices.

In sum, the Western world continues to understand and explain the *Daode jing* in Confucian terms, Protestant terms, theosophical terms, feminist terms, ecological terms, and many other sets of terms—but never, under any circumstances, in Daoist terms. The modern Confucians (from Fung and Chan to their numerous Western disciples) have successfully convinced even highly educated Western intellectuals that there was, for instance, no meaningful Daode thought after the third century C.E.[20] Even leading explicators of "Daoist thought" commonly write as though they have never heard of Daoist minds like Sima Chengzhen or Li Daochun. The writings of such Daoists—people who successfully refined Daoist beliefs and practices to enable them to survive century after century—have never been included in our sourcebooks.[21] Only in the 1990s have sourcebooks begun to include the Great Books of Daoism as they were identified by the Daoists of China themselves.[22] Yet, for the most part, our courses continue to teach Daoism in such a way that students learn that it is necessary and appropriate to ignore such texts. The Confucians co-opted the Western academy so effectively that our classrooms still echo with the Confucian lie that "China had two 'Daoisms'—the noble and intriguing thoughts of the philosophers Laozi and Zhuangzi—and the contemptible su-perstitions of later 'magicians' and 'necromancers.'" To the extent that we allow our students to believe such untruths, we are doing the equivalent of teaching our students that Judaism ceased to exist when Jesus was born. That is, we are promulgating the self-serving lies of the antagonists of our subject and presenting those lies as though they were unquestionable fact.

Thinking the Unthinkable: Teaching the *Daode Jing* as Daoism

So, if we were to do the unthinkable—to teach the *Daode jing* in a manner consistent with its actual place in Daoist tradition—how would we do it? Specialists in the study of Daoism are only now beginning to learn enough about the tradition to enable us to answer such a question. Only a handful of scholars, from Anna Seidel to Livia Kohn, have even begun to pay any at-tention to what Daoist tradition has to say about "Laozi," or about the nature of the *Daode jing*.

Yet one thing that we have known all along is that, in Daoist tradition, the *Daode jing* is a scripture. From one Daoist perspective, the *Daode jing* is "the final intellectual result of practical efforts to achieve longevity, . . . a theoretical treatise referring to these practices and alluding to them in a coded form."[23] From other Daoist perspectives, the text is a potently sacred scripture, revealed by a divinity who has existed from the beginning of the cosmos.[24] In this perspective,

> Laozi is . . . the one who comes down from heaven to earth regularly, like rain, at first to serve as "counselor to the Emperor" . . . and later, after he has transferred this power to the first of the Heavenly

Masters ... in the 2nd century A.D., to serve as divine "lord of the religion."[25]

In other Daoist formulations, Laozi "is the image and the model of the entire universe," and by proper meditation and/or ritual, the practitioner is (re-) united with the universal Dao, assimilating his or her personal reality to the universal reality, according to the model of Laozi himself.[26] In certain contexts, the *Daode jing* is a cosmic reality in itself, a manifestation of realities beyond the ken of ordinary minds, and as such it gives its possessor immense power and corresponding responsibilities.[27]

In sum, from the richly varied perspectives of centuries of Daoists, the *Daode jing* is not just a record of some old man's wise suggestions for living life. Its contents are understood by Daoists not just as musings about the Dao: in some sense, they are the Dao. The scripture is sacred not for what it says, but for what it is.

But one must also beware overestimating this scripture's importance in Daoist life: the *Daode jing* was generally an honored scripture, but it was seldom regarded as the final or ultimate revelation of the Dao. It would therefore be misleading to teach students to think of it as scripture in the sense of the Christians' Bible or the Muslims' Qur'an—that is, as an authoritative revelation of a single great message. In Daoism, there has seldom, if ever, been any belief in a single great message.[28] In Daoism, there is no trace or either orthodoxy or orthopraxy, and Daoists felt little need to conceptualize or justify the absence of either.[29] Our students should be keenly aware of these facts.

Respect for Traditional Religion in Secular Education: Lessons from Laozi

Skeptics might ask: Should educators today really teach the *Daode jing* from a Daoist perspective? After all, biblical scholars in academia do not assume that they ought to teach *Matthew* from a Christian perspective; they teach their students to stand, at least temporarily, outside of Christian tradition, to analyze the text without the interpretive lenses of later "traditional teachings." The goal of such analysis is not to teach students how to be Christian, but merely how to understand Christian texts. Such studies assume the necessity of maintaining a critical perspective.

Yet I believe that we must remain self-critically aware of the secularizing tendencies of academia, wherein the beliefs of religious practitioners are often casually disregarded or explained away as superstition or Freudian illusion.[30]

It is true that we must teach our students to distinguish history from myth: the Jesus who walked in Capernaum and the Christ of Pauline theology or Chartres Cathedral are quite distinguishable. But both are worthy subjects of academic inquiry, and Christian belief that they are ultimately identical may not be gratuitously dismissed. That is to say, while our students should be led to be able to think outside of the terms of the tradition under study, they should not be taught hostility to that tradition; in all my courses, my syllabus explains that our goal is to evaluate religions in a manner that is both properly critical and properly sympathetic. While we are unlikely to wish our students to accept a Daoist understanding of the nature of the *Daode jing*, I can see little objection to the position that we ought to expose our students to such interpretations, and to explain those interpretations sympathetically in terms of the realities of Chinese history and society. Simply to exclude such interpretations as inherently irrelevant—as has almost always been done in our classrooms—seems to leave the educator open to the charge of cultural imperialism, that is, that we arrogate unto ourselves the authority to tell Daoists what parts of their tradition are meaningful and valid and what parts are unworthy of serious attention. Postmodern educators have been as guilty of this secularistic arrogance as their predecessors.

Second, it seems quite possible that at least some later Daoist interpretations of the *Daode jing* might actually shed significant, even vital light upon important elements of its contents. For instance, Westerners have generally been fascinated with passages that encourage the practice of *wuwei*, "nonaction." Indeed, such a practice has widely been assumed to have been the most fundamental and essential element of the Daoist life. But if we can break out of our inherited Orientalist mind-set, we quickly learn that in the actualities of Daoist life, *wuwei* has generally not been a central value to most Daoists of the past or the present: in many segments of Daoism one finds little trace of it.[31]

If we can look past the fetishized idea of *wuwei*, we find that the *Daode jing* recommendations for living "a Daoist life" are actually quite manifold. But at least a few passages clearly suggest the importance of self-cultivation through some biospiritual process, a meditative process that involves manipulating or refining life forces like *jing* (vital essence) and *qi* (life energy). The research of Harold Roth is beginning to suggest possible communities of practitioners of such processes.[32] And clearly, the *Nei ye*, a text with many similarities to the *Daode jing*, is devoted primarily to urging the reader to engage in such practices. But our inherited interpretive models do little to help us understand, or teach, the nature or purpose of such practices, even in the context of the *Daode jing*. However, if we remove our Confucian/Victorian blinders, and look at Daoism honestly, we find an enormous literature on such practices throughout Chinese history, from the *Taiping jing*, an important text of Celestial Master Daoism, through the Tang heyday of the consolidated *Daojiao*, into the "Inner Alchemy" traditions of late imperial times.[33]

Although our students—secularistic like most of their professors—may have trouble dealing with the fact that Daoists often revered the *Daode jing* as a revealed scripture or that Daoists used it in ritual and sacerdotal settings, they should certainly be able to understand it as an early expression of the abiding Daoist principle of self-perfection through the cultivation of our vital life energies. If we fail to include Later Daoism as a meaningful context for understanding the *Daode jing*, we rob our students of the chance to understand (1) that important element of classical Daoism, and therefore (2) the deep-rooted continuities that run through Daoism, from the *Nei ye* and *Daode jing* to the present.[34]

A Zhuangzian Hermeneutic: Liberation by Means of the Facts

From the foregoing it should be clear that I teach my students to study the *Daode jing* by means of a protean hermeneutical process, the structure and contents of which are dictated by the text before us and by the facts of Chinese and Western cultural history. My guiding principles are that interpreting the *Daode jing* requires (1) sound philological and historical training, (2) a willingness to test interpretive models against the realities of the text and its cultural context, and (3) a willingness to modify or discard models that cannot be shown to accord with those realities.

In that sense, my assumption is that the conscientious educator is comparable to a scientist, who honors empirical facts and works cautiously to develop and test hypotheses until a coherent theory seems to be justified by the evidence. In such an endeavor, the scientist is not guided by the emotional needs of his or her students: he or she does not analyze or present the data on the basis of students' desire to find their life's meaning in it, or to compensate them for the fact that other types of data do not satisfy such desires. It does not matter to the astronomer whether her or his students are able to understand mass and gravitation in terms of their own lives (though the inverse might seem desirable). Nor should students be led to imagine that performing spectroscopic analysis can be regarded as optional if they feel that it might interfere with their urge to "find themselves" in the stars. I am willing to be indulgent enough to inform students that they are free to run their private lives as they see fit; if one becomes a happier, more well-adjusted person by following astrological beliefs, perhaps that is all well and good. But any serious astronomer is going to teach her or his students that what we do in this classroom is not astrology, it is science, and that in science we set aside our personal needs and desires, no matter how valid they might be, when we are assessing empirical facts. Our assumption is going to be that we will take the facts seriously, even if they give us no satisfaction, or even make us deeply uncomfortable. And if need be, we allow our understanding of ourselves to be altered, even revolutionized, by the true implications of the facts.

Is it reasonable to follow such principles in teaching a text from ancient China? One may answer that Zhuangzi seems to demand it. Zhuangzi challenged readers to question what they have always assumed to be truth, to question our means of determining truth, and to allow our living to be guided by the true realities of life: unrelenting change, complexity that may well exceed human comprehension, and inevitable death. Following Zhuangzi's path may be baffling and uncomfortable, but he seems to say that doing so is ultimately more fulfilling than attempting to struggle against such realities. His charge to learn to see and respond to life as it is, rather than as we wish it to be, is deeply challenging, and it may be for that reason that he couched his teachings in humorous stories of doves and cicadas and whimsical eccentrics who live life fully, despite the fact that their lives might violate cultural norms—including the assumption that rational analysis leads to truth.

In teaching the *Daode jing*, I challenge students to question cherished beliefs—Confucian, modernist, and postmodernist alike. I challenge them to regard interpretive models as things to be examined critically, not simply applied to the data unreflectively. I challenge them to ask uncomfortable questions about the text, such as whether there is any way we can ultimately know for sure what it might mean. I challenge them to ask whether any interpretive method can reliably reveal the text's meaning, or whether all such methods might merely be cultural constructs, which in the final analysis explain only the interpreters themselves.

Because he leads us to ask such questions, Zhuangzi has often been called a relativist. But as some recent analysts have observed, Zhuangzi does not explicitly deny the validity of particular views: he merely draws them all into question.[35] If we cannot be entirely sure that we are justified in accepting any particular view, we also cannot be entirely sure that we would be justified in rejecting it. Indeed, Zhuangzi seems to maintain that there must be some sound and valid approach to living. The famous parable of the butterfly dream shows a mind doubting the validity of two contrary models of self-identification. Yet the writer does not conclude that all models are necessarily invalid: "Between

Zhou and the butterfly there must be a difference" (*bi you fen yi*). But the writer urges us to look for proper perspective not in any coherent interpretive model, but rather in the indeterminate "transformation of things" (*wuhua*).

To return to my starting point, I repeat that there seems to be no definitively right or wrong way to teach the *Daode jing*. But that fact does not logically lead to the conclusion that all approaches are equally valid. There are clearly better and worse approaches, and some can legitimately be condemned as invalid. After all, Zhuang Zhou might not have been able to be entirely sure whether he was Zhou or a butterfly, but there was no question that his reality lay somewhere within that bipolarity: he did not conclude that he might really be a gourd or a millipede! So our task as educators is to weed out invalid approaches to the *Daode jing* and to work within the remaining possibilities.

For some, this task will mean teaching the text as a product of its time, as a response to a particular set of historical and intellectual realities. In that sense, the *Daode jing* is, in its final form, someone's attempt to provide an alternative to certain patterns of thought and behavior in parts of ancient China. For other educators, it may mean teaching the *Daode jing* as an early expression of key aspects of Daoist practice, pointing out the significance of the text's passages on self-cultivation. To me, it seems necessary to teach our students both of those perspectives, because the text's composer (or at least, its final redactor) gave us a text that includes both. I try to help students cope with the resulting ambiguities by offering them a new hermeneutic model: unraveling a text that is composed in various layers, each the work of different minds, minds that proceeded from different assumptions, values, and concerns. This model, which reflects the textual and historical conclusions of many scholars, helps students understand the importance of historical realities, the importance of textual realities, and the fruitfulness of scholarly analysis as a hermeneutical tool.

This approach also gives students an intelligible reason to reject all the truly silly interpretations of the *Daode jing* that float around today. Just as Zhuang Zhou may or may not have been a butterfly but was certainly not a gourd, so the *Daode jing* is an expression of ancient Chinese sociopolitical thought, an expression of interest in meditational and behavioral self-cultivation, possibly even an expression of popular values of ancient Chu, but it is certainly not the product of a modern or postmodern mind and was certainly not intended to correct the evils of our own age. So, although some educators may not yet feel ready to smash those interpretive gourds, we should help our students see what they are good for—studying the unreflective cultural imperialism that lingers in the postmodern West—and what they are not good for: understanding the *Daode jing*.

NOTES

1. Some of the thoughts presented here were stimulated by a 1993 Minneapolis workshop entitled "Text and Context: Critical Thinking Strategies for Texts in Translation." In that workshop, sponsored by the University of Minnesota, M. J. Abhishaker of Normandale College examined the problems of critical thinking in a culturally diverse interpretive context, and I focused discussion on hermeneutical issues involving the *Daode jing* I am indebted to Dr. Abhishaker and the other participants.

2. For decades, the *Daode jing* has been widely interpreted as offering solutions to problems that modern Westerners see as afflicting their own world. As Steve Bradbury has said, "Because the vast majority of its translators, Western and Chinese, were attracted to it in the first place because of their humanist faith in . . . the *Daode jing* as proto-humanist doctrine compatible with liberal Protestantism, they have usually produced . . . readings of the work that . . . endorse a Western agenda." That agenda generally relates to a modern metanarrative that subordinates textual, historical, and cultural facts to a yearning for a utopian society freed of the evils that supposedly afflict the world under the oppressive yoke of "organized religion," "industrial development," "technology," "patriarchal hegemony," or the linear rationalism of "the Western mind." Educators should acquaint themselves with Bradbury's essay, "The American Conquest of Philosophical Taoism," in *Translation East and West: A Cross-Cultural Approach*, ed. Cornelia N. Moore and Lucy Lower (Honolulu: University of Hawaii College of Languages, Linguistics and Literature, and East-West Center, 1992), 29–41. More generally, see J. J. Clarke, *Oriental Enlightenment: The Encounter between Asian and Western Thought* (London: Routledge, 1997); J. J. Clarke, *The Tao of the West* (London: Routledge, 2000); and Russell Kirkland, "On Coveting Thy Neighbor's Tao: Reflections on J. J. Clarke's *The Tao of the West*," *Religious Studies Review* 28, no. 4 (2002): 309–312.

3. The 1963 Penguin edition of Lau's translation is still useful, though it translates the received text, that is, the traditional version edited by the third-century philosopher Wang Pi. Students today should know that version, but should also be given a reliable translation of the Ma-wang-tui manuscripts, such as that by Robert G. Henricks, *Lao-tzu Te-Tao Ching* (New York: Ballantine Books, 1989). Henricks's version is readable and sinologically sound. In the same year, Lau translated the Ma-wang-tui edition, though the translation was published in Hong Kong, rendering it inaccessible to most students and educators. Fortunately, it has now been published in North America: D. C. Lau, *Lao-tzu: Tao Te Ching* (New York: Knopf, 1994), with a sound introduction by a good scholar, Sarah Allen. There is also a lovely translation of the Ma-wang-tui texts by Victor Mair: *Tao Te Ching* (New York: Bantam Books, 1990). Mair's translation is the most elegant of the reliable minimalist translations, but his explanatory efforts (in his preface, afterword, and appendix) contain so many problems that I recommend it only to advanced students, who may be capable of sorting through them.

4. In the original assignment, I exhibited my personal values by referring to "the writer" as "he/she." Since that time, I have learned not to project my wishes on

history. My colleague Vivian-Lee Nyitray (University of California, Riverside) teaches students to "avoid imposing a modern sensibility on the past," to remember that "people in the past were *not*, for the most part, democratic, tolerant of religious or racial difference, concerned for individual rights . . . , fascinated by the personality . . . , particularly squeamish, or believers in 'Progress.'" I pass these observations along to my students, adding, among other things, that we should beware of logical problems in applying gender-inclusive language to data from ages or cultures that were resolutely gender-exclusive. For instance, the category of "Confucian scholar" (*ju*) has always been closed to women, whether or not *we* believe that it *should* have been. So I urge students to consider such facts when they write; today, for instance, readers of the *Daode jing* come in both genders, but such was not the case in ancient China. See notes 11 and 14 below.

5. Scholars like A. C. Graham and Harold Roth have made clear that, historically, the term "Taoism" was only a bibliographic classification until about the third century c.e. As Roth has put it, "The 'Lao-Zhuang' tradition to which [modern 'tradition'] refers is actually a Wei-Jin literati reconstruction, albeit a powerful and enduring one." Harold Roth, "Some Issues in the Study of Chinese Mysticism: A Review Essay," *China Review International* 2, no. 1 (1995): 157. I address these issues much more fully in *Taoism: The Enduring Tradition* (London: Routledge, 2004), and "Self-Fulfillment through Selflessness: The Moral Teachings of the *Daode jing*," in *Varieties of Ethical Reflection: New Directions for Ethics in a Global Context*, ed. Michael Barnhart (New York: Lexington Books, 2002).

6. On the figure of "Lao-tzu," a rich and constantly evolving cultural construct, see A. C. Graham, "The Origins of the Legend of Lao Tan," in his *Studies in Chinese Philosophy and Philosophical Literature* (Albany: State University of New York Press, 1990), 111–124; Judith Magee Boltz, "Lao-tzu," in *The Encyclopedia of Religion* (New York: Macmillan, 1987), 8:454–459; Livia Kohn, *God of the Dao: Laozi in History and Myth* (Ann Arbor: University of Michigan Center for Chinese Studies, 1998), and "The Lao-tzu Myth," in *Lao-tzu and the Tao-te-ching*, ed. Livia Kohn and Michael LaFargue (Albany: State University of New York Press, 1998), 41–62. The *Western* cultural construct of "Lao-tzu" remains wholly unstudied.

7. See Kirkland, *Taoism: The Enduring Tradition*, 39–52, and "Varieties of 'Taoism' in Ancient China: A Preliminary Comparison of Themes in the *Nei yeh* and Other 'Taoist Classics,'" *Taoist Resources* 7, no. 2 (1997): 73–86.

8. My complete "Historical Outline of Taoism," with explanations of certain interpretive positions, appears in "The Historical Contours of Taoism in China: Thoughts on Issues of Classification and Terminology," *Journal of Chinese Religions* 25 (1997): 57–82; more recent thoughts, and a revised outline, appear in "The History of Taoism: A New Outline," *Journal of Chinese Religions* 30 (2002): 177–193. An exposition of my analysis of the "layers" of the *Daode jing* appears in Kirkland, "The Book of the Way," in *Great Literature of the Eastern World*, ed. Ian P. McGreal (New York: HarperCollins, 1996), 24–29; a new analysis appears in *Taoism: The Enduring Tradition*, 52–67.

9. Again, I employ the masculine pronoun here as a matter of historical accuracy.

10. I am unaware of any study that properly examines the facile modern assumption that the *Daode jing*, or *Zhuangzi*, can or ought to be read in terms of what Westerners understand to be "philosophy." In my "Self-Fulfillment through Selflessness," I suggest some critical perspectives on the interpretive assumptions of Arthur C. Danto and Chad Hansen.

11. Again, I use masculine-gendered language here for a reason. I see evidence in the *Daode jing* that some of its thoughts could have originated in the minds of women, for example, members of local communities of Chu, whose "elders" (*laozi*) may not all have been male. (This analysis originates in ideas of Kimura Eiichi; see my "Book of the Way.") But I also assume that, given the general absence of literacy among women in pre-Han China, the composer or redactor of the *Daode jing* must have been male (albeit possibly with input from female associates).

12. Such is apparently the view of Chad Hansen: "Laozi's position . . . remains a way station in Daoist development . . . We still have no final answer to the question, 'What should we do?' . . . If there is some advice, some point, Laozi could not state it. And so neither can I. But Zhuangzi can! Daoism must still mature more." Hansen, *A Daoist Theory of Chinese Thought: A Philosophical Interpretation* (New York: Oxford University Press, 1992), 202, 230.

13. The happiness of some interpreters to read the *Daode jing*'s teachings as a watery "mysticism"—a category utterly alien to China—can generally be explained in terms of the Western cultural experience. While some traditional cultures did have occasional "mystics" who communed directly with some higher reality, the modern interest in finding new forms of mysticism in old traditions has been propelled by the desperate search for a modern (i.e., nonreligious) religion. No longer willing to take God, Church, or moral absolutes seriously, many moderns yearn for a "Truth" that "liberated" persons can accept and practice without having to yield to any authority outside themselves. To such seekers, the very concept of mysticism involves a de-deified Truth, purged of the premodern cultural baggage that moderns blithely dismiss as "superstition"—that is, all beliefs that deny the autonomy of the individual to dictate what is or is not real, true, or important. In this sense, mysticism is a narcissistic cultural construct, cherished by moderns as a means of escaping God (who, in Western tradition, embarrassingly demands obedience) and sacral community (which embarrassingly suggests that reality exists outside the individual's own "autonomous" consciousness). Though there has still been no critical assessment of the Western cultural notion that the *Daode jing* contains mysticism, a few preliminary reflections in that direction appear in Hansen, *A Daoist Theory of Chinese Thought*. Other reflections on the applicability of concepts of mysticism to Daoist data appear in Lee Yearley, "The Perfected Person in the Radical Chuang-tzu," in *Experimental Essays on Chuang-tzu*, ed. Victor Mair (Honolulu: University of Hawaii Press, 1983), 125–139.

14. Elsewhere I have commented on Tu Wei-ming's effort to facilitate postmodern appropriation of Confucius's teachings by retranslating Confucius's term for the human ideal—*zhun zi*, which originally meant "the sons of the rulers" and was transformed by Confucius to mean "the noble man" rather than "the nobleman"—as "the profound person." Such a translation is intended to render Confucian ideals

accessible and attractive to everyone, male and female alike. However, historical facts clearly reveal that prior to the age of Tu himself, the Confucian tradition was resolutely "sexist." To sanitize for modern consumption a conservative tradition that always rejected, on principle, individual efforts to "improve" tradition seems to be a move well justified in postmodern terms, but illegitimate in Confucian terms. Daoism is a different case, since premodern Daoism welcomed women as practitioners, though it could not fully escape the gender constraints of the surrounding society. See my entry, "Taoism," in *Encyclopedia of Women and World Religion* (New York: Macmillan, 1999), 2: 959–964.

15. See the chapter in this volume by Norman J. Girardot, and his book *The Victorian Translation of China: James Legge's Oriental Pilgrimage* (Berkeley: University of California Press, 2002).

16. As Tu Wei-ming has noted, the Enlightenment mentality is the common heritage of all modern minds, Chinese and Western alike. Liu Xiaogan, for instance, may be Chinese, but he is a product of twentieth-century China, not pre-Han China. The same is true for all living interpreters, none of whom know what it would be like to look at the *Daode jing* as would a pre-Han person, as someone who had never experienced a world without a politically and culturally unified China, Buddhism, Neo-Confucianism, rationalism, democracy, Marxism, Christianity, and all the cultural and intellectual realities of the twentieth century. The text is thus an alien world for Chinese and Western interpreters alike.

17. In this day and age, it is socially unacceptable in most parts of Western society, even in the supposed ivory tower of academia, to provide students with a liberating model for rejecting colonialistic habits by explicitly comparing cultural appropriation to sexual appropriation. That is, no one today would accept that John's needs, however legitimate, could condone his appropriation of Jane. But even postmoderns seem content to look the other way when Westerners argue that their personal needs justify their unauthorized appropriation of Asian texts or Native American rituals. Postmoderns, like moderns, assume that *it is the individual herself or himself who "authorizes,"* so all cultural appropriation is logically acceptable, since such an act is no more than my exercising my unchallengeable individual autonomy. As a matter of fact, postmoderns are as eager as moderns to reject the value of tradition, so ripping cultural artifacts out of their traditional settings is not only innocuous, but virtuous.

18. It should be noted that the "Great Minds"/"Great Books" model for understanding Daoism leads almost inevitably to a total disregard for the lives and thought of the Daoist *women* throughout history. The traditional Chinese canon of Great Books—essentially Confucian—generally excludes works by or about women, though Daoists of various periods valued and preserved records of women's lives and teachings. See my entry in *Encyclopedia of Women and World Religion* (New York: Macmillan, 1999), 2: 959–964.

19. On the reasons for the growing ignorance of, and antipathy toward, Daoism among late imperial Confucians, see Kirkland, "Person and Culture in the Taoist Tradition," *Journal of Chinese Religions* 20 (1992): 77–90.

20. For decades, the standard "scholarly" overview of Daoism was Holmes Welch, *Taoism: The Parting of the Way* (Boston: Beacon Press, 1965), a slightly revised edition of a 1957 book. Welch's chapter "Later Philosophical Taoism" (158–163) disregards all the *Daozang*'s texts of religious thought and (like "authorities" from Fung Yu-lan to Stephen Mitchell) tells the reader that such texts are by people "whom we can only regard as representatives of quaint, but moribund superstition" (163). The "real heirs" of Laozi and Zhuangzi, Welch tells us, were Neo-Confucians, Zen masters, and landscape painters. Meanwhile, in another chapter, Wang Che, whose writings Welch apparently never bothered to read, is ridiculed as "eccentric" and even "fanatical" (145).

21. The long-standard *Sources of Chinese Tradition*, edited by William T. deBary (New York: Columbia University Press, 1960), mentions no such sources, any more than Wing-tsit Chan mentions them in his still standard *Source Book in Chinese Philosophy* (Princeton: Princeton University Press, 1963). See my review of Wm. T. deBary and Irene Bloom, eds., *Sources of Chinese Tradition*, 2nd ed., vol. 1 (New York: Columbia University Press, 1999), in *Education about Asia* 7, no. 1 (2002): 62–66.

22. See especially Livia Kohn, ed., *The Taoist Experience: An Anthology* (Albany: State University of New York Press, 1993). Other "new" Daoist texts appear in Donald S. Lopez Jr., ed., *Religions of China in Practice* (Princeton: Princeton University Press, 1996). However, as noted in my review in *Education about Asia* 2, no. 1 (spring 1997): 58–59, Lopez chose to swing the pendulum fully in the other direction, that is, ignoring all Daoist texts that present "intellectualized" models of the Daoist life, thereby falsifying the reader's image of "Daoism" as gravely as deBary and Chan had done at the other extreme. One should also note that anthologies of Chinese literature continue to follow Confucian paradigms by continuing to exclude most of the literature that originated among Daoists. See, for example, my review of Victor Mair, ed., *The Columbia Anthology of Traditional Chinese Literature* (New York: Columbia University Press, 1995), in *Education about Asia* 3, no. 3 (1998): 64–65.

23. Isabelle Robinet, *Taoism: Growth of a Religion*, trans. Phyllis Brooks (Stanford: Stanford University Press, 1997), 29.

24. See Kohn, "The Lao-tzu Myth," and *God of the Dao*. Some of the roles of Laozi in Daoism are highlighted in Kohn's "Laozi: Ancient Philosopher, Master of Immortality, and God," in Lopez, *Religions of China in Practice*, 52–63; but one should note that the account of Laozi that she translates there, from Ge Hong *Shen-hsien-chuan*, casts him in the role of "a successful practitioner of immortality": Ge "had no interest in stylizing him as the Dao, as the religious followers did" (54).

25. John Lagerwey, *Taoist Ritual in Chinese Society and History* (New York: Macmillan, 1987), 23.

26. These central elements of Daoist thought, generally ignored before the present generation of specialists, are outlined in Kristopher Schipper, *The Taoist Body*, trans. Karen Duval (Berkeley: University of California Press, 1993), 113–119. Another long ignored facet of these beliefs is that "the mystical vision of the body in Taoism" probably "served as a model of reference in Chinese medicine" (124), which focuses on transformations of life energy (*qi*), unlike the more materialistic models of Western medicine, which deny the existence or value of such realities.

27. See Livia Kohn, "The *Tao-te-ching* in Ritual," in Kohn and LaFargue, *Lao-tzu and the Tao-te-ching*, 143–161. "The value and sense which the Taoists attribute to their sacred writings" is usefully summarized in Isabelle Robinet, *Taoist Meditation*, trans. Julian Pas and Norman Girardot (Albany: State University of New York Press, 1993), 19–28.

28. As Timothy Barrett has said concerning Tang times, "The Taoists were not preaching any new religious message about the human condition but offering their expertise in dealing with the world of the supernatural." T. H. Barrett, *Taoism under the T'ang: Religion and Empire during the Golden Age of Chinese History* (London: Wellsweep Press, 1996), 16.

29. See Judith A. Berling, *A Pilgrim in Chinese Culture: Negotiating Religious Diversity* (Maryknoll, N.Y.: Orbis Books, 1997), especially 85–86, 97–98.

30. See Russell Kirkland, "The Study of Religion and Society in Contemporary Asia: Colonialism and Beyond," *Bulletin of Concerned Asian Scholars* 28, nos. 3–4 (1996): 59–63.

31. Indeed, the intellectual history of ancient China suggests that the concept of *wuwei* originated not in "Daoist" circles, but rather among political pragmatists of the fourth century B.C.E. The term was used not only by Confucius, but also by the "Legalist" Shen Buhai (d. 337 B.C.E.). See H. G. Creel, *Shen Pu-hai: A Chinese Political Philosopher of the Fourth Century* B.C. (Chicago: University of Chicago Press, 1974), especially 176–179.

32. See Harold D. Roth, "Redaction Criticism and the Early History of Taoism," *Early China* 19 (1994): 1–46, and *Original Tao: Inward Training (Nei-yeh) and the Foundations of Taoist Mysticism* (New York: Columbia University Press, 1999); and my review, "A Quest for 'The Foundations of Taoist Mysticism,'" *Studies in Central and East Asian Religions*, nos. 12–13 (2001): 203–229.

33. See especially Livia Kohn, ed., *Taoist Meditation and Longevity Techniques* (Ann Arbor: University of Michigan, Center for Chinese Studies, 1989).

34. Scholars like Kristofer Schipper have spent a generation laboring to explicate such continuities, as seen most readily in his book, *The Taoist Body*. Another study of a hitherto ignored continuity between classical and later Daoism, the advocation of altruistic activity, is Russell Kirkland, "The Roots of Altruism in the Taoist Tradition," *Journal of the American Academy of Religion* 54 (1986): 59–77. For more on integrating the data of Later Daoism in the teaching of Daoism, see Russell Kirkland, "Teaching Taoism in the 1990s," *Teaching Theology and Religion* 1, no. 2 (1998): 121–129.

35. See Philip J. Ivanhoe and Paul Kjellberg, eds., *Essays on Skepticism, Relativism and Ethics in the Zhuangzi* (Albany: State University of New York Press, 1996).

Hermeneutics and Pedagogy: Gimme That Old-Time Historicism

Michael LaFargue

My approach to teaching the *Daode jing* is based in part on an approach I've developed to hermeneutics, a subject that I have thought about a lot, beginning in my days as a graduate student in biblical studies.[1] I formulated the beginnings of this hermeneutic theory in my graduate dissertation, in which I thought what I was doing was rescuing gnosticism, and a particular gnostic text (the *Acts of Thomas*), from its misinterpretation by Christian theologians. They were interpreting gnostic texts from a perspective shaped by mainstream Christian assumptions. (Gnosticism traditionally serves as a kind of whipping boy for Christian theologians, a counterpoint that serves to show the obvious superiority of mainstream Christianity by contrast.) I realized early on the implausibility of attacking this kind of interpretation on substantive grounds, that is, on the grounds of substantive weaknesses in the orthodox Christian assumptions it was based on. I needed to focus on developing an interpretive *method*, a method that could derive from a text itself and from historical research the proper framework of assumptions within which it should be interpreted, rather than rely on the interpreter's own views about substantively *correct* assumptions.

At this point I had the good fortune of coming across Jonathan Culler's *Structuralist Poetics*. Culler argued that a text's "structure" does not lie on the surface to be observed by a neutral observer. The key to structure lies in the reader, the assumptions that a reader brings to the text, causing her to construe it as she does. Culler used Chomsky's term "competence" to refer to such assumptions.

Some hermeneutic theorists use notions similar to competence to legitimate a very free reading of texts. Because there are no universal, normative assumptions, every reader should feel empowered to read the text in the light of whatever assumptions she happens to have and like. But in the context of my work at the time, this seemed to me to simply legitimate the practice of orthodox Christian theologians, reading gnostic texts in the light of their own assumptions. I took the notion of competence in a different direction, developing the idea that there are different kinds of competence appropriate to different texts. We arrive at good historical interpretations of a given text, not by reflecting on possible meanings of given sentences, but by trying to discover the nature of competence appropriate to this text. This competence is partly literary, having to do with the textual code and verbal genres being used. Partly it is substantive, having to do with the basic, taken-for-granted assumptions of the original author and audience and the basic concerns, questions, and problems they were addressing. Taken without reference to this specific competence, every text is ambiguous, since a given set of words can be construed in any number of different ways, to address any number of different concerns. But most texts were not so ambiguous to their original authors and audience: the shared competence they brought to the text is what gave their words specific meanings to them. Chiefly by reflecting on indirect indications in the text itself, aided by additional historical research, we can gather clues as to the competence necessary to understand it.

This approach gave me a basis for arguing that the *Acts of Thomas* should be read in a way fundamentally different from the way it was customarily read by Christian theologians[2]—not because the assumptions they brought to the text were questionable in themselves, but because, historically speaking, they did not match the assumptions that the original authors and audience brought to the text.

But this view also set me at odds with a good deal of contemporary hermeneutic theory and practice, allying me much more closely with the historicist hermeneutics of Dilthey and his mentor Schleiermacher, than with their much more popular modern critic H.-G. Gadamer.[3] The works of Gadamer, Paul Ricoeur, and Jacques Derrida seem to me to have inspired a kind of hermeneutics that is a throwback to the pre-Dilthey tradition of scripture interpretation, which was always for the most part ideological warfare conducted by indirect means. Everyone feels supported in trying to capture classical texts for whatever cause they feel strongly about (Christian fundamentalism, feminism, Zen Buddhism, and so on) by simply reading these texts in the light of their own dearly held assumptions, concerns, and values. An interpretation is a "good interpretation" if it accords with the values and assumptions that the interpreter regards as the right ones. The result seems to me very often just propaganda masquerading as "interpretation."

Pedagogy: Why Try to Recover the Original Meaning?

The project of "recovering the original meaning" of classical texts is almost universally associated with the assumption that the original meaning has an authoritative status *because* it is original. I think this is an important assumption to bring to light and argue against when teaching classical texts like the *Daode jing*. I advocate instead a kind of "confrontational" hermeneutics. Classical texts give paradigmatic expression to perfectionist views of the world and of human excellence, based on values that millions have found inspiring. But these are not universal values, and the views of ancient gnostics or ancient Daoists may or may not be appropriate to life today. Interpretation should give us something very challenging, something very strong to wrestle with. Confronting such a challenge can show us some weaknesses in our own conventional and often mediocre views. Meeting this challenge might mean adopting some of the views expressed in the text; it might also mean developing better versions of our own values that contrast with those found in the text.

Confrontational hermeneutics entails two different elements. The first element should aim at understanding the text precisely in its *otherness* from our own views and values, focusing on the ways the basic thought patterns of the text's original authors and audience were fundamentally different from our own. Doing this requires temporarily setting aside our own most cherished assumptions so as to produce for ourselves a strong opponent to wrestle with, so to speak. The second element should be the wrestling itself, considering the pro's and con's of this reconstructed view of the world vis-à-vis our own views or other views we might be attracted to.

I very much believe in "empowering the reader" to challenge the message of a text. Neither the *Daode jing* nor any other text should be regarded as having some intrinsic unquestionable authority. I also believe that an encounter with the text becomes much more productive if one first takes care to understand the text in its otherness, something worth wrestling with.

I should make it clear that I think "understanding" a text is a creative enterprise in itself. It does not mean memorizing some positivistically understood "doctrines" that the text teaches, abstracted from human life and experience. It is a work of disciplined creative imagination. Using parameters given by the text (different from one's own), one must try to construe the text in such a way that it makes sense. "Make sense" means, first, to understand the pragmatic implications of a given idea: what change accepting this idea would bring about in readers, their outlook, or their conduct. It means, second, to understand why a sensible person would adopt these ideas as a principal guide to how to lead one's life.

Following this pedagogical approach, my usual assignment for graded papers (which I use also for other religious texts in other courses) directs students first to choose some challenging idea central to the teaching of the *Daode jing*, some aspect that they think would be difficult for the average person to make sense of. Their paper should address a person unfamiliar with this book, showing their own understanding by their ability to explain their chosen idea in such a way that it would make sense to this person.

Frequently Asked Questions

Are you saying it is *wrong* to ignore the question of original meaning and use the *Daode jing* as a stimulus and guide in one's personal search for the truth?

Absolutely not. This has been the approach of Chinese commentators throughout the ages, and millions have undoubtedly profited greatly from this kind of reading. "American Daoists" such as Benjamin Hoff and Fritjof Capra are simply continuing this tradition—why should it matter that they are not Chinese? The *Daode jing* is public property and people can do with it whatever they want. If it serves to stimulate and inspire, who could object?

I do have trouble with scholars who place great emphasis on some linguistic or historical point they think others have missed, complain about "translations" by unscholarly amateurs like Stephen Mitchell and Witter Bynner, insisting on setting limits to what can be considered a "legitimate" interpretation of the *Daode jing*—but then in the next breath declare their belief that the *Daode jing* is an "open" text, by its very nature inviting multiple interpretations, so that the project of reconstructing its original meaning is misguided from the start. I believe that either one is trying as best one can to reconstruct what the *Daode jing* meant to its original authors and audience, or one is not. If one is not, then there is no basis for placing any limits to what can be considered a legitimate interpretation; historical and linguistic information is at best just one more source of interesting ideas among many. Serious historical and linguistic scholarship is relevant only if one is trying to reconstruct what the text originally meant. And in this case, the idea that the *Daode jing* is an open text with no determinate meaning means that historical research will always be half-hearted, providing an opening for scholars to insert their favorite personal ideas unsupported by historical or textual evidence, while at the same time claiming special status for these personal interpretations because they are somehow connected to expertise in linguistic and historical matters.

Why do you insist that students not take a more free and ahistorical approach in your classes?

Free reading is something all readers can do on their own at home, using whatever version or "translation" of the *Daode jing* gives them the most inspiration and stimulation. Using the *Daode jing* in this way might also be quite appropriate in a creative writing course, for example, where the goal is to give students some stimulus and inspiration for developing their own thoughts on whatever subject interests them.

On the other hand, the project of recovering and engaging with the original meaning of the *Daode jing* is something difficult to do on one's own, and something for which a college classroom is uniquely suited. And there are some things that can be gained from this kind of historical reading that cannot be gained from a more free reading. For example, this kind of reading is more likely to present students with something more foreign to their own present views, therefore something that will require them to stretch their minds further. Also, the *Daode jing* gives paradigmatic expression to some ways of seeing the world that became foundational for many aspects of later East Asian culture (aspects not always specifically associated with the *Daode jing* or Daoism). Free reading interpretations may be more inspirational and useful to modern students in their personal quest for spiritual truth, but they are very misleading if one wants to understand certain foundational aspects of East Asian culture formulated in the Warring States period. I try to give students some sense of how the worldview expressed in the *Daode jing* has influenced other aspects of East Asian culture by including some readings related to Chinese medicine and Qigong and some excerpts from the Daoist meditation manual *The Secret of the Golden Flower*.[4] When time has permitted, I've also used K. Schipper's book about later Daoist religion, *The Taoist Body*, discussing some continuities and discontinuities between the Laoist worldview and the worldview that Schipper describes.

I have found that students from Japan, in particular, find the teachings of the *Daode jing* similar to many elements of Japanese culture (though many have never heard of "Daoism"), which contrast with aspects of culture in the United States that they found jarring on their first encounter. I would like to find ways of drawing out their views on this subject in class discussions.

Why do you present your interpretation to students as representing the original meaning of the *Daode jing*? How do you know that you have transcended all your own cultural biases and recovered the *Daode jing*'s original meaning?

Going by the relevant historical information I presently know about, my interpretation currently seems to me to approximate the *Daode jing*'s original meaning better than any other interpretation I know of. If it were not what I consider to be the best historical approximation, it would not be my interpretation: I would reject it and adopt some other one. I would think this should be the position of any scholar who has done serious research trying to recover the *Daode jing*'s original meaning.

Do I think that my interpretation is free of cultural biases that might prevent me from fully recovering the *Daode jing*'s original meaning? I think most likely it is not. In the course of twenty-five years' study of this work, I have discovered many cases of mistakes due to such biases, and I can only suppose there are more that I have not yet become aware of. I just don't know what they are at this point. If I did, I would try to correct my interpretation to remedy these inadequacies.

If time permits, I do sometimes begin the study of the *Daode jing* by drawing out students' previous associations with "Daoism," derived often from books like Hoff's *The Tao of Pooh* or Capra's *The Tao of Physics*. It is often helpful to have some explicit discussions of this kind of "American Daoism" as a point of contrast with early Chinese Daoist texts such as the *Daode jing* and the *Zhuangzi*, but also to make it clear that this difference does not necessarily and by itself imply that American Daoism is by nature inferior.

I also try to make it clear that students are responsible for understanding the interpretation of the *Daode jing* given in my *commentary*. I don't think there is anything very essential about my *translation* of the *Daode jing*, in contrast to the translations of other competent scholars such as Addiss and Lombardo, Victor Mair, Mary Ellen Chen, Wing-tsit Chan, D. C. Lau, J. J. L Duyvendak, and Arthur Waley. I do advise students against using other "translations," such as those of Stephen Mitchell and Witter Bynner, which may be good for spiritual inspiration but are not appropriate for my courses since they are not informed by historical and linguistic competence. (In collaboration with Julian Pas I've published an essay explaining some of the difficulties one faces in translating the *Daode jing* and some major reasons for variations in translations. This includes some illustrations of cases where Mitchell and Bynner insert lines that bear little or no relation to the Chinese text.)

Doesn't the *Daode jing* itself say that its message can't be put into words? Doesn't this mean that academic analysis is an obstacle to understanding Dao? Your approach to interpretation is not a Daoist approach.

Exactly. The approach to interpretation I am teaching is not a Daoist approach. So far as I can see, Daoists were totally uninterested in the project of recovering the original meanings of texts, or challenging themselves by wrestling with sympathetically reconstructed views of the world fundamentally at odds with their own. The course I teach is not religious instruction aiming to make students into Daoists. If it were, we would need a teacher who would put us through a rigorous training of a different sort.

The fact that *Dao* cannot be put into words does not mean that it has no definite content, that it is vague, or that whatever inspirational meaning anyone attributes to this word gets at the meaning it had for the *Daode jing*'s authors. One should not confuse depth with vagueness. The project of recovering original meanings requires that we develop some clearly articulated proposals about what this text might mean, so that these proposals can be tested. Likewise, the project of confronting ourselves with a challenging text requires that we specify clearly what it is that we are confronting. Leaving the text vague makes it easier to domesticate, reducing it to some views more familiar and more congenial to our own views of the world. There is an important sense in which understanding what *Dao* is requires going beyond what can be expressed straightforwardly in conventional language and concepts. This is due to the limitation of conventional language and concepts, not to the fact that *Dao* is not a definite and precise notion. And this kind of understanding normally takes place *after* struggling with some difficult notions, not as a substitute for such struggle.

Method in Reading

In practice, my pedagogy in courses on the *Daode jing* combines trying to teach students to be "competent" readers of the text, on the one hand, and summarizing for them the main elements of "Laoism"[5] on the other. In courses where I can devote only a brief time to the *Daode jing*, the first assignment I give is usually to read several short essays in the topical glossary that accompanies my translation and commentary on the *Daode jing*.[6]

As to competence, one of the main issues I focus on is the issue of how to understand the proverblike aphorisms contained in the *Daode jing*.[7] When we hear proverbs familiar in our own culture, spoken in contexts where they are appropriate, we have no difficulty understanding their meaning without analysis. But when we are forced to think reflectively on unfamiliar aphorisms from another culture, the usual reaction is to try to read them in a literal-minded way. By "literal-minded" I mean that we construe each word according to a dictionary definition, or simply think of whatever meaning comes to mind, and that we take statements to be enunciating a general principle applicable in an unrestricted way to all situations whatsoever. Literal-minded reading is one of the main sources of misunderstanding of religious texts, and in particular is the source of many objections students immediately think of to many lines in the *Daode jing*. "One who shows off will not shine"—but how about people who get famous by self-advertising (e.g., Madonna)? "One who knows does not speak"—but what about speaking the words of the *Daode jing*? And so on.

I try to go through some common American proverbs to show that they are also generally false if we take them literally. "Slow and steady wins the race"—but did so-and-so win the hundred-yard dash by going slow and steady? "No news is good news"—but last week I had no news about my midterm grade because it was so bad the teacher was afraid to tell me about it. "When it rains, it pours"—but all last week it just drizzled every day.

The opposite of literal-minded understanding is contextual understanding. In regard to proverbs and aphorisms, this means chiefly two things: relating the aphorism to some appropriate *restricted range* of situations and construing the words of the aphorism in a narrow way so that they make sense in relation to each other.

First, any given aphorism makes sense only in relation to a restricted range of circumstances. "Slow and steady wins the race" applies only to some kinds of races or competitions, the kind where pacing oneself is important. This is something we intuitively understand in our common use and understanding of proverbs. It is something we have to explicitly think about when trying to understand aphorisms in the *Daode jing*. When trying to understand "One who shows off will not shine," one should not right away start directly thinking of possible meanings of these words. The *first* thing to do is try to imagine the kind of situations that this aphorism might apply to in such a way that it would make sense.

As Arthur Waley pointed out long ago, much of the *Daode jing* is intensely *polemical*. This means that the "situation" any given proverb addresses is one in which the speaker thinks there is some mistake being made that needs correcting. Identifying the situation to which the aphorism applies means identifying the particular mistake that the speaker means to counteract. This again is true of many proverbs and aphorisms in common use today. For example, "If it ain't broke, don't fix it" is meant to counteract the common tendency to meddle with something even if it is functioning in a reasonably satisfactory way. "It takes two to tango" is usually meant to counteract the tendency to blame one person in a quarrel when both are at fault. If one does not know what the proverb means to counteract, one does not know its meaning.

Hyperbole is a common feature of proverbs related to this counteractive function. "Don't believe anything you hear, and only half of what you see" states its point in a very exaggerated form no one would ever take as a literal rule. It does this because it wants to say something that contrasts in the strongest possible way with the tendency toward gullibility that it means to counteract.

I think this is one of the most important methodological principles that ought to guide a "competent" reading of the *Daode jing*, combating the tendency toward literal-mindedness. Part of the polemic strategy of the *Daode jing's'* authors is to use terms that go against common views in the most flagrant way. "The five colors make men's eyes go blind" (chapter 12) is clearly false if taken literally. It exaggerates the point that overstimulation causes insensitivity in order to counteract people's attraction to stimulating sensations. "Discard wisdom [*sheng*]" (chapter 19) doesn't make literal sense in a text that otherwise idealizes "the wise [*sheng*] person." It exaggerates its opposition to a certain kind of wisdom by the use of flagrantly shocking language. (I think this point must be kept in mind also when interpreting the line "Heaven and Earth are not benevolent... the wise person is not benevolent." "Benevolence" [*ren*] functions in the *Daode jing* as a code word for Confucianism, and I think this passage in chapter 5 is most plausibly read as an exaggerated polemic against the Confucian ideal of the benevolent ruler. It has no parallel elsewhere in the *Daode jing*, which in many places recommends a caring attitude on the part of rulers.)

The other important point in a contextual understanding of aphorisms concerns the way that the words of a saying need to be interpreted in relation to each other in a way that makes sense. The saying "A watched pot never boils" is false if one first interprets each phrase separately and literally, then tries to join them. Literally watching a pot will clearly not prevent it from boiling. We normally don't take each phrase separately and literally. We construe the words in relation to each other in such a way that they make sense. *Anxious* watching will *make it seem as though* the pot will never boil. Not all nice guys finish last, but *a certain kind* of niceness will put one at a competitive disadvantage ("finish last" is hyperbole).

This is important in understanding many paradoxical sayings in the *Daode jing*. In each case, we have to construe the words in relation to each other in such a way that they make sense. Not all kinds of showing off cause people not to shine in all circumstances, (chapter 24), but some kinds of showing off turn other people off and cause dislike rather than admiration. Not all kinds of fine speech are insincere (chapter 81), but in certain cases smooth talk should make one suspect insincerity.

Applying this principle would avoid literal-minded understanding of sayings about "not doing" (*wu wei*) in the *Daode jing*. "Do nothing, and nothing will remain un-done" does not amount to the admittedly "radical" but ultimately silly assertion that things will always work out right if you literally do nothing (the "Pooh Bear" interpretation). The saying invites listeners and readers to stretch their mind to imagine some possible meaning of the phrase "do nothing" in such a way that it could plausibly help in getting things done. We ought to be guided in this imaginative process by other passages in the *Daode jing* giving advice about how to get things done.

Roots and Branches

This methodological principle about competent understanding of aphorisms leads to a further, more substantive set of ideas that recently occurred to me as a way of describing the unique *structure* of the *Daode jing* thought to students. I first thought of this as an answer to a frequent student objection, which goes as follows: The *Daode jing* advocates being humble. But it also says that if you are humble you will become the ruler over all. This is a contradiction. A truly humble person would not want to become ruler over all.

I think the answer to this is that the *Daode jing* advocates rulership *rooted in* humility—or more precisely, rulership rooted in a deferential attitude and style of interaction (I think the word "humility" is misleading in this context). To use a common Chinese metaphor: Deference ought to be the root, rulership the branch ("Not presuming to act like leader of the world, so able to be head of the government"; chapter 67). The problem does not lie in wanting to be a ruler, but in wanting this "branch" unconnected with the root Laoists think it ought to have. ("To act like leader without putting oneself last, this is death"; chapter 67.)

I think this is an example of a more general characteristic of the formal structure of Laoist thought that makes it different from thought-structures we are more accustomed to. We tend to conceive of issues as either/or questions, a choice between opposites. Either you can be humble or you can want to be a ruler; the task is to choose between these rather simple and clear alternatives. Laoist thought is also structured around opposites, but rather than advocating a choice of one over the other, it typically advocates taking the more unconventional choice as the root of the more conventionally attractive one.

Being a ruler is conventionally associated with self-aggrandizing motivation and a self-aggrandizing manner. From a Laoist point of view, this is a branch not properly rooted. It ought to be rooted in a characteristic that is the opposite of a "ruling" attitude as conventionally conceived. The interpretive challenge is to construct a concept with a more unfamiliar set of associations: a kind of self-effacing motive and manner that would also plausibly lead to success as a ruler.

This general idea can be used to explain the basic structure of Laoist thought in various areas, such as the following.

People tend to prefer activity and excitement to stillness. Activity not rooted in stillness wears one out. It is not that activity should be abandoned, but that it should be rooted in stillness. One needs to set aside some periods to cultivate mental stillness, but then carry the spirit of this stillness into one's active life. (This ideal is conveyed by the image of "an infant who screams all day without becoming hoarse," an ability attributed to the infant's having attained "the perfection of [internal] harmony"; chapter 55.)

Some people have the ambition to cultivate personal qualities that others admire. They try to repress qualities and impulses not admired by the society around them. This results in artificial virtues and lack of internal wholeness: branches without proper roots. It is not that one should abandon the quest for personal excellence, or even cut off all caring about what others think. It is rather that genuine personal excellence is rooted in an integrated and natural balance involving the whole person; attaining such excellence requires pay-ing special attention to those qualities in one's own being that might be im-portant in achieving wholeness, but that feel worthless, "empty," "nothing," because they receive no recognition, or might even feel socially embarrass-ing. So chapter 28 advocates cultivating femininity and cultivating what feels embarrassing—parallel notions for men in a male-dominated society—in order to recover one's "uncarved" self. Cultivating what might seem in the conven-tional mind to be the opposite of excellence is the root of true excellence.

Some people prize the ability to be articulate and speak eloquently. Elo-quent speech without sincerity is show without substance (flower without fruit, as chapter 38 puts it). But this is not a rejection of all impressive speaking. The *Daode jing* is after all itself an example of a kind of great verbal artistry and a kind of eloquence. Rather, the most impressive articulation of ideas is the kind that is rooted in inarticulate knowledge. This I think is good advice for students writing papers. They read writings that are finished products of someone else's thought and don't understand the struggles authors have gone through to produce them. Each student feels that other students in the class are very articulate in contrast to her own inability to put her thoughts into words that adequately express her inarticulate feelings and ideas. I think the best kind of writing is rooted in this initially inarticulate kind of knowledge. One of the things students can learn from the *Daode jing* is to value this inarticulate knowledge, while not giving up the attempt to put it into words that communicate it well.

We are familiar with the image of the competitive and aggressive person who wants to prove his superiority in battle. We are also familiar with the opposite of this, the person who advocates gentleness in all human relationships and encounters and has no desire to win out over others. Laoists criticize direct confrontation and love of victory through violence, not because they are adamantly opposed to the desire to win out over others, no matter what the circumstances. Rather, this is an example of branches without proper roots. They admire the "softness" of water precisely because it wins out over what opposes it. They approve of victory won through "soft" tactics (see chapter 36).

This is the same as the doctrine of *yin-yang*, the uniting of opposites, right?

I suppose you could call this a way of integrating opposites, but it doesn't seem to be what most people mean by integrating opposites. It has nothing to do with having yin qualities and yang qualities in equal measure, for example, or alternating between yin and yang. In general, Laoism pictures yin qualities as the proper "root." Yang qualities are branches: okay when they are rooted in yin qualities, not okay when they are not.

Mysticism, Philosophy, Metaphysics, Cosmology

Statements in the *Daode jing* about a transmundane *Dao* that is a world-origin present special difficulties for an interpretative approach aimed at "making sense" of the material. I take "make sense" to mean, first, to understand the pragmatic implications of a given idea: what change accepting this idea would bring about in a person, her outlook, or her conduct. It also means to understand why a sensible person would adopt these ideas as a principal guide to how to lead one's life. A focus on *historical* understanding means in addition that we try to understand what the *Daode jing's* authors most likely took to be the pragmatic implications of the ideas they put forth, the most likely basis they had for believing in these ideas, and the basis on which they hoped these ideas would be accepted by their contemporaries. These kinds of questions have guided my own research efforts, and I try to engage students in asking and trying to answer these kinds of questions.

This is an approach I think one should take to all religious texts. I realize it is not a very common approach taken in published accounts of the *Daode jing's* teaching. One often gets a simple statement about "what Daoists believe" about

Dao. Attempts to give some reason why they believed this are confined to drawing parallels to other religious or philosophical systems. These "doctrines about *Dao*" are assimilated to doctrines various mystics teach about an ineffable transcendent reality, to the Brahman of Hindu thought, or to Hegel's Absolute, to "metaphysical" doctrines held by various Western philosophers, and so on. The established respectability of these parallels appears as an easy substitute for the more difficult task of giving a plausible historical account of why the *Daode jing*'s' authors believed what they believed on this subject. (Is there evidence that these doctrines came to them in mystical ecstasy? On what basis did they then persuade nonmystics to believe them? Is there evidence that they were philosophers speculating on metaphysical issues?) And one can always fall back on the common attitude: It is well known that religious people simply believe what they believe—there is no explanation.

Statements about the pragmatic implications of ideas about a transmundane *Dao* customarily take a similarly ahistorical approach: What conclusions would *I* draw if I held that *Dao* was the origin of the world? Many students who have some previous associations with "Daoism," for example, come with an idea that they also associate with "The Force" in the movie "*Star Wars*": the idea that *Dao* is the origin of the world is translated into the idea that *Dao* is a kind of force or energy that some people can feel pervading the material world. Such people can tap into or unite with this force, and "becoming one with the universe" in this sense is what it means to "become one with *Dao*." This, then, is their version of the pragmatic implications of the cosmogonic statements about *Dao* in the *Daode jing*. So far as I can see, this version finds no support in any statement made in the *Daode jing* itself. It never connects statements about *Dao* as world-origin with the idea that *Dao* is something present in the world around us. It never says we can learn about *Dao* through observations about or perceptions of phenomena or events in the world, or that we can become one with *Dao* by becoming one with the world. When students bring up these ideas, I sometimes make this an occasion for making a distinction central to my approach to interpretation: the fact that we have *two* questions to deal with here. One question is "Is this a *good* idea?" A quite different question is "Is this likely to have been *their* idea?" If there seems to be general interest, I devote some time to spelling out what the "*Star Wars*" view amounts to, and what might be good reasons for relating to the world in this particular way, before going on to look at evidence as to the probable basis for beliefs about *Dao* as world-origin in the *Daode jing* and pragmatic implications its authors associated with these beliefs.

My approach to the question about the basis for these beliefs is determined by one of the results of my research concerning reflections in the *Daode jing* of contemporary self-cultivation practices.[8] To give students some background, I sometimes read with them passages from the proto-Daoist *Nei Ye* and/or from the Mencius relevant to these practices.[9] I also summarize for them the results of my study of special recurrent terms in the *Daode jing*: emptiness, femininity, stillness, steadiness, softness, weakness, clarity, harmony, uncarved, merged, oneness, *Dao*, *De*, and the Mother. Many of these terms are descriptive, describing a quality or state of mind one is advised to cultivate in oneself. They do not describe different states, but different aspects of a single state of mind. There is a tendency to "hypostatize" these states, to speak of them as though they were independent presences or forces inhabiting a person's mind. *Dao* and *De* serve in the *Daode jing* as summary references to this way of being and are similarly hypostatized. *Dao* and *De* are pictured as hypostatized internal presences "welcoming" (chapter 23) or "supporting" (chapter 41) a person, and this is the same presence that is termed "the nourishing Mother" (chapter 20; *Dao* and the Mother are identified in chapter 25).

These observations present us with understandable reasons why Laoists would attribute great importance to *Dao*. It was a hypostatized summary reference to the state of mind Laoists cultivated, associated with attitudes and styles of behavior advocated in Laoist polemic aphorisms, and was thus *existentially* foundational for a way of life that had its own intrinsic attractiveness. (This needs to be distinguished from the view that doctrines about *Dao* serve as an *epistemological* foundation for Laoism; they did not, first, for unknown reasons, begin believing in some doctrines about *Dao*, then use these doctrines as "first principles" from which to derive a "Daoist system of philosophy.") This way of construing Laoist thought is one of the main targets of criticism in my *Tao and Method*.

Also relevant here are two features of ancient Chinese thought and rhetoric. One is the habit of attributing cosmic importance to factors regarded as of central importance in human social life. The Confucian Xunzi, for example, says of the central Confucian virtue *li* (etiquette, ceremony, refined politeness), "By this the sun and moon shine, by this the four seasons proceed, by this the stars take their course . . . by this the myriad things flourish."[10] Chapters 16, 25, and 39 of the *Daode jing* reflect the custom of picturing the Chinese emperor as one of the pillars of the cosmic order along with "Heaven" and "Earth." The other feature of Chinese thought and rhetoric important here is the habit of expressing *evaluative* priority by using images of chronological priority, and "origin" images ("source," "root," "ancestor," etc.). I ask students to imagine equivalent images in our own culture: What kinds of terms and images do we use to express these same things? Some students suggest, for example, terms like "center" or "foundation."

It no longer comes as natural to us to use cosmic imagery as it did to many ancient peoples. One of the closest parallels is love and falling in love, and I try to point to some of these as well. ("Love makes the world go 'round"; "The first time ever I saw your face I thought the stars rose in your eyes"; "I felt the earth shake under my feet and the sky come tumbling down").

I also ask students to think about the pragmatic implications of the idea that *Dao* is the origin of the world. What specific changes in a person's outlook on the world did Laoists associate with this idea?

I think the most important element in an answer to this question is the picture, implicit in several places, of two states or layers of mind. The more original state or deeper layer is completely still, not yet stimulated by exciting or desirable things in the world. There has not yet arisen that outward-directed flow of energy that comes with desiring things in the world, competing for fame in the world, or "working" to make one's mark on the world. In this state one's personality is still "uncarved"; that is, it retains an organic wholeness not yet diminished and distorted by being "carved" to produce qualities admired by the world. This layer of one's mind has a kind of holistic awareness of the world, not distorting reality by pigeon-holing judgments that usually go along with rigid conceptual thought. This layer of one's mind is soft and flexible (see chapter 76), not having yet developed that kind of hardness associated with con-frontationally trying to force the world to conform to one's wishes.[11] This state or layer of one's mind is the primary concrete referent of the term *"Dao."*

The character of the social world we live in is determined by an opposite mentality: by the attraction to exciting and desirable things, to impressive out-ward appearance, to forceful, dominating ways of interaction, to imposing conceptual order on the world, and so on. Social acceptance gives things as they appear from this perspective a certain solidity or "being." But from a Laoist point of view, this is an illusory solidity, false appearances not backed up by any-thing of substantial value. The state or layer of mind that Laoists cultivate, even though it seems like "Nothing" from the conventional perspective, is the basis of all that is truly valuable and important in life, in the sense that one sees things in their true meaning, as important, when one sees them rooted in this "Nothing." "[True] 'Being' is rooted in [this] 'Nothing,'" as chapter 40 expresses it.

This is also what I think it means to say, ""The world has a source, the Mother of the world. Once you get the Mother, then you understand the chil-dren" (chapter 52). To "get the Mother [*Dao*]" is to acquire the state of mind Laoists cultivate. "The children" are circumstances and events in the world. The fact that the state of mind one cultivates is "the origin of the world" means in concrete terms that this state of mind gives one the key to understanding circumstances and events in the world as they should be understood. I take it that this is equivalent to the way things are pictured in the polemic aphorisms; for example, one should understand that being low is the proper foundation of high social status, that fine speech and appearances are typically deceiving, that the most important qualities are ones that are frequently overlooked or looked down upon, that agitation wears one out but stillness enables one to last long.

On this view, "the world" that has *Dao* as its origin is primarily *the socio-logical and psychological human world*. (I think there is no evidence that Laoists turned away from the human social world to become interested in the natural world of trees and animals, rocks and rivers, other than as sources of meta-phorical images representing Laoist themes.)[12] The idea that *Dao* is the "origin" of this world represents a kind of social and axiological ontology. The world perceived by the conventional mentality is in some sense an illusory world: the meanings of phenomena as perceived in this world are false meanings. To see them rooted in *Dao* is to see them quite differently, but to see them as they truly are.

There is then a kind of ontology implicit in the *Daode jing*, but it is not the kind of *theoretical* ontology of the kind developed in Western philosophy and theology. Western thought has generally been much more oriented to devel-oping an objective account of the nature of the external world (in modern times considered quite separately from the human social world) and lacks the strong emphasis on self-cultivation found in Laoism. On my view, the *primary* referent of the word *Dao* in the *Daode jing* remains the state of mind that Laoists cultivate. It is the *Dao* that *some people have as the result of self-cultivation* that is a "world-origin." Statements about *Dao* as world-origin do not yet represent "theories" about the world believed in as the contents of intellectual beliefs in the absence of any concrete self-cultivation.

I arrived at the foregoing understanding of the *Daode jing* prior to any study of Neo-Confucianism, but was struck by seeing how closely this basic pattern of thought, and its connection with self-cultivation, is mirrored in certain strains of Neo-Confucian thought, particularly as represented in the opening chapters of Zhu Xi and Lü Tsu-ch'ien's *Reflections on Things at Hand* and in some of Thomas Metzger's descriptions of basic Neo-Confucian themes in his *Escape from Predicament*.

Since my courses treating Daoism also usually treat Buddhism, one other contrast I have found helpful in pinpointing the precise character of Laoism is the contrast between the use of the term "empty" in the *Daode jing* and "empty" as a key term in certain strands of Mahayana Buddhism. The Ma-hayana Emptiness doctrine is aimed against people who are looking for some unchangingly reliable reality having its own being (*svabhava*) independent of the flux of cause and effect in the world; the point of the Emptiness teaching is to cut off all craving for some particular reality to depend on, by asserting that there are no realities beyond this constantly changing flux. "Emptiness" in the *Daode jing*, on the other hand, is directed against those who are overly impressed by "solid," "full" things, that is, those things that make their presence forcefully felt in the human social world. Laoist "Emptiness" teaching combats this by insisting that the most valuable things in life are those that lack such solidity. They are so subtle that they feel "empty."

Meditation

When I teach courses on Buddhism, I generally introduce students to a simple (*Vipassana*) form of Buddhist meditation, because I think attempts to meditate give students a helpful experiential basis for understanding Buddhist ideas. I've tried to devise also some meditation techniques based on Laoist ideas that might give students some equivalent basis for understanding Laoism, and I devote seven to ten minutes of several class sessions to this. I've thought of three basic guiding ideas for such meditations.

"Bringing about Softness" (chapter 10) seems related to practices described in *The Secret of the Golden Flower* involving attempts to breathe very softly and smoothly, and to Qigong practices involving attempts to locate and dissolve tensions in one's body through a kind of mental massage.

"Working" in Laoism refers I think partly to the sense of strain we associate with "pulling oneself together" in order to go out into public, a strain that makes dealing with the public something that tires one out. Such strained "working" often takes place more or less continually on a preconscious level, so it is helpful to try at meditation to become more conscious of such strain and try to relax it.

In pulling themselves together, most people probably achieve a sense of controlled orderliness in their being, which engenders a certain corresponding fear of the apparent internal disorder that might occur if one lets go of this control and lets oneself "come apart." I think the "chaos" theme in the *Daode jing* (chapters 15 and 25) suggests that one needs to overcome this fear and on occasion yield to apparent internal disorder in order to foster the arising of a less strained, more natural and organic internal harmony. One could use this also as a guide to a meditation practice aimed at relaxing control and letting one's mind become a kind of chaotic mental soup. (I was told once that the term *hun dun*, "chaos," is the origin of the modern "won ton," the name of a kind of soup.)

"But this doesn't apply to me. I'm one of the people, not one of the rulers."

I try to emphasize that a historical approach to the *Daode jing* is not an *alternative* to one that considers its potential relevance to people today. The message of the *Daode jing* is one that can be generalized and applied to many situations other than the specific ones envisioned by the original authors. I often have students break down into small groups to discuss specific chapters of the *Daode jing* and encourage them in these discussions to consider what it might mean if a person wanted to apply these passages to her own life today.

One of the biggest obstacles to this in many students' minds is the fact that so much of the *Daode jing* consists in advice about how to rule a country. I try to point out that much of this advice can be generalized and applied, for example, as advice to parents about how to deal with their children. Still, students typically find this aspect of the *Daode jing* at best irrelevant to their lives, and at worst objectionably elitist. Advice is relevant only if it "applies to the lives of ordinary people like us." There seems to be something objectionable in itself about writing a book advising people in authority on the best way of maintaining and using that authority.

This is an excellent opportunity for illustrating what I mean by "confrontational hermeneutics." That is, the student reactions just mentioned reflect a set of assumptions implicitly taken for granted in much Western thought. Our general tendency is to take these assumptions as a normative framework *within* which to understand and evaluate works like the *Daode jing*. Whatever we can, we interpret in a way that accords with these basic assumptions. Whatever does not accord with these assumptions we reject as fundamentally mistaken. (This is the way that I myself read the *Daode jing* when I first became attracted to it in my hippie days in the 1970s'.) When this is done, our own basic assumptions are protected from any kind of questioning. There is never a confrontation between them and the different assumptions the text's authors may have held. What I think needs to be done instead is to make our own assumptions explicit and hold them at arm's length, temporarily suspending our commitment to them, in order to seriously consider a set of assumptions differing from ours on a very basic level.

In the present case, I try to articulate as a basis for discussion some assumptions prevalent in the United States today, first asking students if my list accurately articulates their sense of things. My list is something like the following:

> All important truths are universal truths, equally applicable to the lives of all.
> The very idea that some people should have authority over others is of
>   questionable legitimacy.

"The people" are in general good. They usually have complaints and want to reverse various decisions made by those in power. Our sympathies should generally lie with the people protesting against the establishment.

The proper way to react to the abuse of authority is to limit the power of authorities and give more power to the people. This applies especially to "bureaucrats," who, being appointed rather than elected, are not directly responsible to the people.

If an idealistic individual finds herself living in a society whose norms she cannot respect, the proper responses are (1) withdrawal, (2) publicly dramatizing one's dissent, or (3) working to undermine the present order and bring about fundamental, revolutionary change. Revolutionaries inevitably represent themselves as working on behalf of the people.

Politics is ideally the struggle for the victory of what is right, and also the struggle for the victory of the people over the powers that be. These are for the most part identical.

One should generally assume that people who aspire to positions of power do so out of egotistic desire to assert that they are "better than other people," one of the worst sins in modern egalitarian democratic societies. Identifying oneself with the people is a basic precondition for moral respectability in this kind of society.

Side by side with this list, we can list a set of assumptions taught or taken for granted by the authors of the *Daode jing*:[13]

What the people most need is an orderly and harmonious social order, an environment conducive to peace and moderate prosperity. Such social order depends on the ability of the government to unify the people under its leadership and on its paternalistic work for the common good, in contrast to individuals striving on behalf of personal and private interests. The government is able to do this only by gaining the willing allegiance and cooperation of the people. So the prime concern of political thought is, first, how to gain this willing allegiance and cooperation and, second, how to wield the power thus gained in a way that will produce a social environment most conducive to human flourishing.

If an idealistic individual finds herself living in a society whose norms she cannot respect, the proper response has two aspects, one personal and one social. First, on a personal level, one must internally free oneself from the distorting influences of social pressure so as to cultivate a more organically harmonious way of being. And one must develop a relation to some reality beyond and superior to the norms of society—thus the importance of developing a relation to a "transcendent" *Dao*. Second, on the social side, one should devote oneself to making society a better place for others. One can be most effective in doing this by gaining positions of responsibility and influence within the present sociopolitical structure or by winning the ear of those who have the most power and influence. The crucial thing is that people in such positions must use those means of gaining allegiance and cooperation and carry out those public policies that are most conducive to harmony and prosperity in society.

These two endeavors are governed by different ideals, described in different aspects of Laoist teaching. Teachings related to self-cultivation are not universal truths applicable to the lives of all, but are intended for idealistic individuals who voluntarily take on the project of self-transformation. This group is open to all, but the general assumption is that not everyone in the society will have this ambition. So this teaching about the mental qualities or states of mind to be cultivated is not the basis for a proposed transformation of the entire society, nor a curriculum to be taught to all the people. (The *Daode jing* shows no interest in the internal state of "the people" [*min*], and never speaks about them as anything other than the objects of rule.) One does not teach the people Daoist values and self-cultivation, but concentrates on fostering unity, harmony, and moderate prosperity in the society. Thus politics is not the struggle for the public victory of those values one believes in most passionately and cultivates in one's personal life. It is the practical attempt to provide an environment conducive to a relatively good life for people not like oneself.

Tendencies commonly found in rulers—exploitation, self-aggrandizement, meddlesomeness, arbitrary imposition of rules, willing resort to armed violence—are regarded as some of the main obstacles in the way of achieving a unified and organically harmonious society, since such a ruler acts as a foreign presence stirring up people's resentment rather than gaining their willing cooperation. But the solution is not to limit the power of rulers and give more power to the people. Instead, the solution is to convert rulers to a style of leadership that will make them both worthy of respect and effective in gaining it.[14]

Setting these two sets of assumptions side by side invites a comparative evaluation of the strengths and weaknesses of each. To stimulate discussion, I try to present a case for integrating some of these ancient Chinese ideas into our own attitudes—not as a substitute for the democratic ethos and institutions, but as a counterbalance correcting some of its weaknesses.

We can start with the problem of alienation. Alienation occurs when the influences that dominate the public realm—influences that determine who receives recognition, status, prestige, wealth, and power—are not correlated with what people regard as true values. Alienation in this sense is widespread today, at both ends of the political spectrum. I think that it is justified: people with good moral sensitivities *should* be alienated. The development of good moral sensitivities requires that one strongly resist the tendency to assume that most successful people in our society deserve their success, that the views and values of the most powerful and influential people in our society actually deserve our respect, that there is some close correlation between yielding to social pressure and actually being a good person.

There is an assumption in modern Western culture that the proper response to alienation is denunciation and opposition. If one feels that the system is corrupt, not publicly taking a stand against it also feels like moral compromise. This I think is ultimately shaped by the "prophetic" strain in the Judeo-Christian tradition.[15] This has been coupled in modern times by a structural and populist utopianism. Structural utopianism is an important element in what is now called "modernism": the confidence that rational political science could discover for us a set of structural reforms and political institutions that would remedy all injustices. By "populist utopianism" I mean a confidence in "the will of the people" as the agent that will actually bring about a just society.

In class discussions, I try to raise questions about the validity of these assumptions and about the practical effects of acting on them.

As to structural utopianism: Does anyone know of a specific set of political and social institutions that will produce a society *fundamentally* more just than our own? Do we have good reasons to think that, in the near future, someone will discover such a revolutionary new system that we could implement? Of course, one cannot rule this out, but is it wise to predicate our behavior on the assumption that this will actually happen? The system we have is a combination of a free market economy, electoral politics, the rule of law, an expansion of areas of individual freedom, and at the same time a counterbalancing expansion of a managerial government called on to remedy many undesirable effects of the free market and the free choices of individuals pursuing their own interests. I argue that, in the absence of any radically different practical alternatives on the horizon, the best we can hope for, in the near future at least, are adjustments in this basic system. Such adjustments could result in major improvements in the system areas, such as wider and more equal availability of health care and education, more genuine equality of opportunity, and so on. But each of these adjustments comes with a cost, generally an expansion of government with an attendant limitation of individual freedoms, increased taxation, increased power for politicians and government bureaucrats, and so on. And I don't see that any amount of adjustment promises to produce a *fundamentally* more just and less alienating society.

Populist utopianism seems likewise predicated on assumptions at odds with reality. The idea that there exists an actual large group whose desires if listened to would revolutionize the social order for the better—such an idea has a great initial appeal. Anyone who questions it is immediately suspect of being an elitist, siding with some elite group and putting down the people. But this should not prevent us from considering how closely this idea matches actual conditions today. The idea of "the will of the people" seems predicated on the further idea that people suffering from domination and injustice will feel solidarity with other victims and will struggle for the common liberation of all. But what we seem to see instead is various interest groups each advancing its own interests that conflict with the interests of other groups. What group of voters feels that their voting should be guided, not by their own interests, but by some consideration of the common good? Some political theorists express confidence that competition among interest groups will itself bring about the common good, but it seems more often just to result in stalemate, or in political compromises that give the word "politics" an exceedingly negative connotation in modern democracies. "Democratic" electoral politics thus becomes a major cause of alienation rather than a solution.

Some might argue that we should keep alive utopian hopes even if they are unrealistic, because this is the most effective way of preventing wholesale and devastating moral compromise, in which people accept the legitimacy of the present order just because of its actual power. I think there is some validity to this, but one must also consider the actual effect of the attitudes and behavior that it leads to. What strikes me most in this respect is the way protest against the system, and especially against the government, has become characteristic of right-wing groups, those least concerned about the plight of the poor and the powerless in society. And indeed, for the most part, weakening the power of the government in favor of "the people" does not actually result in bettering the conditions of the poor and powerless, but in a more Darwinian society favoring the interests of those who are already wealthy and powerful. As bad as it is, the government is the only agency from which we can hope for any reduction in the injustices caused by free market economic forces, free competition for jobs, education, medical services, and so on. The fact that alienation from the system tends to keep the best, brightest, most idealistic individuals out of government service actually works to the detriment of the system itself, in which we all have to live.

In light of these considerations, the alternative reactions to alienation expressed in the *Daode jing* have more to recommend them than one might initially suppose.

Laoists were also obviously alienated from their society. This is expressed, for example, in their love for paradox, praising qualities looked down on in their society and criticizing those qualities most admired. But their reaction to alienation followed a Chinese pattern (shared with their Confucian rivals) that is more bifurcated than the typical Western pattern. It is bifurcated in that it offers a personal program different from the social and political program it also offers. Their personal solution was self-cultivation. Self-cultivation means freeing oneself on a personal level from the influence of the false values that dominate public life in conventional society, and cultivating intensely in one-self those values one thinks are true values. Internalizing these qualities to a very high degree "saves" a person from meaninglessness even in the midst of a corrupt society. It enables him to unite with a reality, *Dao* that transcends the social world. (The fact that *Dao* needs to fulfill this function makes it important that *Dao* not be a vague and indeterminate reality or concept devoid of any real content having specific pragmatic implications.) Laoists wanted to offer this personal solution to all individuals whom they could interest in taking it up. But they did not envision a society in which all individuals would actually engage in this self-cultivation. It was a rather perfectionist project which had to be vol-untarily taken up by individuals willing to invest considerable time and energy on it. It was not envisioned as something already innate in the masses of the people, just waiting to be released by weakening the influence of bad leaders.

But offering this personal, "individualist" solution to alienation indepen-dent of any social change did not lead to abandoning any interest in social reform on behalf of the people. Laoists were interested in making society a better place for the masses of the people outside ruling circles. But this did not lead them to identify themselves with "the people" in opposition to rulers and managers, nor did it lead them to any plans for a radical restructuring of their society. On the contrary, they accepted the hierarchical structure of society and its accompanying paternalistic approach to governing. Their program for social reform was focused on attempts to infuse social leadership with Laoist values, both by elevating good Laoists to influential middle-level administrative posi-tions, and by acting as counselors to higher level princes and kings (who at the time were either the remnants of hereditary nobility or warlords newly come to power). This leadership would not directly teach Laoist values to the people, nor enshrine them in laws to be obeyed by all. Leaders would, rather, personally embody Daoist qualities, qualities that would be felt in their personal presence (*De*) and their style of social interaction, and so would result in a *more* powerful government, assumed to be necessary for a harmonious and prosperous society.

I ask students, in the light of all this, to reconsider their instinctive antipathy to any advice encouraging any ambition to become a representative of the system and to improve and strengthen it, which seems to them to imply rejection of their preferred stance of identification with "ordinary people" in opposition to the system. I point out that, willy nilly, most of them will probably at some time become functionaries in some large organization, private or state-run, with responsibilities that place them in control of other people who are either employees or clients of this organization. Their tendency is to look on this as an unfortunate economic necessity. Laoists would have them look on this as an opportunity to make the world a better place, at least that corner of the world that they are in charge of.

These are all matters to think about. I want students to suspend their own views long enough to take a sympathetic look at different Laoist attitudes, but then to engage in serious critical thought as to the pros and cons of each way of dealing with these issues. If Laoist views on these subjects are applicable today it is not because they are timeless truths possessing some intrinsic and timeless authority, but by coincidence—because current circumstances bring certain issues and problems to the fore today, and Laoism has a better way of dealing with these issues than the responses that most readily come to minds shaped by the Western cultural tradition. This is a good example of the advantages of a historicist approach over a free reading focused most often on finding "universal truths." Historical reconstructions focusing on *particularities* of views from the past and other cultures give us something challenging to chew on. "Universal truths" tend to get their universality by being vague; lacking specific content and specific implications, they offer us nothing challenging to struggle with.

NOTES

1. I've outlined this theory in *Language and Gnosis: Form and Meaning in the Acts of Thomas* (Philadelphia: Fortress Press, 1985), chap. 1; "Socio-historical Research and the Contextualization of Biblical Theology," in *The Social World of Formative Christianity and Judaism: Essays in Honor of Howard Clark Kee*, ed. P. Borger, J. S. Frerichs, R. Horsley, and J. Neusner (Philadelphia: Fortress Press 1988), 3–16; "Are Texts Determinate? Derrida, Barth, and the Role of the Biblical Scholar," *Harvard Theological Review* 81, no. 3 (1988): 341–357; *Tao and Method: A Reasoned Approach to the Tao-te-ching* (Albany: State University of New York Press, 1994), 5–43) and Michael

Lafargue "Recovering the *Tao-te*-Ching's Original Meaning: Some Remarks on Historical Hermeneutics," in *Lao-tzu and the Tao-te-ching*, ed. Livia Kohn and Michael
LaFargue (Albany: State University of New York Press, 1998), 255–276. I owe a great
deal both in hermeneutics and in pedagogy to the mentoring of Dieter Georgi,
and partly through him to his teacher Rudolf Bultmann.

2. My resulting interpretation of the first two chapters of the *Acts of Thomas* was
published as *Language and Gnosis*.

3. See Michael Ermarth, *Wilhelm Dilthey: The Critique of Historical Reason* (Chicago: University of Chicago Press, 1981). For my critique of Gadamer, see LaFargue,
Tao and Method, 7–12; for Derrida, see LaFargue, "Are Texts Determinate?"

4. I've found most helpful Ted Kaptchuk's *The Web That Has No Weaver* (Chicago: Congdon & Weed, 1983) on Chinese medical theory, and B. Frantzis, *Opening
the Energy Gates of Your Body* (Berkeley: North Atlantic Books, 1993).

5. I've adopted A. C. Graham's term "Laoism" as a convenient designation of the
specific teaching of the *Daode jing*, to distinguish this from other teachings associated
with the term "Daoism." See A. C. Graham, *Studies in Chinese Philosophy and Philosophical Literature* (Albany: State University of New York Press, 1990), 118, 124. This
enables me to avoid engaging in struggles over what properly deserves the prestige
name "Daoism." For students concerned about this question, I recommend Nathan
Sivin's very informative article, "On the Word 'Taoist' as a Source of Perplexity, with
Special Reference to the Relations of Science and Religion in Traditional China,"
History of Religions 17 (1978): 303–330, for the situation in China, and Julia Hardy's
"Influential Western Interpretations of the *Tao-te-ching*," and *The Tao of Pooh*, ed.
Benjamin M. Hoff (New York: Penguin Books, 1983), for a history of "Western Daoism."

6. See LaFargue, *The Tao of the Tao Te Ching, A Translation and Commentary*
(Albany: State University of New York Press, 1992), 219–253. I assign the essays
under the following topics: Organic, Natural, Appearances, Self-Promotion, Con-
tending, Confucianism, Empty, Nothing, Uncarved Block, Agitation, Desire, Still,
Naming, Understanding, Impressive, Strict, Hurting, Forcing, Low, Softness, Improvements, Working, *Dao*, and *De*. These give an overview of my attempts to reconstruct the original historical meaning of the *Daode jing*. I sometimes also assign
the longer and more systematic essay on "Organic Harmony" in LaFargue, *Tao and
Method*, 160–172. I think organic harmony as there defined is the core value in
Laoism.

7. More complete explanation of my theory about how proverbs mean is given in
LaFargue, *Tao and Method*, chaps. 6–7. See also my "Understanding the Aphorisms
in the *Tao-te-ching*," *Journal of Chinese Religions*, no. 18 (fall 1990): 25–43.

8. LaFargue, *Tao and Method*.

9. Ibid., 104–112, 181–195. My attention was first drawn to parallels between the
Daode jing and the *Nei Ye* by the work of Hal Roth; see "Psychology and Self-Cultivation in Early *Taoistic* Thought," *Harvard Journal of Asiatic Studies* 51 (December
1991): 599–650.

10. A. C. Graham, *Disputers of the Tao: Philosophical Argument in Ancient China*
(LaSalle, Ill.: Open Court Press, 1989), 243.

11. Many of these ideas are implied in passages using the key recurrent term "turn back." For example chapter 16 speaks of "turning back to the root," which it says is equivalent to achieving a mental stillness (*jing*) that is the opposite of activity (*zuo*); this implies that stillness is a kind of primary or "root" state, compared to which activity is secondary and derivative. The common tendency is to flee this "root" and involve oneself in outward-directed activity. Laoist advice to "turn back" is advice to reverse this outward flow and turn back to this neglected root. Similarly, chapter 64 says one should "desire [to be] desire-less, learn [to be] un-learned . . . turn back to the place all others have gone on from"; chapter 28 speaks of "turning back to an infant [-like state], turning back to [being] uncarved"; chapter 52 speaks of "turning back to the [internal] Mother," in contrast to occupying oneself with phenomena in the world, the Mother's "children"; chapter 32 says that the "naming" involved in legalistic rule making is a result of "cutting up" an initially "uncarved" *Dao*. I think the end of chapter 1 also pictures conceptual naming as something that arises out of a prior "merged" state of mind, that is, a state of mind prior to the emergence of well-defined concepts. If my understanding is correct, this aspect of Laoist thought is probably summed up in the rather cryptic passage in chapter 25: "One can call it [*Dao*] 'Great.' Great means going forth, going forth means going far away, going far away means turning back." ' The social world we see is the result of a "going forth" from *Dao*, a movement that initially alienates this world from *Dao*. Overcoming this alienation is the object of Laoist self-cultivation, which is a reversal ("turning back") of this cosmic movement away from Dao.

12. LaFargue, *Tao and Method*, 172–174.

13. Some elements in this list are the result of my attempts to situate the *Daode jing* in its social setting in ancient China, spelled out in LaFargue, *Tao and Method*, chaps. 3–5. Many of these assumptions are not specifically Laoist, but were elements of a political culture that Laoists shared with other thinkers of the time, including their Confucian rivals. The tendency among Western scholars is to try to assimilate divisions between different Chinese schools to modern divisions we are familiar with (right vs. left, religious vs. secular, etc.). I think n historical reading should focus instead on the way that the shared political culture of ancient Chinese thinkers differs from the shared political culture that shapes modern thought.

14. See the remarks by A. C. Graham on what he calls "hierarchical anarchism": the utopias of even the most "primitivist," anticivilization thinkers in ancient China were presided over by a sage emperor. *Disputers of the Tao*, 299–311.

15. This attitude is well represented, I believe, in the *Gospel of Mark*, another of my favorites among religious classics, though its message is in many ways directly opposed to the *Daode jing*. See my "The Authority of the Excluded: Mark's Challenge to a Rational Hermeneutics," in *Religious Propaganda and Missionary Competition in the New Testament World: Essays Honoring Dieter Georgi*, supplement to *Novum Testamentum*, no. 74, ed. Lukas Borman, Kelly DelTredici, and Angela Standhartinger (Leiden: Brill, 1994), 229–255.

Selected Bibliography

Abram, David. *The Spell of the Sensuous: Perception and Language in a More-Than Human World*. New York: Vintage Books, 1996.

Allan, Sarah, and Crispin Williams, eds. *The Guodian Laozi: Proceedings of the International Conference, Dartmouth College, May, 1998*. Early China Special Monograph Series no. 5. Institute for East Asian Studies, University of California, Berkeley, 2000.

Barnhart, Michael, ed. *Varieties of Ethical Reflection: New Directions for Ethics in a Global Context*. New York: Lexington Books, 2002.

Barrett, T. H. *Taoism under the T'ang: Religion and Empire during the Golden Age of Chinese History*. London: Wellsweep Press, 1996.

Bell, Catherine. *Ritual: Perspective and Dimensions*. New York: Oxford University Press, 1997.

Berling, Judith A. *A Pilgrim in Chinese Culture: Negotiating Religious Diversity*. Maryknoll, N.Y.: Orbis Books, 1997.

Bilsky, Lester J. "The State Religion of Ancient China." PhD diss., University of Washington, 1971.

Birrell, Anne M. "Studies on Chinese Myth Since 1970: An Appraisal." Part I. *History of Religions* 33 (1994): 380–393.

———. "Studies on Chinese Myth Since 1970: An Appraisal." Part II. *History of Religions* 34 (1994): 70–94.

Blofeld, John. *The Secret and Subiime: Taoist Mysteries and Magic*. London: Allen & Unwin, 1973.

———. *Taoist Road to Immortality*. Boston: Shambhala, 1985.

Bradbury, Steven. "The American Conquest of Philosophical Taoism." In *Translation East and West: A Cross-Cultural Approach*, ed. Cornelia N. Moore and Lucy Lower. Honolulu: University of Hawaii College of Languages, Linguistics and Literature, and East-West Center, 1992.

Bynam, Caroline Walker. *Fragmentation and Redemption: Essays on Gender and the Human Body in Medieval Religion*. Boston: Beacon, 1992.

Capra, Fritjof. *The Tao of Physics*. Boston: Shambala, 1975 (1983, 1991, 1999).

Chan, Alan K. *Two Visions of the Way: A Study of the Wang Pi and Ho-Shang Kung Commentaries of the Lao-tzu*. Albany: State University of New York Press, 1991.

Chan, Wing-tsit. "Influences of Taoist Classics on Chinese Philosophy." In *Literature of Belief: Sacred Scripture and Religious Experience*, Neal E. Lambert, Provo, Utah: Brigham Young University Press, 1981.

———. *Source Book in Chinese Philosophy*. Princeton: Princeton University Press, 1963.

Chang Chung-yuan. *Creativity and Taoism: A Study of Chinese Philosophy, Art and Poetry*. New York: Harper & Row, 1970.

Ch'en, Ellen. "Is There a Doctrine of Physical Immortality in the *Tao-te-ching*?" *History of Religions* 12, no. 3 (1973): 231–247.

Chen, Ellen Marie. *The Tao Te Ching: A New Translation with Commentary*. New York: Paragon House, 1989.

Chen, Guying. *Lao Zhuang xinlun*. Hong Kong: Zhonghua shuju, 1991.

Chu Hsi. *Reflections on Things at Hand*. Trans. Wing-tsit Chan. New York: Columbia University Press, 1967.

Clarke, J. J. *Oriental Enlightenment: The Encounter between Asian and Western Thought*. London: Routledge, 1997.

———. *The Tao of the West: Western Transformations of Taoist Thought*. London: Routledge, 2000.

Creel, H. C. *The Birth of China*. New York: Frederick Ungar, 1937.

———. *The Origins of Statecraft in China*. Vol. 1: *The Western Chou Empire*. Chicago: University of Chicago Press, 1970.

———. *Shen Pu-hai: A Chinese Political Philosopher of the Fourth Century B.C.* Chicago: University of Chicago Press, 1974.

———. *What Is Taoism? And Other Studies in Chinese Cultural History*. Chicago: University of Chicago Press, 1970.

Csikszentmihalyi, Mark, and Philip J. Ivanhoe, eds. *Religious and Philosophical Aspects of the Laozi*. Albany: State University of New York Press, 1999.

Csikszentmihalyi, Mihaly. *Flow: The Psychology of Optimal Experience*. New York: Harper & Row, 1990.

Culler, Jonathan. *Structuralist Poetics: Structuralism, Linguistics, and the Study of Literature*. Ithaca, N.Y.: Cornell University Press, 2002.

Davis, Lydia. "The Professor." *Harpers'*, February 1992, 56–59.

deBary, William Theodore. *The Buddhist Tradition in India, China and Japan*. New York: Random House, 1972.

———, ed. *Sources of Chinese Tradition*. New York: Columbia University Press, 1960.

Eliade, Mircea. *The Sacred and the Profane*. New York: Harper & Row, 1967.

Ermarth, Michael. *Wilhelm Dilthey: The Critique of Historical Reason*. Chicago: University of Chicago Press, 1981.

Fish, Stanley. *Is There a Text in This Class? The Authority of Interpretive Communities.* Cambridge, Mass.: Harvard University Press, 1980.

Frantzis, B. *Opening the Energy Gates of Your Body.* Berkeley: North Atlantic Books, 1993.

Girardot, Norman. "Behaving Cosmogonically in Early Taoism." In *Cosmogony and Ethical Order*, ed. R. Lovin and F. Reynolds. Chicago: University of Chicago Press, 1985.

———. "Chinese Religion: History of Study." *Encyclopedia of Religions* 3, ed. Mircea Eliade. New York: Macmillan, 1987, 312–323.

———. *Disputers of the Tao: Philosophical Argument in Ancient China.* LaSalle, Ill.: Open Court Press, 1989.

———. "Kristofer Schipper and the Resurrection of the Taoist Body." In *The Taoist Body*, by Kristofer Schipper. Berkeley: University of California Press, 1993.

———. *Myth and Meaning in Early Taoism.* Berkeley: University of California Press, 1983.

———. "Part of the Way: Four Studies on Taoism." *History of Religions* 11 (1972): 319–337.

———. *Studies in Chinese Philosophy and Philosophical Literature.* Albany: State University of New York Press, 1990.

———. " 'Very Small Books about Very Large Subjects': A Prefatory Appreciation of the Enduring Legacy of Laurence G. Thompson's *Chinese Religion: An Introduction.*" *Journal of Chinese Religions* 20 (fall 1992): 9–15.

———. *The Victorian Translation of China: James Legge's Oriental Pilgrimage.* Berkeley: University of California Press, 2002.

———. "Whispers and Smiles: Nostalgic Reflections on Mircea Eliade's Significance for the Study of Religion." Ed. Bryan Rennie. Albany: State University of New York Press, forthcoming.

———. *"The Whole Duty of Man": James Legge and the Victorian Translation of China. 19th Century Transformations of Missionary Tradition, Sinological Orientalism, and the Comparative Science of Religions.* Berkeley: University of California Press, forthcoming.

Girardot, N.J., James Miller, and Liu Xiaogan, eds. *Daoism and Ecology: Ways within a Cosmic Landscape.* Cambridge, Mass.: Center for the Study of World Religions, Harvard Divinity School, 2001. Distributed by Harvard University.

Goodspeed, Bennett W. *The Tao Jones Averages: A Guide to Whole-Brained Investing.* New York: Dutton, 1983.

Guodian. Ed. Guodian Chumu zhujian.Wenwu chubanshe. Beijing: Jingmen Museum, 1998.

Hall, David, and Roger Ames. "Daoism." In *Routledge Encyclopedia of Philosophy*, ed. Edward Craig. London: Routledge, 1998.

———. *Thinking from the Han.* Albany: State University of New York Press, 1998.

Hansen, Chad. *A Daoist Theory of Chinese Thought: A Philosophical Interpretation.* New York: Oxford University Press, 1992.

———. *Language and Logic in Ancient China.* Ann Arbor: University of Michigan Press, 1983.

Hardy, Julia. "Influential Western Interpretations of the Tao-te-ching." In *Lao-tzu and the Tao-te-ching*, ed. L. Kohn and Michael LaFargue. Albany: State University of New York Press, 1998.

Hu, Shi(h). *Zhongguo gudai zhexueshi.* 1919. Taipei: Shangwu, 1961.

Ivanhoe, Philip J., and Paul Kjellberg, eds. *Essays on Skepticism, Relativism and Ethics in the Zhuangzi.* Albany: State University of New York Press, 1996.

Kaltenmark, Max. *Lao Tzu and Taoism.* Trans. Roger Greaves. Stanford: Stanford University Press, 1969.

Kaptchuk, Ted. *The Web That Has No Weaver.* Chicago: Congdon & Weed, 1983.

Kirkland, Russell. "The Book of the Way." In *Great Literature of the Eastern World*, ed. Ian P. McGreal. New York: Harper Collins, 1996.

———. "The Historical Contours of Taoism in China: Thoughts on Issues of Classification and Terminology." *Journal of Chinese Religions* 25 (1997): 57–82.

———. "The History of Taoism: A New Outline." *Journal of Chinese Religions* 30 (2002): 177–193.

———. "On Coveting Thy Neighbor's Tao: Reflections on J. J. Clarke' s *The Tao of the West.*" *Religious Studies Review* 28, no. 4 (2002): 309–312.

———. "Person and Culture in the Taoist Tradition." *Journal of Chinese Religions* 20 (1992): 77–90.

———. "A Quest for 'The Foundations of Taoist Mysticism.' " *Studies in Central and East Asian Religions*, nos. 12–13 (2001): 203–229.

———. Review of *The Columbia Anthology of Traditional Chinese Literature*, ed. Victor Mair. *Education about Asia* 3, no. 3 (1998): 64–65.

———. Review of *Sources of Chinese Tradition*, ed. William T. deBary and Irene Bloom. 2nd ed., vol. 1. *Education about Asia* 7, no. 1 (2002): 62–66.

———. "The Roots of Altruism in the Taoist Tradition." *Journal of the American Academy of Religion* 54 (1986): 59–77.

———. "Self-Fulfillment through Selflessness: The Moral Teachings of the *Daode jing*." In *Varieties of Ethical Reflection: New Directions for Ethics in a Global Context*, ed. Michael Barnhart. New York: Lexington Books, 2002.

———. "The Study of Religion and Society in Contemporary Asia: Colonialism and Beyond." *Bulletin of Concerned Asian Scholars* 28, nos. 3–4 (1996): 59–63.

———. *Taoism: The Enduring Tradition.* London: Routledge, 2004.

———. "The Taoism of the Western Imagination and the Taoism of China: De-Colonizing the Exotic Teachings of the East" unpublished lecture, University of Tennessee, 1997.

———. "Teaching Taoism in the 1990s." *Teaching Theology and Religion*, vol. 1, no. 2 (1998): 177–89.

———. "Varieties of Taoism in Ancient China: A Preliminary Comparison of Themes in the *Nei yeh* and Other Taoist Classics." *Taoist Resources* 7, no. 2 (1997): 73–86.

Kohn, Livia. *Early Chinese Mysticism: Philosophy and Soteriology in the Taoist Tradition.* Princeton: Princeton University Press, 1992.

———. *God of the Dao: Lord Lao in History and Myth.* Ann Arbor: University of Michgan, Center for Chinese Studies, 1998.

———. "Laozi: Ancient Philosopher, Master of Immortality, and God." In *Lao-tzu and the Tao-te-ching,* ed. Livia Kohn and Michael LaFargue. Albany: State University of New York Press, 1998.

———, ed. *The Taoist Experience: An Anthology.* Albany: State University of New York Press, 1993.

———, ed. *Taoist Meditation and Longevity Techniques.* Ann Arbor: University of Michigan, Center for Chinese Studies, 1989.

LaFargue, Michael, ed. *Lao Tzu and Taoism.* Albany: State University of New York Press, 1998.

———. *Tao and Method: A Reasoned Approach to the Tao-te-ching.* Albany: State University of New York Press, 1994.

———. "Understanding the Aphorisms in the *Tao-te-ching.*" *Journal of Chinese Religions,* no. 18 (fall 1990): 25–43.

Lagerwey, John. *Taoist Ritual in Chinese Society and History.* New York: Macmillan, 1987.

Lambert, Neal E., ed. *Literature of Belief: Sacred Scripture and Religious Experience.* Salt Lake City: Religious Studies Center, Brigham Young University, 1981.

Lao, Siguang. *Xinbian Zhongguo zhexueshi.* 3 vols. Taipei: Sanmin shuju, 1981.

Laozizhu. *Laozizhu fu Laozi xinkao shulue.* 2nd ed. Ed. Yang Jialuo. Taipei: Shijie shuju, 1958.

Lin, Paul J. *A Translation of Lao Tzu's Tao Te Ching and Wang Pi's Commentary.* Ann Arbor: Michigan Papers in Chinese Studies, 1977.

Loewe, Michael, ed. *Early Chinese Texts: A Bibliographical Guide.* Berkeley: Society for the Study of Early China and Institute of East Asian Studies, University of California, 1993.

Lopez, Donald S., Jr., ed. *Religions of China in Practice.* Princeton: Princeton University Press, 1996.

Lu, Ji. "The Art of Writing." In *The Art of Writing, Teachings of the Chinese Masters.* Trans. Anthony Barstone and Chou Ping. Boston: Shambhala, 1996.

Mair, Victor, ed. *The Columbia Anthology of Traditional Chinese Literature.* New York: Columbia University Press, 1995.

Mawangdui. *Mawangdui boshu Laozi shitan.* Ed. Yan Lingfeng. Taipei: Heluo tushu chubanshe, 1976.

Metzger, Thomas. *Escape from Predicament: Neo-Confucianism and China's Evolving Political Culture.* New York: Columbia University Press, 1977.

Mote, Frederick W. *The Intellectual Foundations of Ancient China.* 2nd ed. New York: McGraw-Hill, 1989.

Munro, Donald J. *The Concept of Man in Early China.* Stanford: Stanford University Press, 1969.

Nachmanovitch, Stephen. *Free Play: The Power of Improvisation in Life and the Arts.* New York: G. P. Putnam's Sons, 1990.

Needham, Joseph. *Science and Civilisation in China.* Cambridge: Cambridge University Press, 1954–.

Neihardt, John G. *Black Elk Speaks: Being the Life Story of a Holy Man of the Oglala Sioux.* Lincoln: University of Nebraska Press, 1961.

Neumann, Erich. "Mystical Man." In *The Mystic Vision: Papers from the Eranos Yearbooks.* Vol. 6. Bolingen Series. Princeton: Princeton University Press, 1968.

Neville, Robert C. *Behind the Masks of God.* Albany: State University of New York Press, 1991.

Nivison, David S. *The Ways of Confucianism: Investigations in Chinese Philosophy.* Ed. Bryan W. Van Norden. La Salle, Ill.: Open Court, 1996.

Noll, Richard. *The Aryan Christ: The Secret Life of Carl Jung.* New York: Random House, 1997.

Pas, Julian. *A Select Bibliography on Taoism.* 2nd enlarged ed. Saskatoon, Canada: China Pavilion, 1997.

Payne, David. *Confessions of a Taoist on Wall Street.* Boston: Houghton Mifflin, 1984.

Qian, Zhongshu. *Guanzhuibian.* 4 vols. Beijing: Zhonghua shuju, 1979.

———. *Limited Views: Essays on Ideas and Letters.* Selected and translated by Ronald Egan. Cambridge, Mass.: Harvard University Asia Center, Harvard University Press, 1998.

Robinet, Isabelle. *Les commentaires du Tao To King jusqu'au VIIième siècle.* Paris: Collège de France, 1977.

Roth, Harold. "The Laozi in the Context of Early Daoist Mystical Praxis." In *Religious and Philosophical Aspects of the Laozi,* ed. Mark Csikszentmihaly and Philip J. Ivanhoe. Albany: State University of New York Press, 1999.

———. *Original Tao: Inward Training (Nei-yeh) and the Foundations of Taoist Mysticism.* New York: Columbia University Press, 1999.

———. "Psychology and Self-Cultivation in Early Taoistic Thought." *Harvard Journal of Asiatic Studies* 51 (December 1991): 599–650.

———. "Redaction Criticism and the Early History of Taoism." *Early China* 19 (1994): 1–46.

———. *Taoism: Growth of a Religion.* Trans. Phyllis Brooks. Stanford: Stanford University Press, 1997.

———. *Taoist Meditation: The Mao-shan Tradition of Great Purity.* Trans. Julian Pas and N. J. Girardot. Albany: State University of New York Press, 1993.

Rump, Ariane. *Commentary on the Lao Tzu by Wang Pi.* Honolulu: University of Hawaii Press, 1979.

Saso, Michael. *The Teachings of Master Chuang.* New Haven: Yale University Press, 1978.

Schipper, Kristofer. "The History of Taoist Studies in Europe." In *Europe Studies China: Papers from an International Conference on the History of European Sinology,* ed. Ming Wilson and John Cayley. London: Han-Shan Tang Books, 1995.

————. *The Taoist Body*. Berkeley: University of California Press, 1993.

Schopen, Gregory. "Archaeology and Protestant Presuppositions in the Study of Indian Buddhism." *History of Religions* 31 (1991): 1–23.

Schwartz, Benjamin I. *The World of Thought in Ancient China*. Cambridge, Mass.: Harvard University Press, 1985.

Segal, Robert A., ed. *In Quest of the Hero*. Princeton: Princeton University Press, 1990.

Seidel, Anna. "Chronicle of Taoist Studies in the West." *Cahiers d'Extreme-Asie* 5 (1990): 223–347.

Sivin, Nathan. "On the Word 'Taoist' as a Source of Perplexity, with Special Reference to the Relations of Science and Religion in Traditional China." *History of Religions* 17 (1978): 303–330.

Smart, Ninian. "Understanding Religious Experience." In *Mysticism and Philosophical Analysis*, ed. Steven Katz. New York: Oxford University Press, 1978.

Smith, D. Howard. *Chinese Religions from 1000 B.C. to the Present Day*. London: Holt, Rinehart and Winston, 1968.

Smullyan, Raymond. *The Tao Is Silent*. New York: Harper & Row, 1977.

Thompson, Laurence. *Chinese Religions: An Introduction*. 5th ed. Belmont, N.Y.: Wadsworth, 1996.

Towler, Solala. *A Gathering of Cranes: Bring the Tao to the West*. Eugene, Ore.: Abode of the Eternal *Tao*, 1996.

Underhill, Evelyn. *Mysticism*. London: Methuen, 1911.

Watson, Burton. *Chuang Tzu: Basic Writings*. New York: Columbia University Press, 1964.

————, trans. *The Complete Works of Chuang Tzu*. New York: Columbia University Press, 1968.

Welch, Holmes. *Taoism: The Parting of the Way*. 2nd ed. Boston: Beacon Press, 1965.

Wong, Eva. *Shambhala Guide to Taoism*. Boston: Shambhala, 1997.

————. *The Teachings of the Tao*. Boston: Shambhala, 1997.

Xiao, Gongquan. *Zhongguo zhengzhi sixiang shi*. 2 vols. Taipei: Zhongguo wenhua xueyuan chanbanshe, 1980.

Xu, Fuguan. *Zhongguo sixiangshi lunji xubian*. Taipei: Shibao wenhua, 1982.

Yates, Robin. *Five Lost Classics: Taao, Huanglao and Yin-yang in Han China*. New York: Ballantine Books, 1997.

Yearley, Lee. "The Perfected Person in the Radical Chuang-tzu." In *Experimental Essays on Chuang-tzu*, ed. Victor Mair. Honolulu: University of Hawaii Press, 1983.

TRANSLATIONS AND COMMENTARIES ON THE *DAODEJING*

Addis, Stephen, and Stanley Lombardo. *Tao Te Ching*. Indianapolis: Hackett, 1993.

Chan, Wing-tsit. *The Way of Lao Tzu*. Indianapolis: Bobbs-Merrill, 1963.

Chang, Chung-yuan. *Tao: A New Way of Thinking*. New York: Harper & Row, 1975.

Chen, Ellen. *The Tao Te Ching: A New Translation with Commentary*. New York: Paragon, 1989.

Ch'en, Ku-ying. *Lao Tzu: Text, Notes, and Comments.* Translated and adapted by Rhett Y. W. Young and Roger T. Ames. San Fransisco: Chinese Materials Center, 1977.

Creel, H. G. *What Is Taoism?* Chicago: University of Chicago Press, 1970.

Feng, Gia-fu, and Jane English. *Tao Te Ching.* New York: Vintage Books, 1972.

Graham, A. C., trans. *The Book of Lieh-tzu.* London: Lewis Reprints, 1973.

Henricks, Robert G. *Lao Tzu's Tao Te Ching: A Translation of the Startling New Documents Found at Guodian.* New York: Columbia University Press, 2000.

———. *Lao-Tzu Te-Tao Ching: A New Translation Based on the Recently Discovered Ma-wang-tui Texts.* New York: Ballantine Books, 1989.

———, trans. *Te-Tao Ching.* New York: Modern Library, 1993.

Kwok, Man-Ho, Martin Palmer, and Jay Ramsay, trans. *Tao Te Ching.* Rockport, Mass.: Element, 1993.

LaFargue, Michael. *The Tao of the Tao Te Ching: A Translation and Commentary.* Albany: State University of New York Press, 1992.

Laozizhu. *Laozizhu fu Laozi xinkao shulüe.* 2nd ed. Ed. Yang Jialuo. Taipei: Shijie shuju, 1958.

Lau, D. C. *Chinese Classics: Tao Te Ching.* Hong Kong: Chinese University of Hong Kong Press, 1982.

———. *Lau Tzu, Tao Te Ching.* New York: Penguin Books, 1963.

Le Guin, Ursula. *Lao Tzu: Tao Te Ching. A Book about the Way and the Power of the Way.* Boston: Shambhala, 1997.

Lu, Dongbin. *The Secret of the Golden Flower: A Chinese Book of Life.* Translated and explained by Richard Wilhelm; commentary by C. G. Jung [translated into English by Cary Baynes]. New York: Causeway Books, 1975.

Mair, Victor. *Tao Te Ching: Lao Tzu.* New York: Bantam Books, 1990.

Mitchell, Stephen. *Tao Te Ching.* New York: Harper Perennial, 1992.

Waley, Arthur. *The Way and Its Power.* New York: Grove Press, 1958.

Walf, Knut. *Westliche Taoismus-Bibliographie: Western Bibliography of Taoism.* Essen, Germany: Verlag Die Blaue Eule, 1992.

Wu, John C., trans. *Tao Teh Ching.* Boston: Shambhala Press, 2003.

Wong, Eva. *Lieh-tzu.* Boston: Shambhala, 1995.

Index